LARRY WISE ON COACHING ARCHERY

Advance Praise for
Larry Wise on Coaching Archery

The archery equipment available today is on the whole substantially better than when we launched *ArrowTrade Magazine* back in 1997, but the individual shooter's skill continues to play a larger role in accuracy. The experience Larry Wise has as a bowhunter, pro shop owner, coach and competitor means he can assist archers of every level to improve their shooting. More than any article describing the latest equipment advances, his columns for this magazine have helped readers and their customers continue to enjoy the sport of archery.

Tim Dehn
Editor of *ArrowTrade Magazine*

After sponsoring the "Core Archery School," which was devloped and is taught by Mr. Larry Wise, 16 separate times our archery shop was put on the map, so to speak. His genuine interest and concern for individual archer's progress and enjoyment of the sport of archery at all levels is unsurpassed. His one on one coaching during these sessions, actually touches the very heart of what archery is all about, fun, self awareness, and a sense of accomplishment, cannot be matched.

His Core Archery system is, in essence, a repeatable shooting system that teaches archers to use their skelatal structures to support the stress of long term shooting, thus providing a more relaxed posture to the muscles needed to complete the shot accurately.

Les & Gail Wynne
N.F.A.A. Master Coaches, Right-On-Target Family Archery, Waynesville, N.C.

Larry Wise, as a life-long educator, has an incredible ability to teach archers using a comprehensive understanding of back tension, advanced biomechanics, and a championship archer's mental game. Larry has been a professional archer himself along with working with intermediate and elite archers for decades as he continues to stay on the cutting edge with the latest equipment and shooting techniques. This new book is his best and most complete compilation of decades of expertise and experience that's easy to read, understand, and implement."

Rob Kaufhold
President of Lancaster Archery Supply, Inc.

LARRY WISE ON COACHING ARCHERY

by
Larry Wise

Library of Congress Cataloging-in Publication Data

Larry Wise on Coaching Archery / Larry Wise.
   p. cm
   Includes bibliographic references and index.
   ISBN 978-0-9913326-2-5 (softcover)
   1. Archery. 2. Coaching. I Larry Wise, 1947-

ISBN: 978-0-9913326-2-5

Copyright © 2014 by Watching Arrows Fly

All rights reserved. Except for use in a review, the reproduction or utilization of this work in any form or by any electronic, mechanical, or other means, now known or hereafter invented, including xerography, photocopying, and recording, and in any information storage and retrieval system, is forbidden without written permission of the publisher.

The web addresses cited in this text were current as of January 2014, unless otherwise noted.

Writer: Larry Wise; **Developmental Editor**: Steve Ruis; **Copy Editor**: Steve Ruis; **Proofreader**: Michèle Hansen; **Graphic Artist**: Steve Ruis; **Cover Designer**: Steve Ruis; **Photographers** (cover and interior): Larry Wise and Steve Ruis unless otherwise noted

Printed in the United States of America 10 9 8 7 6 5 4 3 2 1

Watching Arrows Fly
3712 North Broadway, #285
Chicago, IL 60613
312.505.9770

Contents

Introduction vii

Section 1 Observing Your Student-Archers
1. Information Gathering 1
2. Still Pictures 5
3. Video Images 9

Section 2 Evaluating Your Student-Archers
4. Introduction to Compound/Release Form and Execution 13

Section 3 Planning Corrections
5. The Stickman Chart 31
6. Practice with a Purpose 33
7. Why We Miss Deer 37
8. Aiming Better 47

Section 4 Implementing Plans of Correction
9. The Compound Bow Stance 57
10. The Bow Hand 63
11. Full-Draw-Position 69
12. The Ten Minute Coach 75
13. How to Properly Shoot and Train with a Release Aid 83
14. How To Cope With Target Panic/Release Aid Management Skills ... 93
15. Matching the Bow to the Archer: Selecting a Correct Length Bow ... 105

Section 5 Parts of The Mental Game: Thinking in the Present and Thinking About Goals
16. Shooting Better with Brain Power 117
17. Present Process Thinking 125
18. Thinking About Goals: Much Ado About Something 131

Section 6 The Structures of Coaching and Competing
19. Training Cycles 139
20. Coaching Proper Archery Technique: Are You Certified? 143
21. Tournament Preparation 155
22. Tournament Site Practice 161

| 23 | Post-Tournament Evaluation | 165 |
| 24 | Fostering Young Talent | 169 |

Section 7 On Equipment

25	Arrows in Action: Dynamic Arrow Spine	181
26	Putting Your Bow In Balance	191
27	Installing and Calibrating Target Sights	199
28	Powder and Paper Testing	209
29	Getting Looped	217
	About the Author	224
	Notes	230

Introduction

Coaching is teaching and teaching is coaching. They are one and the same. This means that when coaches intend to teach archery students those coaches should know and use the same basic educational methods that all good teachers use. Coaches should learn "standard teaching practices" so they can be most effective in creating a good learning environment for their students. I believe that education is hard work, that it must be organized, objective-based and, above all else, student centered.

Teaching in public school classrooms for thirty-five years enabled me to learn some good teaching techniques. I've further developed those techniques and adapted them to coaching archery over the past twenty years. There's always room for improvement, I know, but my experience affords me the opportunity of presenting here a sketch of what a good coach should do in an effective coaching session. Archery students expect their needs to be met by us coaches so we must make every effort to meet those needs in an effective manner.

The Coaching Routine
Every time an archery student comes to me for a learning session I cycle through the same four activities. It's the routine or algorithm that I use to be thorough. First, I must observe my student. Second, I must evaluate their skill and, third, I must write a plan of correction for the skill areas that need remediation. Fourth, I must help them implement the changes that will lead them to improvements.

Here's my simple and effective routine:
Step 1 Observe Your Student
Step 2 Evaluate Your Student
Step 3 Write a Plan of Correction
Step 4 Implement Your Plan

Every time a student comes to me I follow this routine—no exceptions. It's only effective if you do it all . . . in order . . . every time!

There's More
If your students develop their skills to a level that allows them to think about competing in tournaments then there is much more for to do. Coaches must then help

their students set some goals, write training plans that help accomplish those goals, and then monitor and adjust that plan as needed.

This gets us to three additional steps to the basic coaching routine:

Step 5 Set Goals
Step 6 Write a Training Plan
Step 7 Monitor the Plan

This Book

My purpose in writing this book is to help coaches organize their processes by following a sequence of effective coaching actions. The topics covered in the following chapters are designed to help you to begin building skills in those areas.

Repetition is at the heart of all good teaching (and archery is a repetition sport), so some of what you read will be repeated, perhaps quite a few times. I did this because the things that get repeated (like the importance of full-draw-position) are that important and secondly, I don't know that you will read this book from cover to cover. I often skip over sections of a book I am reading to look at the parts that are relevant to what I want to know. So, feel free to jump around as your interests take you.

The chapters include some new writing exclusive to this book but most are adapted from *Arrow Trade* magazine articles I have written previously. They are a beginning. You will always be adding to those skills as you gain coaching experience.

Read,
Learn,
Practice,
Coach!

Larry Wise

Section 1
Observing Your Student-Archers

From your first sight of your student or from your first phone conversation with them you are observing. You are observing his/her body actions or voice inflections and forming opinions. Collecting as much information about your student from that first contact impacts your relationship with them and, consequently, your reaction to them and your ability to affect their shooting progress.

Your eyes and ears are your information-gathering tools that enable you to interpret what your student is doing and how they are feeling about what they are doing. Using your eyes and ears along with the technology available today gives you a wealth of information about your student so that you can apply your knowledge about proper shooting form to assist them in their quest to "shoot better."

Following are the major methods you can use to collect information about your student. I'll include a few tips about when and how to use them as well. Remember, coaching begins and continues with observation.

Chapter 1
Information Gathering

The Information Form

A lot happens before I give anyone the information form that I require all of my students to fill out. We talk. As soon as they arrive at my house or we meet at a shooting range, we talk. I ask how their drive was on their way to my home or the range. I ask lots of questions about their car, their bow, their hunting, or other interests. If I have been to their home area I ask about that or about a mutual friend.

I ask all of these questions for two reasons: first I must get to know them and second, we have to establish a relaxed atmosphere between us if we are to work together to get the best results. I want to be sure that my student knows that I am going to be working "with" them and that we will be going on a journey "together" while we improve their shooting form or mental skills. I guess you could say that we are building trust between us and with that trust established my student can believe in the plan of correction that we will make for his or her shooting.

At some point in our conversation I must give them the basic personal information form that I've developed. It's not fancy or complex. You can probably make a better one – one that works better for your teaching style or the way you use technology to process the information.

My information form has the usual lines for name, age, years of experience, equipment, and some scores on various standardized rounds. These simple items help me get to know my student and tell me about their ability level.

I have found that the two most important items are their years of archery experience and their 20-yard indoor target score. If their experience is low then I know the terms I have to define and that I should skip nothing in my presentation about shooting form.

Their indoor score tells me their skill level under fixed and ideal conditions. Outdoor rounds are difficult to compare because of terrain and weather conditions so I rely on their indoor scores to make estimates of ability level.

The last item, the objective for this lesson, is the most important. Discussing why this student decided to come for this lesson helps us come to a mutual agreement on the objective, so I can make plans for the rest of our time together.

You have to know if your student is coming to learn basic shooting form, or advanced skills, or to deal with some release-dysfunction issue. At the end of the les-

Core Archery
Coach—Larry Wise
Archer Profile

Location _____ Date _____

Name _____

Street Address _____

City _____ State _____ Zip _____

Email _____

Years In Archery _____ Age _____

Equipment

Bow _____ Sight _____

Arrows: _____ Release _____

Scores

Indoor Vegas Face _____ 3-D _____

Field Round _____ FITA _____

Goal For This Lesson _____
_____
_____
_____

I collect information from each of my students so that I can contact them later. The number of years they have been shooting and how well they have been scoring tell me their level of archery knowledge and help me plan our first two hours together. I can also contact them later to learn how they are progressing and what questions they might have.

son your student will be judging his lesson by how well this objective was achieved. Or, at the least, he will judge the worth of the plan that you've built to achieve that goal.

Without this clear and agreed-upon objective your lesson will most likely be wasted time. Without it your lesson will be like driving your car around town just to kill time with no real place to go. Don't be that driver. Set an objective, discuss it, and build a plan to reach it. Revise the plan along the way if necessary but build a plan and get started executing it.

I save that information form in a large notebook with all the others I have from years of coaching. When students return for additional lessons I review their information before they arrive. I'll also have his information available in case I may have to contact them for some reason. Collect the information, use it, and save it.

Listening and Questioning

My conversation with each student continues throughout the coaching session and uncovers other important facts. I watch them complete their form to determine if they write with their right or left hand and compare that to their shooting side. Some students write with one side and shoot with the other and I have to know that and determine if their dominant eye matches their aiming eye. If there is no match then I have to deal with that issue to be sure it is not affecting performance.

If they wear glasses then their sight reticule and peep-sight aperture are issues that need to be discussed and corrected. Not seeing the target is not an option.

Just observing how a student walks can be helpful. If they have a noticeable tilt to their posture while walking, that may affect their posture for archery. Noting their strength level while they are drawing their bow is just as important as is determining if they have any physical challenges that will affect posture and their execution process.

I need to know if they are shooting archery for hunting, target, or both. Some students are only shooting for personal recreation in their backyard. Learning how often they practice can help you in drafting their training plan for the coming months.

Job and family information is necessary when decisions about training have to be made. Time and support for an archer's training make reaching goals easier – lack of support makes it more difficult and frustrating.

Equipment Assembly

Either during or after they have completed the information form we have to assess and assemble their equipment. Learning what bow they have and the accessories they have selected for it gives you some insight into their level of expertise and shooting purpose.

From your first viewing of their bow and accessories you can get a feeling if their setup is a good match for their needs and abilities. Most of all I'm looking at draw weight and draw length wondering if both suit the student when they are in full-draw-position.

Some students have spent too much money and others have spent too little on their equipment. I see this rather quickly when they open their bow case but have to be very judicious in my comments so as to guide them in future choices for their equipment and not insult their choices – most students are quite proud of their equipment.

Sometimes it's difficult to avoid commenting upon obviously wrong cam-size/draw length selections. In those cases I have to be honest at some point and guide them to the proper selection. Sometimes I can rectify the situation on site. It's really easy to do when I'm teaching at Lancaster Archery.

Experience is a great teacher when observing your archery students. When you've had the benefit of working with a hundred men, women, and youths you develop more and better skills at seeing and listening. Make a list of the topics I've mentioned here, and develop your own information form. Revise that list, customize it for your coaching and then collect the information. Having and using that information will allow you to do the job better. And we're never done "getting better." Never.

Chapter 2
Still Pictures

Digital photos, "still" pictures, are an extremely important part of my initial evaluation of any archery student. I find it essential that I record exactly what it is that my student has constructed as his full-draw-position. It is like taking a picture of your new house when it is finally finished and comparing it to the original plans. How good does it look? How close to the "plan" did your contractor come in his efforts to build what you wanted? Does it look more like the Leaning Tower of Pisa than it does a well-built house?

The evaluation of the pictures comes later. For now you need to know what pictures to take. That is, from what angles do you need to take those still pics and how many will serve your subsequent evaluation procedure?

I like to take at least five pictures of each student I work with. My "basic five" are as follows:

1. **Face View** – taken full view as you look directly at your student's face or front.

Face View Viewing your student's front or face tells you lots about his/her posture at full draw. I look for alignment of his spine, shoulders, head/chin, holding elbow and bow arm. Showing this view to your student often requires no words from me; they see the issue of misalignment and correct it themselves.

2. **Bow Hand** – taken close up as you zoom in on your student's bow hand.
3. **Elbow View** – taken full view from behind the archer's holding elbow as your see the target in the background.

Elbow View *From this vantage point I can read in an instant if my student's full draw position is correct by noting if his holding elbow/arm is in line with the arrow. A top view here is also very useful. I can also note if his head and body are aligned correctly.*

4. **Back View** – taken full view as you look at your student's back.

Back View *I use this view to verify most of what I saw from the front view. In addition I can determine if his shoulders are indeed level and his holding elbow is at least as high as the arrow and if his hips are staying in vertical alignment with his torso.*

5. **Bow Hand (Front)** – taken close up as you look at the back of your student's bow hand.

These five views of my student mark the beginning for his pictoral record. You can take more as your student progresses in later coaching sessions but even then I always come back to these five, even for top professionals. I always have to know if the building has been erected to the specified plan because even top professionals develop bad habits over time and those habits usually show up in these basic five pictures.

If I were to add a sixth picture to this group it would be a close up of the archer's release hand. Their release hand is visible in the Face View photo and you can always zoom in on it to note its position. However, later on when you are helping to correct the release hand it is helpful to take a close up of it to show your student their progress or lack thereof.

Here's what I look for in each of my five still pictures.

Face View Our most basic teaching tool in archery is the "Archer's T" position. We teach this to all archers and archery coaches and now is the time to use it. Visualize the letter "T" laid over the archer's body to check their core (spine) for vertical alignment. I also compare their head position to the vertical and their chin and shoulders to the horizontal.

With the "T" visualized on their body you can note if their hips are in line with their body and centered over their feet. I can also see if their holding elbow is at least as high as the arrow, but not too high, and if they are properly aligning the bones in their bow arm. I can also see any misuse of their hands.

Bow Hand Close Up I'm looking for both position and tension in this picture. Your bow hand has to be first positioned correctly with contact on the thumb pad (the *thenar eminence*) only. Following that, you must release all unnecessary tension out of the fingers and hand so the bow is unaffected by your bow hand during its power stroke (the movement of the string from loose to the arrow disconnecting). Compound bows and recurve bows differ in the amount of tension desired in the bow hand, so follow the appropriate model when assessing your student's hand. In either case, the thumb will point toward the target when it is properly positioned.

Elbow View My first look at an archer from this viewpoint tells me that they are or are not in optimal full-draw-position for efficiently holding (and releasing) the bowstring. It only takes a second to determine if their holding forearm (top view) is in line with the arrow or not. This position is essential for sound biomechanics for anyone shooting a hand-held bow of any kind: long bow, recurve, or compound.

I'm taller than most of my students so I have a bit of an upper view of their arm as it relates to the bowstring and arrow. If you need to stand on a chair or ladder to have this view I recommend that you do so.

I can also see the archer's head position and release aid angle from this view behind their elbow.

Back View The next view that I prefer is of the shooter's back as I am standing on the shooting line. From this view point I can again see the "T" overlaid on their posture and whether their shoulders are level or raised. I can also check head and/or chin tilt as well as hip/spine alignment and their holding elbow elevation. A bent bow arm is also easily detected.

Bow Hand (Back) I take a close-up picture of the back of each student's bow hand. A little experience viewing bow hand backs will teach you to notice tenseness and knuckle angles.

In additon to the above, occassionally I find these other viewpoints useful:

Distance Views Standing at a distance is also helpful when taking still pictures. Stand about eight to ten yards from the archer to take pictures from the Face, Elbow and Back views and use them to assess posture; you'll see some things that you may have missed from the closer views.

Top View I rarely use this view because I don't have an easy way to establish it. Getting directly over the top of an archer requires a balcony or scaffold arrangement of some kind and I don't have that at my home. Some indoor 3-D ranges do have this feature that they use mostly for simulating tree stand shots and so, in a few cases, I've been able to get overhead pics of archers to see shoulder, head, arm, and stance alignment.

I use mostly the first five viewpoints for my first analysis of an archery student. The other views come into play when I work with more advanced archers who may have a very specific issue they are working to improve.

A digital camera that allows you to connect to a large monitor/TV screen is helpful. Viewing in the small camera screen is okay when working with more advanced archers who you've worked with before but for new students use a larger screen. The larger image makes it easy for all to "see" the flaws that you see so easily and realize that they "need" to make a correction.

Last, all the pictures in the world won't help you make decisions about what form issues a student needs to improve unless you have a firm understanding of a biomechanically efficient form model. Without this model in your mind and in your student's mind you are running a lottery when choosing what issue to correct. Hence, you must learn and understand both the compound and recurve form models before you can do meaningful coaching.

Chapter 3
Video Images

If you want to study how things change, you use the methods of Calculus and/or record video images. In studying archery shooting form we mostly use video. (You can breathe out now.) We record videos from various angles, replay them and observe how the archer is "changing" from step to step throughout the entire shot process.

I use the same angles as listed in the previous chapter for still images with the addition of the Target View. The Target View is a tripod-mounted camera set between the target and archer viewing the archer's aiming face. Set the camera in place, turn it on and then proceed to shoot several shots when all are safely back at or behind the shooting line (except the camera).

Target View *Setting a still camera or video recorder between the archer and target gives you a perspective you don't usually get. A video can show you when misalignments occur and how they affect the followthrough of the shot.*

Following are some things to look for from the three main viewing positions listed previously.

Face View The camera-to-face video record of an archer's shot will indicate when his head position gets out of line, when he drops his chin, when he shifts shoulders and when in the sequence of steps he bends his elbow. You can also see when he leans his upper body away from the target and how he is drawing the bow. I also look for when an archer changes his release hand position and how he stabilizes it for the release action. Now that I have established that we can see execution in videos that we can't see in still forms, I will stop emphasizing the words "when" and "how."

Elbow View From this vantage point I can use video to determine when and how she is drawing the bow by watching the drawing shoulder. I can see if and when she is getting her holding forearm in line with the arrow and how her elbow/forearm reacts during followthrough. I can also watch her head reaction at the end of the shot.

How a student holds his release aid is of great importance to good biomechanics of the shoulder so I look for that angle and if/when it changes, as well as how it changes.

Back View I'm always visualizing the letter "T" superimposed on an archer's back so I see that throughout the video sequence of an archer's shot. How they manage their shoulders through time is an important biomechanical issue so watch for changes in shoulder elevation. Hip management and weight balance are other issues to watch.

Multi-Camera Sets If you have the advantage of having several cameras to set then you can get two, three or four views of the very same shot and greatly enhance your assessment. Seeing four views simultaneously on a split screen is maybe the best video tool but not available to many coaches.

I'm sure there are many more issues to look for in video recordings – you'll decide that for yourself based on your students' needs. Saving videos for future reference is an important tool if you are working long-term with a student. Consider a memory stick for each student while you maintain a library of files on your own computer hard drive. Comparing new with old every few months is a good teaching tool.

Of course, close-up views of hands and head are also important as well as any other view that you think might be helpful for analyzing a form issue. With our digital technology these days the sky is the limit.

Section 2
Evaluating Your Student-Archers

Before you can begin to evaluate any student's technique you must have a "standard" model in mind, a model that has been tested and proved worthy and effective for accomplishing the task or action you have in mind.

This is especially true for archery technique. Taking pictures and videos and watching your student shoot arrows is not of any use if you don't have a form model to use for comparison. Most archers do not have any model in mind when they watch others shoot or view videos of their own shooting.

A Compound Bow Form Model

To effectively evaluate shooting form you must first learn a biomechanically sound and thoroughly tested model. I offer my own Core Archery form model for shooting your compound bow with a mechanical release aid (see the book of the same name as well as some other chapters of this book). The twelve steps of this model have been tested and proven as a winning model for more than thirty years – I've used them since 1978. These steps use your body and its mechanics to shoot efficiently in a set of actions that are designed to "repeat" themselves with minimum muscular effort and maximum skeletal involvement.

You can see the principles of my Core Archery form model at work in today's top professionals. Learn this model and then watch the professionals. Begin to "see" good form at work.

A Recurve Bow Form Model

If you are interested in learning a form model for shooting a recurve bow then I recommend reading Coach Kisik Lee's second book **Inside the Archer**. I won't try to summarize or discuss this model in this book although I am certified to teach it. Read Coach Lee's book and use it for your recurve model.

Two Models?

It is important to learn both models if you plan to be a good coach. There are similarities to both and also some differences – you must know all of those to be effective. Studying both models increases your understanding of the biomechanics we use in archery and you need to know that so your students can excel.

Shooting Form For The Compound Bow & Release Aid

I remind every archery student that the compound bow does not reduce the number of shooting challenges you experience compared to the recurve bow or any other type of bow. What it does do is present a different set of challenges caused by a force-draw curve that peaks at mid-draw—instead of at full draw—and then reduces the holding weight to a range of 10 to 20 pounds. In addition, the hand-held release aid presents challenges of conscious versus subconscious operation.

These features make shooting the compound bow with a release aid highly accurate but also vulnerable to mental dysfunctions. This section targets the physical and mental form techniques needed to properly execute the archery shot. Dealing with the release-aid-related mental dysfunctions is the subject of another section of the book.

Study ➤ Learn ➤ Practice ➤ Succeed!

Chapter 4
Introduction to Compound/Release Form and Execution

It's important to note here that as with any shooting form, the setup steps are critical to achieving the final outcome desired. If the final execution is flawed then it is probable that one of the setup steps was flawed and for that reason we separate these steps and study them in order. We know, however, that they are not executed separately but in an interrelated flow that links all the steps into an "archery ballet." We can use digital pictures to study each step and video to study the flow that links the steps. But first, we have to investigate each step individually.

The Shot Objective
When you nock an arrow, raise and draw your bow, what is it that you want to do? To hit the ten-ring? Hit the "X?" Or hit the "gold?" Each of these is a worthy outcome but they are just that, outcomes. They are but future results as you the archer prepare to draw, aim and release the bow. However, to perform at our best we must be "present minded." To reach our full performance potential our conscious thinking must be present with the physical actions and focused on the process of shooting.

In compound/release-aid archery, that means that we should be focused on executing the shot with back tension. If we establish this process as our shot objective then we have the best chance of executing it with success. Thoughts of future or past results keep us from our "present" task of building our bodies into the proper position for executing the shot with the back tension process. It's like reaching for your dropped cell phone while you're driving your car – look away from the road for a second and you'll find yourself turning the car into the ditch.

To reach full potential you must foster your "present thinking" skills. And that thinking must invoke the best process for shooting with a release aid; your thinking must be upon executing the shot with back tension and only upon that.

Full Draw Position Defined
Executing shots with back tension has physical requirements. The dynamic loads placed on the body by the force-draw characteristics of a compound bow and the capabilities of the human anatomy dictate those requirements. Compound bows reach peak weight just a few inches into the draw stroke which then reduce significantly at

full-draw-position. Therefore, an upright posture with level shoulders offers a stable platform from which an archer can use the necessary back muscles to most effectively operate a mechanical release aid.

You should be aware that in order to use the appropriate back muscles an archer must place his or her draw-side shoulder and scapula in the optimum position to use those muscles. Therefore we must define both this full-draw-position and back tension.

Teaching the "Archer's T" Position

With the price of gas at an all-time high these days none of us jumps in our car and drives around aimlessly. In our driving we make sure we have a firm objective/destination so we don't waste precious gasoline. But many archers you know shoot archery without a firm objective position to reach at full draw. Instead they just nock an arrow, draw their bow and get to a different position each time and shoot their arrows. Obviously, if we set out to attain the same full-draw position each and every time we draw the bow then we have a better chance of repeating our performance. Better yet, we should set out to draw our bow to the optimum position for reaching the back-tension-process objective we have set for ourselves.

You can easily teach or learn this position through the use of the "Archer's T." Most coaches have learned this but a quick run-through here is good review. It's simple, takes very little time (five minutes) and leaves a big impression on every archer regardless of his or her learning style or level of experience.

The "Archer's T" Drill Script

Step One Begin with your feet straddling the shooting line with your heels together. Next, raise your arms to form a "T," with your head facing down shooting line. Close your eyes and after several seconds you should feel some degree of swaying. This unstable feeling forces you to trigger many small leg muscles to maintain your balance.

Archer's T I teach every one of my students how to build proper full-draw-position by using the Archer's T which is essential to my coaching. Begin with this T position so that your student can become fully aware how their body feels with their arms outstretched and their head resting over their spine.

Step Two With your eyes still closed spread your feet to hip width. The swaying should diminish and you should feel a more relaxed and stable feeling in your legs and body core. Spreading your feet provides stability.

Step Three Next, roll your shoulders up and forward toward you chin. Because you employ so many upper body muscles to hold this position you cannot reasonably hold or aim a bow with your shoulders elevated. Set them back and downward to feel the more stable and steadier position needed for holding a bow.

Step Four Hold your release hand in the palm-down position and form a hook with the two end-segments of your index, middle and ring fingers. Curl your thumb and pinky finger under your palm and relax them. While still looking forward (not at the target) bend your release-arm elbow so that your hooked fingers rotate under the point of your chin. Your release forearm and elbow are now in line with and behind your imaginary arrow with the elbow at least as high as the imaginary nock. Your shoulders must remain level as first established in the "T" position and the head held erect over the spine with your chin level.

Step Five Now turn your head toward the target. Do not move your release hand or forearm from their alignment with your imaginary arrow. Be sure to hold your chin level with your head directly over the top of your spine.

T Completed *The student completes his T position by bending his holding arm at the elbow and placing his second knuckle under the point of his chin to align his arm with the arrow. Then he can turn his head to the target, form a "stop" sign with his bow hand and relax his bow hand fingers to complete the T position. Once learned you can review and refer to this "objective position" during the remainder of your instruction with this student.*

Step Six Now, to complete the T position make a "stop sign" toward the target with your bow hand. Be sure to hold your hand so that your knuckles are at the recommended forty-five degree angle to the vertical. Relax your fingers and thumb and you'll see that your thumb points toward the target. Your body is now in position to be stable, steady and repeatable.

This is full-draw-position for the compound/release shooter.

Back Tension Defined

From the full-draw-position defined above it is possible to optimize the use of one's back muscles for the purpose of shooting a compound bow with release aid. The muscles to be used are the rhomboids, levator scapulae, and trapezius; their use will promote repeat performances and the best results with the least amount of effort.

These muscles must work in a synchronized manner. To best achieve this, the archer's drawing forearm must be in line with the arrow (top view) with the elbow at least as high as the nock. The archer's head must be held erect, chin level, with the shoulders held down (not shrugged up) and at the same level. The bow arm must also be held with the bones in line to resist the force of the bow.

From this full-draw-position back tension can then be defined as the contraction of the draw-side or dominant-side rhomboids, levator scapulae, and trapezius muscles that results in a force that rotates the draw-side elbow about the shoulder joint in a plane tilted about thirty-degrees to horizontal. Further, this rotational force causes a position change on a hand-held release aid that can and should be harnessed to activate the release aid.

It is significant to note here that if the archer's head is tilted away from its position on top of the spine then some neck and back muscles, most notably the levator scapulae, will be recruited to hold it in that tilted position. You can feel this to the extreme as you tuck your chin to your chest. To ensure that all back muscles are available for back tension an archer must maintain erect head position and allow the levator scapulae muscle to synchronize with the rhomboids and trapezius.

Building Form Step by Step

Achieving full-draw-position as outlined previously is the necessary condition that immediately precedes the execution of back tension. How an archer gets into that position is important to getting the most efficient repeat performances. Therefore, every archer must examine each form element required in building this full-draw-position and determine exactly when it should be set into place. That's why we study form in a step-by-step format – good timing is critical to repeating your actions.

As mentioned, each form element is set in place at its appropriate time and its effectiveness can be measured by how well an archer achieves their shot objective of back tension execution. If the execution is not satisfactory then one or more of the building elements was not effectively put in place and they must search through those elements to find the breakdown point.

If the coach and student have not built those steps as a team and are not communicating with the same language and same form steps then locating deficiencies and improving form elements is hampered. Therefore, learning the following form steps is necessary for both the coach and student. Both must be working with the same standard form model.

It must be emphasized here that each form element is executed at the time when it is most effective. Just as nocking the arrow must be done before raising the bow (this is an obvious one) the other elements must be set in place at the appropriate time and then maintained until the arrow has been released. An important example would be the bow hand – it must be set in correct position in step three when it first touches the bow handle and never changed until the arrow is free from the bow. In other words, the archer must know "what to do, how to do it, and when to do it" in order to get the best results he or she is capable of getting.

Step One The Stance

Stability and balance are key ingredients to successful archery. They both begin with and are influenced by the placement of the archer's feet. The alignment of the feet relative to the target, the spread distance of the feet and the weight balance placed on the feet must all be considered in the stance if consistency in upper body performance is going to be achieved. In other words, you draw your strength and stability from the ground.

Alignment It is usual to first consider the alignment of the feet relative to a direct line to the target. Our position of reference is the "even" or "square" stance that aligns the archer's toes to this line and points the archer's hips and chest perpendicular to the target; at full-draw a line across the shoulders will be parallel to the arrow.

The most popular compound archer stance is the "open" stance. This is achieved by setting the target-side foot several inches from the line to the target thus opening the hips and chest slightly, three or four degrees, to the target. Most could place two or three fingers between the line to the target and their toes on the target side foot.

The opposite of the open stance is the "closed" stance where the drawing-side foot is pulled away from the line to the target. This would point the hips and chest slightly away from the target.

Spread The spread of the feet should be hip to shoulder width. This allows the use of fewer leg muscles to keep your upper body still. By testing one's stance spread in the archer's "T" with heels together and eyes closed any archer can feel how leg muscles must be constantly triggered to maintain balance but as soon as the feet are spread 10 to 15 inches many of those leg muscles can be relaxed. The result is calmer and steadier legs and a nearly still upper body. A model stance, then, has the feet spread to at least hip width.

Balance There are two balance issues to consider: one is left-to-right and the other is heel-to-toe. Both have an effect on maintaining a steady upper body.

The left/right balance should be 50% left and 50% right to prevent leaning toward or away from the target while aiming. Leaning one way or the other will result in high or low missed arrows.

It is highly unstable to have more than 50% of your weight on your heels. To prevent this it is recommended to place about 55-60% of your weight toward the toes on the balls of your feet. Lean slightly forward until you feel your balance-controlling toes doing their work.

Closed-Eye Test A standard test for stance openness is the Closed-Eye Test. This can be done with a drawn bow by aiming normally then closing your eyes, counting

Stance *The most common stance is slightly open to the target as shown here with the toes aligned at about a ten-degree angle from the target line. Toes aligned with the target line form the "even" or "square" stance.*

to ten and opening your eyes. A left or right drift indicates that the upper body is rotating itself over the hips to its natural position. Once this natural position is established you can shift your stance to be more or less open so that your bow arm and bow are naturally pointed directly at the target. This is the recommended starting position for compound bow stance.

Another test that will help define your final stance employs a horizontal line of five spots and your normal stance set to the middle spot. Over several days and fifty arrows shoot the spots from right-to-left, left-to-right and in a random sequence. The patterns in the target spots will show evidence of best performance. Some, for instance, will shoot their best pattern on the far right spot indicating that they shoot best with a more open stance – right-handers are more open to the spot on the right. Others will have the best pattern in the center, etc. Adjust your stance to take this into account.

Step Two Nocking The Arrow

Bow Position While nocking an arrow it is important for you to hold the bow in or near the vertical plane in which you will raise and draw. This will minimize the effort needed to nock the arrow and avoid turning the bow into someone else's shooting space.

Posture Although as an archer you must bend your head to watch what you are doing while nocking the arrow you must take care not to bend your upper body too much. Keeping the upper torso vertical saves the time and effort needed to reestablish vertical posture. Keeping your torso upright also aids breathing that, in turn, helps muscle recovery and relaxation.

Arm Extension Allowing the bow arm to extend while nocking the arrow aids in relaxing your arm muscles. Keeping it bent to hold the bow up continues to work the arm muscles that you need for steady aiming. Rest your bow arm while nocking your arrow.

Step Three Bow Hand Placement

Because the bow hand is the first body part to touch the bow and the last part of the body touching the bow as the arrow crosses the arrow rest it can be said that the shot begins and ends with bow hand placement. Getting it correct at first touch is essential to shooting consistency – if it's correct at first touch then it will not need to be,

Bow Hand *The bow hand should be set onto the bow grip so that only the thumb pad makes contact with the bow. Your knuckles should form a 45-degree angle with the bow and your fingers should be relaxed freeing the bow to repeat its dynamic action.*

nor should it be, changed later in the shot sequence.

Release Aid Hook Up Your bow hand placement begins by hooking the release aid to the bowstring or D-loop. Your release hand can then support the mass of the bow allowing your bow hand to be free for placement on the grip section.

Tape Strip On Hand To save a lot of questions about which part of the hand should be placed on the grip section I recommended that you place a tape strip on your bow hand. The tape strip will cross the thenar eminence (thumb pad) and run roughly parallel to the lifeline in the palm; it should not cross the lifeline. It will also be at a forty-five degree angle to the large knuckle-creases where the fingers join the palm.

Now all you have to do is place the tape strip and only the tape strip on the bow grip. Sounds simple but you'll have to oversee the application to be sure your student does it correctly.

Radius Bone The major purpose of bow hand placement is to allow the draw-force of the bow to be resisted by the radius bone in the forearm. This can only occur if your thumb-pad (thenar eminence) and only your thumb pad contacts the bow grip. If other hand parts contact the grip then you risk transferring torque to the handle.

Placement Routine Develop a simple routine for setting your bow hand on the grip. Do it the same way every time and you can begin expecting the same result on every shot. Routine quickly becomes habit and less effort will be needed doing it right.

Begin by touching the base of your lifeline to the sharp left edge (for right-handers) of the lower grip section.

Next, slide the hand upward until a learned amount of touch is felt between the index knuckle and the top of the bow grip section. A touch may also be felt on the thumb side.

Now is the correct time to lay or roll your thumb pad (the tape strip) onto the grip section. Do this without creating any amount of false pressure and while keeping your fingers and thumb relaxed. Your bow hand is now correctly placed (the release hand continues to support the mass of the bow).

Step Four Release Hand Position

Since the release has already been hooked to the bowstring or D-loop before setting the bow hand, all that remains is to flatten the large knuckles. In anatomy terms, the release hand metacarpo-phalangeal joints (the knuckles connecting the fingers and palm) must be straightened and the release aid held by the second and third phalanges. In other words, use a hard hook with the two end segments of your fingers to hold the release aid.

The little finger and the thumb should be allowed to relax and naturally curl under the palm. These two work independent of the other three fingers and are controlled by the deep flexor muscles that extend up through the forearm. That allows your other three fingers to hold the back-tension release aid with their two end phalanges and, most importantly, with a relaxed wrist.

Any time the little finger and/or thumb get used wrist relaxation is compromised and your back tension effort must be elevated to get the same result. To learn back tension properly the beginning and intermediate student must use a standard two-fin-

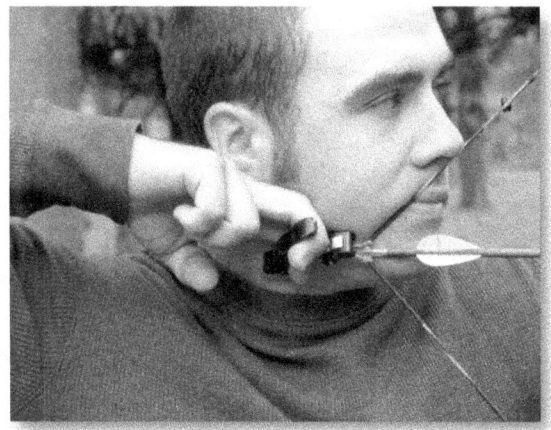

Release Hand A flat-knuckle, straight-wristed bow hand is desired so that your forearm can be relaxed at full draw. That enhances transfer of holding into your back muscles and promotes release hand consistency.

ger or three-finger back tension/triggerless release aid. The student archer must learn with a true back tension/triggerless release aid before using other types.

Step Five Posture Set

Throughout the first four form elements you have been watching what you have been doing with the bow and arrow. That means your head has been tilted downward and must now be repositioned over your spine. Your shoulders must be set back, down and level with each other so that your framework – your skeleton – can most efficiently carry the loads thus giving the utilized muscle groups optimum leverage and as much muscle as possible to relax. In short, you must now erect your launching platform for the shot.

From this upright position you need only turn your head, chin level, toward the target. Tilting the head or tucking the chin must be avoided from this point on because as soon as the head is tilted from directly over the spine, back muscles must be recruited to hold the head in that tilted position. That means those same muscles will not be fully available for back tension making your shot objective more difficult to achieve.

Posture After you set your hands you must make a final adjustment to your upper body posture. You must be sure that your shoulders and chin are level and your head turned to the target. From here the bow must be raised and drawn without changing your head position and to do that the bow must fit you correctly.

Step Six Raising The Bow

Bow Arm Your bow arm should be extended during the nocking element and should have been maintained in that position. Your hands are also in position and only about twelve inches apart with the release hand holding most of the bow mass with moderate pulling tension that pressures the bow lightly into the bow hand (so as not to lose your bow hand position).

The Raise The bow, both hands, and both arms should be raised as a unit without raising either shoulder. Shoulders must be maintained in the "down" and level position set in the previous step so that the upper body skeleton has its optimum stability and muscles have their optimum leveraging capability. If you allow the drawing shoulder to roll outward toward the bowstring then you will increase the chances of injury to delicate shoulder muscles. Keep it rolled back so you can load back muscles from the beginning of the draw effort.

It is important to maintain an extended bow arm and to have the release forearm as much in line with the arrow as is possible. The bow arm raise is accomplished from the shoulder ball/socket joint and below; no shoulder elevation should occur. This prepares the arms for the drawing step.

Raise *Raise the bow and arms as a unit. Protect your shoulder position so you can begin loading your back muscles properly during the draw stroke. Raise the bow until your sight pin appears just above the target spot.*

Many archers are unable to do this due to excessive draw weights and/or mass weights of their bows. If you have difficulty drawing your bow properly then lower the peak weight so that you can perform each form step, including this one, with ease. After you can execute each step correctly then undertake a conditioning program that will enable you to increase the draw weight and/or to hold more bow mass.

Target Elevation The raise should continue until the bow sight can be seen just above the target spot level. Many see their sight pin/scope dot near the one o'clock position on the target face while others prefer to be slightly higher but still on the face. This elevates the bow into a position that will allow it to fall down into the spot as the bow is drawn. In other words, allow gravity to assist with your effort in reaching a final aim. Starting below the spot requires that you raise your bow after you reach full draw and that's a more difficult task by far.

Raising the bow too high will often lead to shoulders raised out of position. Some raise their bow shoulder to an excessive level while others raise the drawing shoulder too high. Once raised too high it is unlikely that you will get it back to the proper level required at optimum full-draw-position. Again, the most likely culprit for this habit is excessive draw weight.

The Arms Your drawing forearm should be at least as high as the arrow at this point. This prepares the arm to be at the same level as the arrow instead of below it. The bow arm is fully extended with the forearm radius bone lined up in front of the upper arm humerus bone preparing both to resist the draw force of the bow thus reducing the need for muscle recruitment.

Visual Spot Contact Throughout the raise visual contact should be maintained on the target spot. Intense focus is not necessary but looking at the spot in general is important for maintaining body and head orientation to the target. If you look away from the intended spot then your body will change alignment much like a golfer who looks away from the ball during some part of the swing and therefore miss-hits the ball.

The sight pin/scope is seen in the archer's unfocused vision as it comes into view at the conclusion of the raise. Watching the pin/scope during the raise not only gets your body out of line with the target it also promotes shooting the wrong target face, a mental error that should never occur.

Bow Hand Your bow hand must remain relaxed through out this bow raising action. There is no need for your bow hand to hold the bow as the release hand/arm have been pulling some to keep the bow slightly pressured into your bow hand. Your bow arm needs only raise the bow mass. Creating excessive hand pressure during the raise leads to inconsistencies in bow hand pressure at full draw and, therefore, in arrow impact locations.

Step Seven **The Draw**

Shoulder Position Great emphasis has been made to this point to protect your shoulder position so that both shoulders are down and level. If at this point in the shot sequence your draw shoulder is allowed to rotate forward then drawing will over stress the upper arm muscles and tendons causing soreness and injury. Keeping your draw shoulder back so your upper arm is near your chest while drawing will promote an eas-

Draw Draw your bow while maintaining a level shoulder position. Raising one shoulder higher than another to get the bow drawn lessens your chances to establish proper and strong full-draw-position.

ier draw and prepare you for proper transfer of the holding effort into the your back-muscles.

The bow shoulder must remain in the down position so that the skeleton can efficiently resist the draw force. Raising the bow shoulder will necessarily recruit most, if not all, of the muscles of the shoulder to resist the draw force of the bow leading to fatigue and aiming inconsistency; bone doesn't fatigue, muscle does.

Bow Hand As the draw force elevates quickly toward peak weight the bow handle presses into your bow hand. It is important to note that having the bow elevated to target level promotes consistent bow hand pressure during the draw, especially as the bow reaches peak weight and remains there for most of the draw stroke.

Maintaining a relaxed bow hand during this peak weight event is critical to having it relaxed at full draw. If you allow tension to build up in your bow hand during peak weight your fingers will stiffen and extend and stay in that position for the remainder of the shot. Blank-bale practice is a must-do part of practice until the bow hand stays relaxed through the draw.

Draw Arm During the draw stroke, your drawing arm elbow should be held at arrow level or slightly higher so long as your draw-side shoulder position is not compromised. Execute your draw motion smoothly on this level so that your release hand moves level just below your chin and into its touch-point along side the neck or jaw.

Keep your wrist straight so your forearm can remain relaxed. Tightening your thumb or pinky finger will recruit muscles in your wrist and forearm hampering your back tension effort, so do neither. Bending your wrist to project your thumb toward a more forward thumb-trigger will also tighten the forearm muscles; use a longer trigger extension that enables you to keep your wrist straight.

Rhomboid Contraction Level As the draw arm and shoulder are used to draw the bow through the peak weight distance of the draw stroke (as much as six inches in some cases) your back muscles must contract to hold the bow. This contraction involves the rhomboids, levator scapulae, and trapezius muscle groups throughout the draw stroke even after peak weight has been passed.

Allowing your back muscles to relax as the bow's draw weight reduces to the lower holding weight promotes back tension failure. Once you relax your back muscles you must then regenerate that holding tension after full-draw-position has been reached and that is a source of inconsistency, shot to shot. Once started, your back muscle loading should always be smooth and never decrease.

Sighting Devices During the final quarter of the draw stroke your bow sighting devices will come into view between your eye and the target. The peep will move into place directly in front of your eye while the front sight/scope will move into your line of vision to the target. Your visual eye line with the target spot must be maintained even as that sightline is momentarily blocked when the peep and scope cross in front of your aiming eye; moving your eyes to see your scope and then back to the target moves your head position from its optimum placement and requires additional time and effort to reset.

Draw Length Setting At the very end of the draw stroke the compound draw length setting comes into play. If the setting is too short for you then your drawing elbow will not reach its intended full-draw-position directly in line with and behind the arrow. This prevents you from fully transferring the bow's holding force from your arm into your back muscles, a critical error seen in far too many compound archers. As a coach you must be able to visually identify this condition and ensure that it is corrected.

If your draw length setting is too long you will rotate your elbow too far. In this over-rotated position the draw-side scapula is pushed so close to the spine that your rhomboid muscles will not have their optimum leverage thus severely limiting your back tension effort.

Step Eight Full-Draw-Position

Full-draw-position is reached the instant your drawing forearm and elbow are rotated in line with the arrow. Your elbow should be as high as or slightly higher than the arrow to promote optimum scapula position and thereby giving your back muscles optimum leverage for back tension.

Full-Draw-Position This is the position taught using the Archer's T earlier. Reaching it with head, arms and shoulders aligned so you can transfer the holding force of the bow into your back is essential. Aligning any other way increases your muscle workload and reduces your chances of repeating your performance. Aligning your holding arm with the arrow makes you most efficient and allows you to repeat more often.

Holding/Transfer Once your full-draw-position has been established you can complete the transfer of the holding force into your back muscles. That means your drawing-side rhomboids, levator scapulae, and trapezius must not relax during the draw stroke. In fact, their contraction level must continue to elevate after peak weight has been passed and into this "transfer" action.

As this transfer is completed your drawing forearm can be relaxed to its optimum level. In this condition your drawing elbow can be most easily and efficiently rotated as a result of your back muscle contraction during the final seconds of aiming.

Sighting Devices The peep is now directly in front of your aiming eye, allowing you to clearly see through it and the scope to focus on the target spot. In other words, aiming has reached a new and higher level where all of the sighting devices are placed on your sightline. The level bubble can also be seen in your unfocused vision.

Relax Your bow hand has remained relaxed, as has your bow arm. Use only enough bow arm muscle to keep your radius and humerus bones in line. Your draw arm is relaxed as the hold transfers to your back but your release hand fingers remain contracted (hooked) with equal tension in each finger. Your neck must also be relaxed and part of your last full breath exhaled.

String & Nose Many archers are adamant about touching the string to their nose at full draw. It needs to be pointed out here that with the very short compound bows being made now, most being less than thirty-eight inches axle-to-axle, the string angle is so sharp at the nock that you will most likely be forced to bend your neck and distort your head position in order to touch your nose to the bowstring. As mentioned before, a distorted head position can only be held in place with neck and back muscles and you should be using those muscles for back tension. Instead of such distortions, maintain proper head position and remember, with compound bows the minimum aiming requirement at full draw is to have the peep in front of the aiming eye. Don't let the bow dictate your body position; make the bow fit you instead.

Step Nine Aim & Contract

Sight Picture As the transfer of the hold is completed into your back muscles, the sight pin/scope settles to the middle of the target spot. This settling needs to end up at a satisfactory level of stillness but don't try to be perfectly still. Aiming while "perfectly still" will lead to the expectation that every shot "must" be aimed perfectly and that promotes unnecessary tension and unrealistic expectations. Relax and allow a small degree of floating or movement of your ring or dot; don't micromanage your aim.

You must learn that on occasion your aim does reach the perfectly still condition but only on occasion. It should be enjoyed when it happens but never expected. An adequate aim is the norm.

Contraction As your aim is visually established your conscious should focus on your back tension process while your trained subconscious back muscle tightening produces the shot release.

If for some reason the aim is perceived to be less than adequate the shot must be terminated with a let down. This often occurs as your conscious mind is interrupted from its normal shot routine by a nonstandard action or sensory input (a loud noise, a bump, a wind gust, bad feeling bow hand, etc.).

The increasing back muscle contraction causes the draw elbow to rotate about the shoulder ball/socket joint in a plane tilted about thirty degrees from horizontal. This in turn causes the release hand and the release handle to rotate a tiny amount that may or may not be visible to an observer.

Eye Focus As the sight settles into the target spot your focus on the spot must intensify. This focus must establish a clear image on the spot with the sight pin/scope reticle somewhat out of focus but remaining adequately within/around the spot.

Your conscious mental focus, as mentioned earlier, must be in the present moment and on the shot-making process that you are using to produce the release of the arrow. If you allow this process to be unattended by the conscious mind then you cannot and will not get the results you want. The process is all important.

Step Ten The Release

Release Aid When properly executed, the rotation of your release elbow will cause the back tension release aid handle to rotate. When it rotates enough, perhaps as little as half a degree, the two hooked parts, the half-moon and the ledge, will separate causing the release of the bowstring.

When held properly, a thumb trigger style release will also rotate so that the trigger is pressed into the base of your thumb (as opposed to squeezing the trigger with the thumb tip). If you avoid using your sensitive thumb tip you will lessen the chances for your conscious mind to link to the release aid trigger. "Trigger thoughts" can lead to poor shot execution and some mental dysfunctions regarding the release aid.

The index finger trigger should be activated with this same rotation force. Again, don't use the fingertip on the trigger but, rather, wrap your index finger around the trigger so the trigger contacts the finger in the second crease. The other three fingers should be curled loosely around the release handle and contracted during the rotational action of the elbow. Set the trigger tension to medium or medium-heavy, never light.

Step Eleven The Followthrough

Release Hand Following the instant of release (the separating of the metal parts) the release hand will spring directly away from behind the arrow. The release elbow and arm will also spring away a short distance in the 30-degree plane of rotation. This short spring-away is the result of using only the short muscles in the back to cause the required rotational force (they only allow for a short motion, any longer motion means other muscles were used to create it).

Followthrough *Proper alignment and back muscle use will generate a proper followthrough where your elbow rotates about your shoulder joint in a slightly downward angle. It is a short motion because only a few small back muscles are at work. A big motion indicates too much arm muscle action.*

Bow Arm The bow arm remains extended during the followthrough. It may fall downward slightly as some shoulder muscles relax. A wild sideways motion is an indication of excessive arm tension.

Vision The archer's visual contact with the target spot should be maintained until the arrow impacts the target. The bow and sight may have fallen away and the eyes may blink after the release but visual contact should remain on the spot.

Step Twelve **System Reset**

Relax Take a relaxation breath after the arrow impacts the target. Also allow your bow and bow arm to fall downward and rest the bow stabilizer on the ground or the bottom cam on your leg. As this breath escapes allow your shoulders to fall down slightly before resetting them with the next inhale.

Shot Assessment Make a quick shot assessment. Avoid value judgments of yourself and of the arrow impact point/score. Do determine any form element that may need attention for the next shot and any sight adjustment that may be needed. Accept the shot for what it was, only one of many that has to be made.

Clear The Mind Remove the shot from your current thinking just as you do when you type "CTRL-ALT-DEL" on your computer. Eliminate the current data but keep the program available so you can begin running it again with fresh information and renewed action.

Summary

Working through the above steps over and over will pay dividends as you progress in both skill and knowledge. You must build a model form that you understand and, therefore, are better able to achieve.

When both coach and student have the same vocabulary and the same form model, the student has a better chance of actually putting into action the requests of the coach. Once the requested changes become actions, that student will have the greatest chance for achieving his/her most efficient form and, in time, garner higher scores.

Section 3
Planning Corrections

You can talk about a plan, think about a plan, even dream about it, but nothing is as effective as writing it. When you write it on paper for both you and your student to see the plan becomes real.

Written plans can be revised with the stroke of a pen. You and your student can see the plan and its revisions and, more importantly, your student can take a copy with him to guide his practice over the coming days and weeks.

A written plan makes it abundantly clear what both of you are trying to accomplish. When you meet again you can both review the plan, measure progress, and revise it for the upcoming series of practices. A written plan is the student's plan – he takes ownership of it when he takes it with him. Don't keep it in your head as though it is some "top secret" plan that only you know. Write it down and help the student "own" it.

Practice
A student has to learn how to practice if she is to be successful. Mostly, your student has to learn to set an objective for each and every practice session and to keep notes about that session. You, as coach, have to teach them how to organize a practice session so their "correction plan" can be implemented.

Why We Miss
If you gain an understanding of why most archers don't hit the target center then you can better observe them and help them plan more effectively. Read about why we miss in this chapter with that in mind.

Aiming Better
Everyone wants to aim better. Learn about how we can do that and you'll be able to write a better correction plan for each of your students. Most of aiming better is, of course, dependent on body position at full draw and how we get to that position in a step-by-step sequence of steps.

Experience
Knowing which body action and or anatomy element to fix first comes with experience. You can probably guess that those beginning form elements of stance and hand

positions must be dealt with first and you'd be correct. Building repeatable shooting form is like building a house – start with the foundation. Experience will teach you the rest.

Chapter 5
The Stickman Chart

Very few of the students who come to me bring a notebook with them. They have not been writing anything down in the form of a "Shooters Log" and so it is up to us to get them started in that effort. To that purpose I have devised and use my now infamous "Stickman" chart for the purpose of recording what form corrections I want my students to make. It serves as a written record that they can take away with them and is the most important piece of paper that I give them.

I designed it to keep things simple. It is not a work of art but it is effective. I recommend that you use something like it with your students.

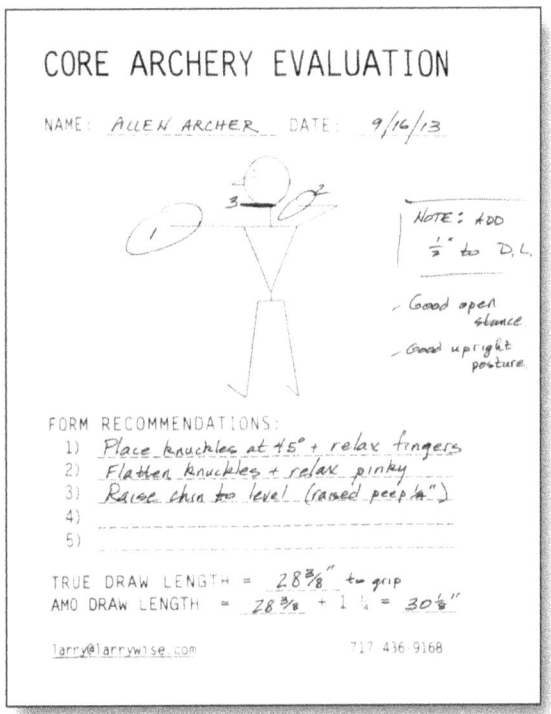

How To Use The Chart
Part of a new-student information form that I require each student complete is a space for them to write their coaching session objective. I have to know why they came to see me and what they hope to accomplish.

They come to me for many reasons. Some come for assistance with target panic, others for getting started with a back tension release aid and others for basic form instruction. We discuss their objective so we both are clear as to what we need to accomplish. This discussion is also a chance for me to get to know this new student.

Another form among the new-student packet I give everyone is the "Stickman" chart (*see example*). From the outset I tell each student that this chart is the most important documant they now have. I then describe exactly how we will use this chart to mark any identified anatomical positions that need to be improved and give each a priority. This order dictates which issue we will repair first, second, and third. Usually I mark only three on the first visit so my student is not overwhelmed—three is enough to fix over the next six to eight weeks. This order must also help us accomplish the objective the student listed on his/her information sheet.

Next, after developing the Core Archery Form Elements, we compare the student's pictures to that model form. Together we can decide what body parts need repositioning and write instructions as to how to do it. These simple written instructions on the stickman chart become the guide for the student's practice sessions for the next six to eight weeks. It also guides us over the next two hours as we begin to make the corrections listed.

We can also record any bow tuning changes that need to be made or that we actually make during the coaching session. I also make sure that when our session is complete and my student is in proper full-draw-position that we record the True Draw measurement of the bow being used, as well as the ATA standard draw length.

At the end of our coaching/learning session my student is ready to use this form to guide his/her practice sessions. He will know exactly what to work on, how to do it and how to structure a practice session that will enable him to get it done. This form is a vital part of my coaching and should be a part of yours as well.

Chapter 6
Practice with a Purpose

Can you answer these questions?
- Why did you practice last Wednesday?
- What did you accomplish?
- What part of your form did you work on?
- What bow tuning did you do?
- Are you better now than you were two weeks ago?
    And the really big one,
- Why don't you know the answers to the first five questions?

If your student is serious about improving his/her archery skill level then, of course, they know the answers to all of these questions. They know them because they build organized practice sessions and keep records of your progress. They know the "whats" and "whys" for all the practice they do because they have it in a notebook.

A Model Practice Structure
A good practice session has the following parts
- A short warm up/stretching period.
- A blank bale/no sight/no target period.
- A scoring round at least twice a week.
- Bow tuning as needed.
- A practice-ending blank bale session.
- Stretching/cool down.

Let's look at each of these ingredients to see how many arrows need to be shot, what scoring needs to be done and the record keeping needed to hold it together so you keep moving in the right direction.

The Warm Up
Starting cold is your enemy. Starting time is the most likely time you'll injure yourself because your muscles aren't ready to work at their highest efficiency. To shoot your best at tournaments you must practice at your best and that means warming your muscles a little before your first arrow.

I like to take a short walk before practice. Other times I use a rubber exercise band to warm up. There are lots of articles already in print on how to use the stretch band to prepare for practice and tournaments – check them out. Having the discipline to do it is what you have to work on. It's up to you to make it happen.

Blank Bale Practice

This is where real archers are made, in front of a bale with no target, no sight, and a plan. Without a plan of what to work on, blank bale shooting will only build endurance. Your biggest job is to make a plan for each practice session. In fact, you should have a plan for the full week of practice and much longer if you have a tournament to prepare for.

Your plan, of course, must be geared toward form improvement. I find that 98% of my students need to improve their bow hand so I suggest you start with that form element. Of course, to do this you must have your form steps written in a sequential list. If you don't have a list now is the time to write it down in your notebook. If you need help with this please see the list in my book "Core Archery" (2004, Target Communications Corp.).

Build form step-by-step until each step is correct. Build one step correctly (it will take you 20-30 days) and then, and only then, move to the next step. For example, my students working on bow hand position will have a written plan to follow for the first four weeks. That plan will focus on hand position and shooting 30 blank-bale arrows to open each practice session and ten more to end the session – all with intense conscious focus on correctly using the bow hand. During these practices you must focus only on hand position. You must make sure you set your hand properly at the first touch to the grip area. "Feeling" is what you must establish and engrain into your subconscious and it can't be done well while aiming. It is best done while shooting without a bow sight and no target. In fact, you should even practice with your eyes closed to be most effective – don't let your vision distract your conscious guidance of your bow hand.

After three or four weeks of progress you may move to a second form element. It should be the form element next in line in your sequence. Always build in sequence like building a house from the ground up. Build in front of a blank bale.

Thirty to forty arrows are sufficient for a blank bale opening practice. More can be shot after you do bow tuning and shoot a scoring round. High quantity is not your priority here, high quality is.

Scoring Rounds

We practice to get better. And if we practice with purpose we will get better but we won't realize it unless we shoot for score regularly and keep records. Scoring is the ultimate measure we have of our shooting improvement (or decline) so we must have a place for it in our short-term and long-term practice plans.

Indoor archery offers some good standard rounds to use and I'd recommend using one of those when indoor practice is all you can do. For outdoor scoring you can choose ot even invent your own standard round. I like shooting 30 arrows at fifty yards using the NFAA hunter target with a four-inch spot. I also like shooting 36 arrows at fifty meters at a 80cm FITA target. Whatever the round, keep records and when you shoot perfect scores on that round, switch to a longer distance or use a smaller spot.

Practice Log Keep some kind of practice log. It doesn't matter if you make a form like this one or just use a spiral notebook as long as you keep records of what you do in practice. Be sure to begin and end with arrows shot at a blank bale with an objective that helps you improve your one form element. Finish on a good shot if you can, if not quit after a ten at the end – don't continue practicing bad habits. It is okay to just throw in the towel at the end of some practices.

A score doesn't need to be shot every practice session. Two scores a week are sufficient to monitor progress as long as you record the scores honestly. Don't shoot archery the way some guys play golf – they roll the ball into a better position when they're in the fairway and don't record the stroke! Honest practice makes for honest progress.

End-Of-Practice Blank Bale Shooting

Every practice session should end as it began, shooting at a blank bale. You start each session working on a certain form element and when ending that session you once again work on that same element. As before, no target or sight should be used during this practice phase so the desired "feel" of the new skill being learned can be gradually engrained into the subconscious mind. Total focus needs to be placed on that one form element and getting the correct "feel" for it.

This closing phase doesn't need to be long. Ten well-executed shots are sufficient to pass along the muscle actions to the subconscious. I always recommend to my students that if the second or third shot feels really good, then quit. Quit on a good one.

If you get to ten shots and can't get a good one, quit also. It is perfectly acceptable to throw in the towel when it just doesn't feel "right" instead of continuing to practice "bad" feeling shots. Some days just don't go well so quit before you regress and look forward to the next practice with confidence that it will go well and the "good" feel will come to you.

Closing with that "feeling" is important and doing it four or five times a week over twenty days will enable you to learn and retain that new habit. Build your "core form elements" and then you will build your score!

Cool Down

When you're all done shooting arrows you need to stretch your warm muscles before quitting. This can be done with stretch bands or with isometric type stretches. A short walk, run, or bike ride are good ways to deprogram and relax.

Bow Tuning During Each Practice

Testing and tuning can be done before scoring, during scoring, or after but not while shooting at a blank bale. You can make changes to the bow and test it before you score and if the score is significantly worse you'll know to reverse that adjustment and make another tuning change. If your bow is performing better then the score will show it.

Record Keeping

Record keeping is the glue that holds all of your hard work together. Good records, when used, prevent you from wasting time relearning a lesson you learned six months ago. You can't remember everything so write it down. Here's a form I've developed. Feel free to use it and make changes to it to suit your own needs.

Daily Practice Log

Date _____ Bow _____

Objective _____

Distance	# Shots	Score & Comments	Bow Tuning
Blank Bale			
Blank Bale			

Chapter 7
Why We Miss Deer

There's not one bow hunter reading this who hasn't missed a deer or hit one poorly.

Now that we have the facts established let's get on with why we miss. David Letterman has his "Top Ten" every week so, not to be outdone, I have my own. Mine aren't so funny. We don't like missing or wounding deer so use this Top Ten list with your customers to start them on the path to fewer bad shots and more game animals recovered.

The Top Ten Reasons Why We Miss Deer

10 Arrow Rest Dysfunction

"Clink"! That's the sound I used to hear all too often when drawing on a deer. "Clink" is the sound the arrow makes when it falls off the arrow rest. I hate it! It's almost always followed by a "Snort" and a white tail disappearing into the distance. Then I get that heart-sinking feeling of failure and frustration at having blown another chance on a good buck.

You always ask yourself Why? What caused the arrow to fall off the rest this time? The answer was and is always the same: lack of preparation! When my arrow rest–arrow combination failed it was my fault! There was no one else to blame. I know that some of them feel that when that happens to them it's someone else's fault but they are wrong; it's their own fault. It's their own fault because they choose to use the rest as it was and either didn't set it up properly or failed to maintain it properly. They thought it was going to work well forever. After all, the shop tech installed it for them and it worked well last year, and the year before that, and the year before that. Right? So who would think that this year there would be a problem? Never the less, you get the blame.

With the technology available in the arrow rest market today there should be no reason for an arrow to fall off the rest. Today's drop-away style rests, like the QAD *Ultra Rest* (*see photo*) and others like it, are so good that I haven't put my arrow back on the rest one time in the past four years.

As soon as I get into my stand, I nock an arrow onto the bowstring and onto the rest. Then I prop up the rest so the arrow is in the shooting position and trapped in place by the trap-arm over top of the arrow. It never comes off! Ever! This is critical because the hardest part of bow hunting is getting to full draw. That means that the arrow has to stay in place on the rest during the very critical raise-and-draw of the bow while your heart is pounding and the deer is close.

A hunting rest has to be/do all of the following:
- Quiet
- Accurate
- Easy To Maintain
- Hold The Arrow In Place
- Properly Installed

Today's drop-away rests have those functions. You must make sure that they are properly installed with the correct nocking point level so the bottom of the arrow is level or slightly higher. You must set the center-shot adjustment so that the arrow is directly in front of the bowstring.

Then you must check these measurements during your preseason preparation and during the season when the bow is getting constant abuse.

Today's drop-away rests that trap the arrow in an upright shooting position are worth the money. Do your best to convince your customers to buy one because they come without the "Clink!"

#9 Shooting Downhill

You've heard this one, "I can't believe I missed that deer high! He was only twenty-five yards away and I held my 25-yd pin right-on!" This hunter probably made a good shot but most likely failed to compensate for the downhill angle between him and his target. He missed because of a little trigonometry issue that I'm well aware of having taught mathematics for 35 years.

Shooting downhill – or uphill – requires a small compensation in your aiming. You must aim for just the horizontal distance between you and your target and not the distance between your eye and the target. The horizontal distance is always less than the eye-to-target distance . . . always! The shooter in the example here needed to aim for 22, 23, or 24 yards instead of 25-yards depending on the angle of depression (decline). Two or three yards off at 25-yds makes a difference. It makes a difference at 20-yards as well.

Angle-compensating range finders tell you this but they cost $250 or more. Use the range finder you have and range level to the trees around you and not to spots on the ground. Or just subtract a few yards and aim accordingly.

Close shots less than eight yards can result in low misses. When targets are under ten-yards from you then your arrow has not yet climbed up to your line of sight to the target. Remember, your arrow always travels in a parabolic arc where it rises up to and then above the line of sight before falling into the target center. For really close shots you have to know to aim with your 35 or 40-yard pin. The only way to learn how to aim your bow is to practice at 8, 7, 6, 5, 4, 3 and 2-yards. In my own case, to hit the X-ring at four yards I must use my 44-yard pin.

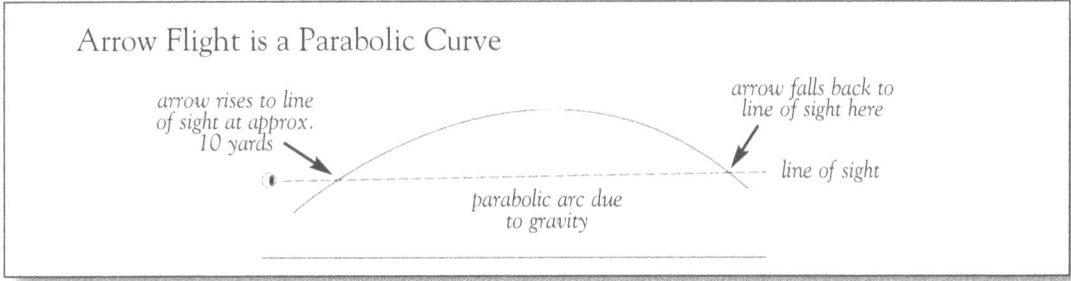

Parabolic Arc *The force of gravity acting on the arrow causes it to fly in a curved path as shown. To hit a target at some distance the arrow must be pointed uphill so it rises up to the level sight line, then above the sight line and when correctly sighted it falls back to the sight line and into the intended target. No arrow (or bullet) flies flat so knowing the distance to the target is essential to hitting it. When the target is less than ten yards away then knowing how to aim/compensate for an arrow below the line of sight requires practice at close range.*

#8 Shooting Lane Clearance

After fifty-three years of bow hunting it finally happened: my arrow hit a branch. Understand that I didn't miss the buck I shot at but by the time the arrow cut off the 3/8″ sapling it had only enough energy to stick the point into the ribs. The deer ran off and I found the arrow about thirty yards down the trail with only a few drops of blood on the tip. I heard the buck stop about sixty yards out and give a big "Snort" of displeasure in my direction. He wasn't very happy and neither was I.

A brief inspection of my shooting lane revealed the cut-off branch end and all of my questions were answered. In simple terms, I just didn't do a thorough job of scoping out the various lanes around me. I looked at several places at first light and should have checked when the light got better but didn't. Lesson learned!

Two things stick in my mind about this. First, I should have done more preseason clearing of that spot. Second, I should have rechecked those lanes during the season and trimmed a few more branches.

At any rate, next time I'll be more thorough and know for sure if the lane is clear. Last, if the lane has any branches in it at all, don't shoot! The rule is as follows: any object that takes up 1% of the space will get hit 99% of the time! Golf is also like this.

#7 Effective Range

Shooting beyond your effective range is a losing proposition every time. The problem is most bow hunters don't know or won't admit to their own personal limited effective range.

Paper Plate *The nine-inch paper plate is a great practice target as it is about the same size as the vital area on a deer's rib cage. I put a dot in the middle of the plate and practice shooting it with my 22-yd pin. At ten and fifteen yards my arrows hit two or three inches high while at 30 yards they hit two or three inches low but always on the plate. I keep it simple with my single sight pin and don't shoot at deer beyond 30 yards.*

Your effective range is the span of distance over which you can shoot at a 9″ paper plate with one pin and hit it. Mine is about thirty yards because I can set a 22-yard pin, aim at the middle of the paper plate and hit it from 5 yards to 30 yards. Beyond 30 yards my 260-fps arrow falls below the plate.

I don't shoot at deer beyond that distance. I range 30-yards around my tree stand and when the deer comes within that circle I aim at the middle of the rib cage and shoot. I don't try to micromanage my process at that point, I keep it simple and effective – one pin in the middle of the rib cage. The arrow may hit a pinch high if the deer is close or a bit low if he's nearly 30 yards away but it will hit the lungs because I'm able to stick to my shot process that I know is consistent. Get cute with your aiming and your muscles will get tense producing a poor shot and a poor hit.

Sound is against you beyond thirty-yards. The speed of sound is about 740 mph or approximately 1100 fps. It takes sound only 0.11 seconds to travel 40 yards or 120 feet. Your arrow traveling at 300 fps will take 0.40 seconds to travel 40 yards. This all means that with a fast arrow the deer still has 0.3 seconds of time to hear the sound and react. Arrows traveling at 260 fps, a more realistic value, will take 0.46 seconds to travel 40 yards giving the deer even more time to disappear. Believe it or not, as long as arrows are slower than sound the bow will remain a primitive weapon! Use it accordingly.

#6 Distance Judging

If you haven't missed a deer high or low then you haven't hunted much. It's going to happen if you hunt.

The first step I take to prevent this is to range a 30-yard perimeter around my tree stand or blind location. As mentioned already, that's my effective range so I have to know it as soon as I get in the stand or as soon as there is enough light to operate my range finder.

Before season I spend time relearning how to estimate 20 and 30 yards from the ground. I also do that from a tree stand because when I get elevated my surroundings look entirely different. Everything looks farther away for some reason and I over-estimate distances so I practice judging from different heights.

Sight pins can be used as a range finder. I have three pins on my own sight arranged so that all three fit onto the deer's body at twenty-five yards. So, if all three pins don't fit on the body I know the deer is most likely out of my range. I often tell hunters at my bow hunting seminars to wait until all of their pins fit on the deer then shoot – you have to hit it because it's close!

Long shots are just not an option for me. I'd sooner wait for another chance at a closer distance. If you do plan to take a long shot over 30 yards then be sure you have the time to take these steps. First, range the deer to the nearest one yard because 43 yards is significantly different than 42 or 44. At that distance a 280 fps arrow is dropping 14 inches between forty and fifty-yards.

Second, the deer must be standing still – and stay still for at least twenty seconds while you range the distance, raise and draw your bow. Then, third, you have to aim and execute your best shot.

The odds are against you. Consider also the fact that sound is working against you and your chances of making the shot are near zero. I like luck to be on my side when I'm shooting targets but I can't ethically rely on it when I'm shooting deer at long range. Long, empty-ended blood trails are far down the list of things I like to do. Passing the shot is the better choice.

#5 Peep & Pin Visibility

I'll tell a story on my good friend Les who came to hunt with me for the first time seven years ago. I have enough property to put out about eight good stands so I gave Les my best one – not too high with good deer traffic.

The very first morning a buck came by on the lower side of the stand. Les took a shot. We named that one "Old Scarback" and still talk about him today. That evening he missed a doe. Needless to say Les was disappointed and a bit apologetic.

The next day we checked over his bow setup and discovered the root of his problem – a small-holed target peep. Les couldn't see! The small hole wasn't letting enough light through so he could clearly make out his sight pins. After removing the peep from the bowstring I used a 3/16″ drill bit to correct the problem. That evening he made an excellent shot on the first doe that crossed by his stand.

The peep housing I use for hunting is a *Super Peep* by Specialty Archery. It's the same one I use for target except that I remove the screw-in peep aperture entirely leaving a nearly ¼″ hole. Through this hole I can see the outer ring of my sight-pin housing and can center it inside my peep when I aim. After that I can choose any pin and have good accuracy.

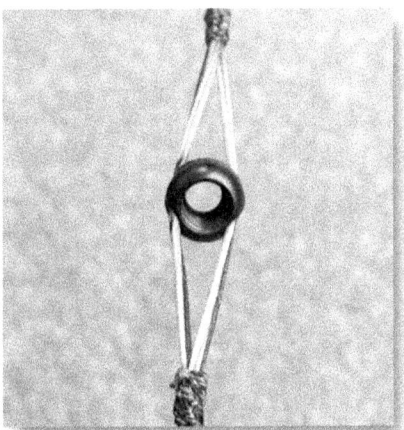

Big-Hole Peep *Use a big hole peep sight for hunting so you can see when the light conditions are poor. A big hole reduces accuracy slightly but you can get that back by using a white-ring around your sight housing. Center the white ring in the peep hole and then pick the pin you need to make the shot (you must practice this at home). I find that three fiber optic pins with a light for after sunset is the best combination for making shots in low light. If you can't see a lighted fiber optic pin then it's time to get out of the woods.*

Fiber optic pins make a world of difference. I was sorting out an old box of parts the other day and came across some old metal sight pins. They had white paint on the ends – that was high-tech back in 1978 when I used them. Today you have your choice of a hundred different kinds of fiber optic pins that are visible after sunset. Some have lights that shine on them so there is no excuse for you to not see your pins.

The main problem I have with the sights that bowhunters use today is they have too many pins. I have no idea how a guy can use five or six pins on his hunting bow unless he's going after mule deer in wide open country. Three is more than enough for white tail deer and makes aiming less stressful because you have fewer decisions to make. One pin is enough for most folks while some hunters shouldn't be allowed to have more than that – you know the ones I'm talking about! The fewer decisions a hunter has to make while under duress the better – make it complicated for yourself and you'll surely fail at "crunch time."

And another thing, if you hunters are using a battery-operated lighted sight be sure to carry an extra battery. Can you tell that this is "experience" talking here? Been there, done that, didn't have an extra battery!

#4 Buck Fever

The "shakes," the "choke," "buck fever," or whatever else you call it affects lots of hunters every year. Some never get over it and just quit hunting. I remember having it so bad when I was a teen that my knees were actually knocking together – if it had been any worse I'd have been changing my pants.

I still get that rush of adrenaline when a buck comes my way. The rush is why we continue chasing deer, turkey, elk, bear or whatever. We go hunting because it holds our interest and gets our heart pumping but when it pumps too hard we can't seem to function well enough to make the shot. So, how do we deal with it?

My tournament shooting has helped me learn how to deal with my "nerves". Notice that I didn't say "eliminate" them because if you eliminate the nerves then you'll stop hunting – you just won't care anymore! I deal with it by knowing how to breathe! Yes, you read that correctly, breathing gets you through the tough spots in tournaments and in the woods.

What happens to most people when they get excited is they tense all of their muscles. Tensed muscles in your neck, chest and gut areas restrict your breathing – constricted muscles make you breathe shallow and in the top half of your lungs only. You tend to suck in your gut and fill the top of your lungs with air – that's only about half a breath or less.

Shooting hundreds of tournaments taught me how to recognize this constriction and deal with it. As soon as I recognize my shallow breathing I now know to inhale while expanding my gut and lowering my diaphragm, thereby filling the lower half of my lungs with air first. Next, I can fill the top of my lungs by inhaling more while expanding my chest. Now I have lungs completely filled with air and the maximum amount of oxygen being extracted from that air.

Two really important things happen at this point. First and foremost my muscles are now getting a full supply of oxygen instead of a half-supply. Oxygenated muscles act more like they do in practice and will, therefore, produce a shot sequence more like your practice shots. This is a good thing if you practiced correct form during the weeks leading up to and throughout the season.

The second thing that happens when you focus on your breathing is you get your mind back in the present. You breathe in the present and so consciously engaging in the breathing activity is a good thing. If your conscious mind is already seeing this big buck hanging on the game pole – a future result - then it's not likely to happen. You have to shoot the arrow in the present and you can't do that if your conscious mind is somewhere else. By the same token, your conscious may be thinking about that buck you missed several days ago or the target panic issues you've had and once again is not in the present where you must shoot your arrow. Keeping your mind present process thinking is how you succeed in tournaments and in bow hunting when it's time to make the shot. Follow this rule:

$$O_2 \text{ (In)} + CO_2 \text{ (Out)} \rightarrow \text{Good Shots Released !}$$

#3 Proper Full-Draw-Position

"Whaaacckkk!" That's not the sound you want to hear. That's an arrow that has hit too much bone. That's the sound you hear when your broadhead hits shoulder or hip bone. And that isn't good! It's usually followed by lots of tracking and eventual loss of the blood trail – and no deer.

The culprit is most likely poor posture at full draw. I'm certain of this because of all the hundreds and hundreds of students that I've worked with over the years, most of them (70%) have bows with draw length settings that are too short. What this means then is they are holding their bows with their arms and not transferring the holding into their back muscles.

Full-Draw-Position Get your drawing/holding arm in line with the arrow. This posture allows you to hold with your back muscles instead of your arm and thereby get a smoother release. Arm holding makes a followthrough out to the side and causes left-right misses. Set your posture correctly as shown and then make the bow fit you and you'll get consistent results on your first shot.

Holding your bow at full draw with tensed arm muscles results in right or left arrow impacts. A quick look at an archer "set up short" shows you exactly what I mean. The holding arm is not in line behind the arrow, it's outside that line. Failure to rotate the holding forearm in line with the arrow requires that your forearm and upper arm muscles must remain contracted and do the holding. Therefore, releasing from this position yields a release hand followthrough that is outward to the right and not directly away from behind the arrow. The results of this followthrough style are arrows that impact left or right of the intended target. In other words you hit the deer in the shoulder or the rump!

Proper full-draw-position requires a bow having its draw length set long enough so that the holding forearm is in line with the arrow. This position allows you to transfer the holding force into your back muscles thereby relaxing your forearm. The result is a proper followthrough with the release hand escaping straight away from behind the arrow with no left/right influence.

#2 Release Technique

"Whoooooosssshhhh!" Yep, you just missed one completely! The arrow sailed right over the deer's back . . . again! It happens all too often according to my friend Danny who does some guiding . . . and tracking . . . late at night! That's also my conclusion from talking with many of my students and seeing them shoot their first few arrows.

The overwhelming majority of the misses and bad hits that Danny's hunters experience are high – either over the back or in the spine. The spine-hit deer are easy to find but then the unpleasant task of killing them has to be completed. The complete misses are no problem but the other high hits must be tracked. It's frustrating for both the hunter and guide.

Danny and I have discussed this often and come to the same conclusion. The blame for the high shots lies with the release technique. It lies first with how the release aid is held and then on how the shot develops after the archer reaches full draw.

Here's the deal. Most bowhunters, about 90%, use an index finger style trigger release aid. That's not the problem. The problem begins when the bowhunter holds the release aid and places the tip of his/her index finger on the trigger. That's no fault of their own, that's just what they see being done by most everyone they know and by most of the bowhunters on the TV shows. They're just doing what seems to be the most common thing and, therefore, must be the "best" way to hold the release. After all, that's how they operate the trigger on their guns!

There's a better way. Touching the most sensitive fingertip to the trigger connects the conscious mind to the trigger. Your mind connects to your index fingertip hundreds of times every day when you touch something. You know when something is smooth, rough, sharp, cold, or hot as soon as your fingertip makes contact with it.

Finger Around the Trigger Wrap your index finger around the trigger and you'll shoot more consistently. Don't use the sensitive fingertip that draws your conscious thinking to the trigger. Instead, establish back muscle holding, then, as you increase that holding tension, also gently tighten all of your release hand fingers. Tighten both your back and your fingers until the release aid discharges – don't give up your back control until the arrow hits the target. Back muscle control on your dominant side is the key to consistent shooting on all of your shots, especially the first.

The problem with touching the release aid trigger is we don't want to be consciously connected to the release of the arrow. If we are thinking about the trigger or the release moment then we anticipate it and our body develops unwanted and harmful reactions to it. For instance, our bow hand is not disconnected from the release event and if we consciously know when we're setting off the trigger so does the bow hand and it may react at the instant of release, before it happens or just after it happens – none of these is a good thing.

Therefore, don't touch the fingertip to the trigger. Surround the trigger with your index finger. Completely surround it up to the second crease of your finger which is far less sensitive to "touch" than the tip. Touch both the side of the release barrel as well as the trigger – it's called full-contact archery! Curl the other fingers as well so that at full draw you can gently tighten all fingers in order to set off the release aid and avoid the conscious focus on a single point.

Something else has to happen first. Before you gently tighten your release fingers you must build your body into proper full-draw-position so you can hold the force of the bow with your draw-side back muscles. Once you establish this holding contraction in your back muscles you must then gently increase it until the release occurs. This back contraction has to start first and then be joined by the fingers. The release arm remains relaxed. Continued gentle tightening of both back muscles and finger muscles will cause enough trigger movement to set off the release aid and discharge the bowstring. Your conscious is focused on the "tightening" process and the actual release occurs totally outside of your conscious thought. In other words, if you're not consciously involved you can't screw it up!

#1 The Top Reason We Miss Deer Is . . . The Bow Hand

About 99% of the students that come to me for coaching must learn to properly place their bow hand on the bow. Notice that I did not say grip the bow. The "grip" is a section of the bow handle where you place your hand and not an action that you do with your hand. Nevertheless, most archers grip the bow handle in some way or another and pay the consequences during the fifteen-thousandths (0.015) of a second that it takes the bowstring to propel the arrow out of the bow.

The instant that the bowstring becomes free from the release aid is when torque

Bow Hand This is the root of most accuracy problems. Don't "grip" your bow handle – in fact, refuse to grip it and your bow will do its job with greater reliability. Place only your thumb pad on the bow grip as shown by the tape strip. Use a wrist or bow sling to prevent the bow from falling out of your hand and be sure to rotate your knuckles to a 45-degree angle to the handle so your relaxed thumb can point to the target.

force in the bow hand affects the bow handle. This is not a good thing because it's so very inconsistent – gripping is very difficult to repeat. Every shot has a different hand tension or torque force and produces different results.

Since the bow hand is the first body part to touch the bow handle and the last to be still touching it as the arrow is launched we had better get it correct at first touch. It's vitally important to your shooting success – get it right and you take the biggest step of all to getting consistent arrow groupings in the target. Get the bow hand correct and you'll make that "first" shot count every time!

Without your bow, raise your bow arm and hand to the target and make a "Stop Sign." Be sure your knuckles are at a forty-five degree angle to the bow and then relax your fingers and thumb. The bow hand is now ready to correctly receive the bow's grip section.

This hand position places only the thumb pad on the bow grip section. I prefer to have a flat spot on my bow grips to receive my thumb pad (the thenar eminence). The bow handle is now directly in front of the radius bone in your forearm. Our radius bone should be in line with the humerus bone in the upper arm so that together they can resist the load of the bow at full draw – like a stick. It's less about the hand and more about the in-line arm bones.

Vertically aligned knuckles that go with a gripping bow hand will rotate the inside of the forearm into the path of the bowstring. This can yield a painful lesson and a big welt on your forearm – I've seen some really ugly ones!

Your fingers must be relaxed from the first touch of the hand onto the bow. Your whole hand should start relaxed and stay relaxed throughout the remainder of the shot process. If you start with tension in your hand or let that tension build as you draw the bow then you'll have to make your hand relax at full draw and that is a "no repeat" situation. You won't be able to do that the same way for two shots in succession. Hunting is a first-shot situation so refuse to grip your bow and start getting reliable effective shots every time.

The results from an improper bow hand are erratic. Some impact left and others to the right if you're torquing the bow – rotating it left or right. Other arrows hit low or high if you're high- or low-wristing the bow grip. Use the relaxed hand and you'll create the best chance you have to repeat your hand placement. From the start, set it correctly and relaxed and keep it that way during the draw and you'll hit that first shot.

Conclusion

If you can get your bowhunting students to fix just one of these ten issues then you've done something important. Copy this list and put it out for everyone to read. Force it on them – we'll all appreciate it and so will they when their success rate goes up.

Chapter 8
Aiming Better

Successful archery requires aiming skill. It doesn't matter if you're shooting the Vegas Tournament, 3-D World Championships, or shooting in your backyard. You must have the complete package of form, vision, and concentration all blended together to enable you to reach your archery scoring potential.

As a coach or archer you will hear many archers say, "I wish I could aim better!" So here's part of the answer you can give those who are willing to listen . . . and hear. This article presents the necessary prerequisite ingredients it takes to aim better including some mental focus skills.

Please note that at no time do I discuss or advocate "aiming perfectly." Trying to aim perfectly builds unnecessary mental and muscle tension which inhibit one's ability to hit the target center. In fact, good form enables you to be relaxed so the sight "floats gently" and that's the secret to aiming better and scoring higher.

On the subject of aiming better your first job as a coach is to teach motivated archers how to improve their body position. This ingredient, once developed and practiced, will lead them to have a more stable and relaxed body position and that is the first requirement for better aiming.

Aiming and Sighting

There's a difference between aiming and sighting. Aiming begins first. Sighting joins the aiming process after you get to full draw. Here's a pair of definitions for you:

Aiming is the act of acquiring and maintaining eye contact with the intended target spot.

Sighting occurs when you involve a reference device(s) like a sight pin, arrow point, scope and/or a peep sight within your aiming.

To do it right you should always begin aiming before sighting and continue doing aiming well after the arrow has been released. I train myself and teach my students to visually acquire the center of the target in Step 5 of their form, which is just before they raise their bow. Visual acquisition is then followed by constant visual contact throughout the remainder of your form steps until the arrow impacts the target.

Sighting begins later, when the archer reaches full-draw-position when the bow sight slides into view in front of the archer's aiming eye. The sight apparatus is placed in line with the archer's line of sight while his eye's focus remains on the target.

You need to be able to draw and establish full-draw-position without losing visual contact with the spot. If your bow's draw weight is too heavy to allow this then lower the draw weight. If you lose visual contact on the target for any reason you'll need to make changes to draw length, peep size, peep location, sight aperture and maybe the prescription of your glasses.

Once you reach your full-draw-position you must slide your sight device into your sight line to the target spot. Don't look to the sight and then try to reacquire the spot, as this tends to realign your body away from your aiming line. Just slide the sight into your established aiming sightline.

When you're aiming and sighting you have both your body and your bow unit synchronized. You are visually and physically focused on the small spot you desire to hit.

Finish the shot by doing what you do to execute the release of the bowstring. Hopefully, you use back tension and during this execution you never lose visual connection to your target. Aiming continues during and after the release moment and long after the sight has fallen out of view. It ends when the arrow falls into your view of the target center and your followthrough has been completed. Looking away earlier will move your head and other body parts that in turn affect the shot.

Aiming Better

Five conditions that affect your ability to aim are:
- Body Position
- Bow Fit
- Sight picture
- Physical conditioning and
- Practice
- Conscious Mental State.

Optimizing these conditions will enable you to aim better and thereby improve your scores and establish that first-shot accuracy you need for all forms of archery. We'll look at each of these in turn.

Body Position Establishing the proper body position can improve your ability to relax which in turn can improve your steadiness. Proper full-draw-position demands that you have erect posture. That means that your shoulders are level, bow arm extended, elbow straight and bow hand relaxed. Your head must be erect and directly

Head and Shoulders Stand erect and allow the bones of your bow arm to resist the force of the bow by putting them in line. This allows most of your arm muscle to relax. In-line leg bones support your body all day so arm bones should have no trouble resisting the force of the drawn bow. Maintain your shoulders so that a line across their tops points to the target.

over your spine with your chin level so that your back muscles can be better used for back tension and not used to hold up your head.

You must have a straight drawing wrist and relaxed forearm and upper arm. You must carry the draw load of the bow with your back muscles not your arm muscles. As mentioned before, the best full-draw-position places your forearm in line with the arrow shaft.

The Core Archery form model that I teach has all of these attributes. With them you can get optimum performance from your body because you are using your skeleton to its best advantage. If you are doing it right you will carry most of the load with your skeleton while most of your muscles relax.

Bow Fit Draw length, draw weight, and grip compatibility affect how the bow fits you. You must be sure to make the proper adjustments to all of them in order to optimize your biomechanical position and, therefore, aiming.

Bow Arm A major part of full-draw-position is your bow arm. To maximize use of your bone structure you must line up the bones of your upper and lower bow arm so they can resist the force of the drawn bow. Elsewhere in your body this alignment technique works quite well for your leg bones as they support your upper body weight all day long as you walk and stand. It takes far less muscle to align the bones than it does to hold your legs in a bent-knee position or your bow arm in a bent-elbow form. Set the draw length of your bow to allow proper arm bone alignment.

Release/Drawing Arm Another major component is the drawing arm position. Proper draw length will place your drawing forearm in line with the arrow shaft. If the forearm is not drawn far enough to allow your elbow to rotate into this position then increase the draw length of your bow. If your drawing arm/elbow is rotated beyond the arrow line, shorten the draw length of the bow. Adjust the bow so you can put your arm/elbow in this optimum position to transfer the bow-holding force from your forearm muscles into the muscles of your back. A relaxed forearm is yields the best release technique.

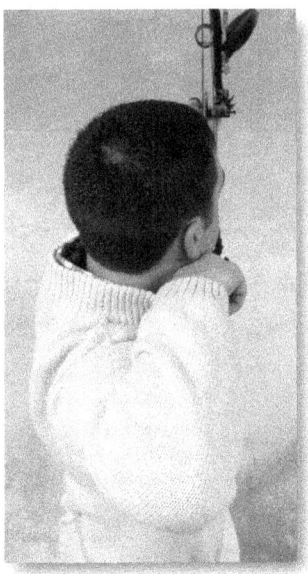

Full-Draw-Position *At full draw your drawing forearm (top view) should be in line with the arrow shaft. In this position your back muscles are able to receive the transfer of holding weight from the drawing arm. With your holding arm relaxed, your aiming gets steadier and your release consistency increases.*

Draw length can be adjusted by using string anchor pins, cable anchor pins, D-loop length, and adding or deleting twists from your bowstring or cables. You may also have a rotating module that allows for adjustments. Switching one-inch modules is not a bad idea either, as it will tell you rather quickly if you're on the correct module before you make fine adjustments.

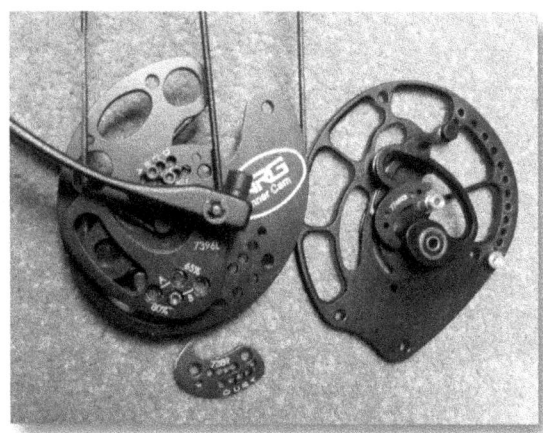

Modules *Draw length adjustment modules make it easy to change the draw length in one-inch or one-half inch increments. Rotating modules are even easier to use when properly fitting a bow to a customer.*

If you have to make a shorter or longer string to change draw length then do it. Spending time here is a must if you expect to take full advantage of your skeleton and use it to produce good form. Once again, I repeat, that without proper body position you can't transfer the "holding force" into your back muscles.

Adjust your bow's draw weight and test the setting by drawing your bow while seated in a chair. Start high or low and make small adjustments until you find your upper and lower limits. Don't let the bow dictate to you what you have to do with your form. If you can't shoot 70 pounds (I can't) then don't force it upon yourself. Set a comfortable weight and select a weaker arrow spine/size to match that weight. I'm reminded here of my favorite quote by Wyatt Earp, "Fast is fine, but accuracy is final." Shoot the draw weight that allows you to be accurate.

When you get draw length set to match proper arm position and your draw weight is manageable you'll find that your aiming ability improves. If you are using your skeleton to do most of the work then you are using less muscle. Less muscle involvement makes you more comfortable – more comfort produces better relaxation and that translates to better aiming.

Bow Hand Placement How your hand fits the grip area of the handle is of great importance. Present your bow hand toward the target like a "stop" sign. This arranges your knuckles at a forty-five degree angle to the bow. Now, relax your fingers and thumb so they don't grip the handle, just place your thumb pad on it. A relaxed hand is the easiest to repeat and delivers the least torque to the handle. In other words, your relaxed hand also allows the bow to repeat its action. Note here that when properly placed your thumb will point to the target.

If the bow grip section does not fit the hand properly then change it. Reshape it, make a new one or buy an after-market grip that fits you so you can place your relaxed hand (thumb pad only) onto the grip with comfort. Comfort promotes the relaxed hand position during the shot that is vital to your success. I prefer a narrow flat grip section so I can establish pressure between the bow grip and my thumb pad and thumb pad only!

Sight Picture When you both aim and sight, eye performance reaches its maximum level. This performance level involves placing a front sight and a peep sight in line between your eye and the target. With these three at different distances only one can be in focus. "Which one?" is the question you have to deal with and how you answer it can make aiming more or less difficult.

The first principle of aiming is:

Your best chance of hitting a target occurs when you are looking at it.

Sounds simple, doesn't it? But to understand it fully you have to define "looking at it." My definition is to focus your vision on the target surface and not your sight pin or scope reticle.

My setup has always been to use the "circle" aiming reticle for target shooting. My eye tends to center the aiming ring with the scoring rings on the target allowing my eye to focus on the target spot. I can see through the circle reticle to the target and maintain that focus through the release of the arrow and beyond.

Reticules *Test several types of sight reticules to find which shape and color gives you a relaxed view and best focus of the target center. Squinting leads to face tightness which, in turn, leads to neck and shoulder tightness. Get relaxed and stay relaxed when aiming and sighting.*

At any rate, you need to find the reticle that puts your eye at ease while you're aiming. Eye tension can lead to squinting, contorting your face muscles, and eventually to tightening neck and shoulder muscles. Reduce eye tension by using the reticle that allows you to relax your eyes and enables you to focus easily on the target spot.

Some factors to consider are the size and color of your aiming reticle, whether it's a circle or a dot, the magnification power of your lens, the housing diameter of your scope/pin sight, the distance between the sight and your eye, distance of the peep from your eye, size of the hole in your peep sight, and the hat you wear to shade your eyes. You must experiment with all of these to find what works best for you in all light conditions.

Cooler colors like blue and green work better for those like me who are far-sighted. After learning this I switched my scope-aiming ring to green or yellow with good success. Near-sighted folks may see the hotter colors better. Experiment to learn what is best for you.

Physical Conditioning

If your heart is pounding at 150 beats-per-minute it's difficult to aim. If you're breathing so fast you can barely draw your bow then it's also difficult to aim. So what do you do? My answer is "get in shape" for archery by doing a few simple but effective exercises.

Walking One of the best activities is walking. Making the time to walk two miles every other day, about 30 minutes, is the difficult part. In fact, if you can walk five days a week you'd be better fit for life in general and your archery would also improve. Getting your pulse and respiration under control will give you great confidence at the beginning or end of any competitive round.

If you are able, elevate your walking to some mixed treadmill walking and running. Or you could work out on a stationary bike. This training, taking just 30 minutes three or four times a week, will improve your heart and respiration rates while not pounding your legs and back like running on a road surface does. Obviously, you can do the stationary bike and treadmill regardless of the weather outside.

Stretch Bands I have a set of four stretch bands that I train with daily. I keep them on my work table in my archery room so I am reminded to actually pick them up and workout with them. If I store them out of sight I forget to use them. Keep them visible and use them regularly.

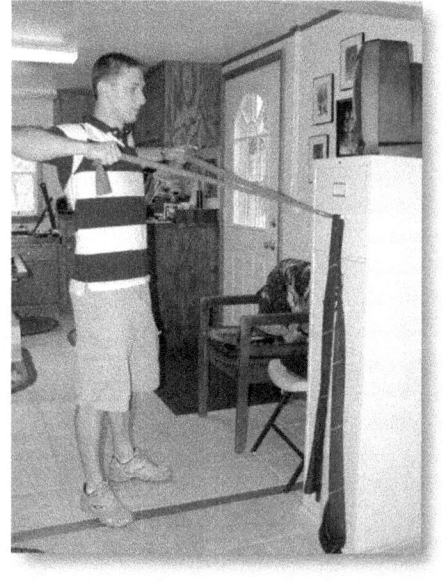

If you have a file cabinet you can hook your bands through the handles and begin your workout. I do pulling-type exercises using the three different handle levels on my file drawers. I face the cabinet for some and then face away for others. You can stand on the band and do upward presses and arm extensions for others. If you have a ceiling hook you can do pull-downs. This is a great way to loosen those old muscles before you start shooting every day.

Pulling Arrows Pulling arrows with your bow arm is a great exercise. In two or three weeks you can significantly increase the strength in your bow arm, shoulder and oblique abs by pulling arrows with that side. Just remember to contract all of those muscles when pulling and not just your arm muscles; using more of your body makes the task easier and conditions more muscles.

Drawing Your Bow Another simple exercise that yields great results is drawing with your non-dominant side or bow arm. Start with a stretch band and draw it a few times before and after each practice session. Gradually you'll be able to increase that to twenty draw strokes before and after practice. When you've built your strength significantly you will be able to draw your bow with that side.

Walking Stick Exercises While you're walking you can do some upper body exercises with a walking stick. Cut a stick about 80% of your body height and 1.5 – 2.0 inches in diameter. It can be thicker at one end if you like or you can use a long shovel handle or a broomstick. While walking I focus on strengthening my bow arm side while stretching and extending my drawing side. You can practice your golf swing as well.

Practice

Most of you practice on a target to build stamina but there's much more to practice than that. In practice you must spend time consciously micro-managing each individual form element, like bow hand position, so that it becomes a habit run by your subconscious mind.

The best way to do this is to stand three yards from a blank target butt. Close your eyes thereby removing any visual distractions from your conscious mind. Then, through the course of shooting 30 arrows for each of twenty days (average human learning time) your subconscious mind will take control over the physical action making it a learned habit. When this occurs with one of your form elements then move to another that needs improving. Through time (months) you will build up each and every form element you need and make yourself a better archer and a better aimer.

Without this blank bale practice you won't improve your form. Introduce this vital practice component into your training regimen – and keep there.

Your Conscious Mind

Aiming better requires better focus of your conscious mind on the proper objective for your shot. When I ask my archery students what their shot objective is most of them – about 70% - tell me that they want to "hit the X" in the target. I beg to differ.

Focusing on the arrow "hitting the X" means that you are focusing on a future event/result. The fact of the matter is that we must execute the shot "in the present." To achieve high level athletic performance we must, therefore, use present process thinking.

We have to be consciously engaged with our shooting process during the time that our body is making the shot. If our conscious thought is in the past, the future or somewhere else then how will the shot process be repeated or even performed once correctly? The fact is that it can't be consistently performed without conscious focus on it and commitment to it.

The process thought that gets the best results for the longest period of time is "executing this shot with back tension."

Using back tension to generate the release of the arrow is important because of the thoughts you don't have while aiming and executing. Many archers are caught in the circumstance of consciously thinking about touching the trigger at the time of release and, therefore, lose conscious contact with their objective process centered in their back – their conscious is distracted to the trigger. Proficiency with back tension keeps your conscious mind in the present and engaged in the process that produces good shots. If your mind is focused on what it takes to make the shot then it won't/can't be focused on other things like the "trigger" or what happened on the previous shot.

It requires some time, several seconds, to complete the shot using back tension and during this time the conscious mind must maintain focus on this process. Any interference will bring about a conflict of interest and result in failure to execute the shot properly. Remember the following proverb: "Man who chases two rabbits catches neither." Chase one rabbit only – back tension.

If you maintain this one goal of "executing this shot with back tension" then you are more likely to attain that goal. During this time your aiming will get steadier and more consistent – your aiming will float gently on the target center section. It may never get perfectly still but it will get better. It most always will not be perfect so we must get comfortable with establishing a "good" aim and rely on our body position and our form to get the job done because form is more important than aiming. Good form produces repeat performances.

Summary

To aim consistently steady you need the whole package body: mind and bow. If any one of these is deficient then aiming falters. As a coach you have to promote this "package" deal to your students who want to aim better. Yep, a good bow can help but that alone will not complete the deal so encourage all of your archers to also improve their form, sight picture, physical condition, practice routine and mental focus.

Section 4
Implementing Plans of Correction

The topics in this section are all designed to help you "help your student" implement their plans of correction. The more you know about how to properly execute each form element the better you will be able to help your student.

If you know how to stand at full draw in order to get the most from your body, the more you can help your student do the same. The same is true for your student's stance, bow hand, and release hand.

Some of your students will face difficulties with their release aid. I call that Release Dysfunction and have developed a sequence of steps to help them develop what I call Release Aid Management Skills (RAM Skills). Of course, part of that is that a bow fits properly. The topics of this chapter help you learn more about those skills.

The more knowledge you acquire about these issues the better able you will be to help your students implement their plans of correction.

Chapter 9
The Compound Bow Stance

Really good field archers do two things exceptionally well: first, they place their bodies in proper full-draw-position and, second, they stay focused on the present while properly executing a shot. Pairing these two skills enables them to stay relaxed so in tournaments they can shoot more like they do in practice. Using both their biomechanics and their mind to full capacity enables the better archers to get that "repeat" performance we are all looking for and keep it working during a tournament.

Upper Body Position
Now, if you plan to use the present-process-thinking objective of "executing this shot with back tension" then you'll be concerned about getting your upper body in the best possible position for using the required back muscles. Proper posture at full draw is essential to using your skeleton to its best advantage thereby allowing most of your muscles to relax which in turn results in your steadiest aim and most consistent release.

Therefore, in this chapter we will be going a little deeper on stances. Yes, on stance. Using your skeleton properly begins when you stand properly. How you connect yourself to the ground affects every step of form that follows and that makes your stance really important. You must know your full-draw-position so you can "set your stance" to best achieve that position.

In fact, the first eight form elements that I teach are all evaluated by how well they enable you to establish full-draw-position and execute your shot with back tension.

We don't build a single form element independent of the other form elements or independent of the final desired objective. Your beginning form elements must relate to and prepare for your full-draw-position and to your final shot objective "executing this shot with back tension". If a particular action prior to the release doesn't set up your full-draw-position and also promote back tension then it must be altered so it does . . . . or eliminated.

Building a Base Scaffold
It is likely that you have an intuitive understanding that your upper body stability will best be served by a steady and sturdy base. After all, most of you work on your feet for some part of the day and know that proper leg use reduces fatigue. With proper leg use you can stand or walk for hours and effectively get your work done.

All day, every day, you rely on your leg bones to hold your body upright. You don't use a lot of leg muscle. You only use enough small muscle groups to keep your leg bones lined up so they support your body weight. In archery, you use your leg bones to build the scaffold for your upper body and a few back muscles to hold the force of the bow. A properly erected base scaffold will promote sound upper body archery technique.

Here's a simple test to try: stand for a few minutes with your knees slightly bent. Tired yet? You get the picture quickly with this test because bent knees recruit most of your leg muscles and after only two minutes fatigue sets in.

Feature 1 Stance Spread

Leg bones and how we position them are the first step to achieving proper execution with back tension. You have to get this part correct from the beginning or your success will be limited. Build the scaffold too narrow and the top will teeter-totter back and forth. Build it too wide and it places too much stress on your lower back and also recruits more muscle to hold the position.

How far you spread your feet, distribute your weight and how you angle your torso relative to the target are the main features of the form element called stance. Following is what I teach beginners, as well as advanced archers.

Determining spread is easily taught using the beginners "T" body position. Stand with your heels together, eyes closed and arms raised to form the archer's "T" as illustrated. In this position it takes only a few seconds to feel your body swaying back and forth. When your heels are together you must use lots of small leg muscles to keep your balance – it's close to the feel you get when standing on just one foot.

Repeat the closed eye "T" position again. This time after a few seconds spread your feet to hip width. You should immediately feel most of your leg muscles relax and the wobbling dissipate. At this point you can experiment with different spread distances – from ten inches to eighteen inches – to find what feels most comfortable, most stable and allows your body core to be most steady.

T Form Spread *Spreading your feet to hip width while standing in this "T" position demonstrates how many leg muscles can be relaxed while maintaining stability. Try this little test for yourself and you'll know what I mean and then be willing to pass it along to your students.*

You can bend your knees for a few seconds to remind yourself about leg bone alignment. Repeating a point made earlier, the leg bones should be in line so they are supporting the weight of your upper body. To keep them in line requires only a few small muscles and there's no need to "lock" your knees, use just enough small muscle groups to keep the bones in line. Therefore a quality stance will have feet spread to a "comfortable" stable width, leg bones lined up and most of your leg muscles relaxed.

Feature 2 **Stance Angle To The Target**

The second aspect of stance is body presentation to the target. At what angle to the target do you want your hips, chest and shoulders so that you can aim most effectively inline with the target center?

Even/Square Stance The even or square stance aligns the feet so that the toes are even with a line to the target. A line through your shoulders will be parallel to this line as would the line through your hips.

Open Stance The open stance for right-handers presents more of your hips and chest to the target by setting the target-side foot a short distance from the straight line to the target. Your toes would touch a line that is angled about ten degrees to the left of the target.

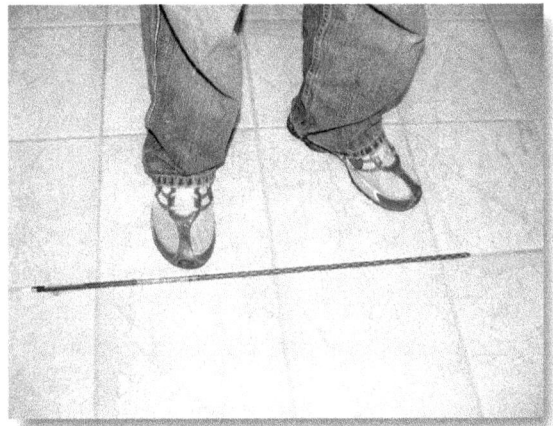

Open Stance The most commonly used stance turns your hips slightly towards the target or "open" to the target. This right-hander shows how your left foot is pulled several inches away from the line to the target to form the open stance. Most archers find that their upper body wants to hold this position naturally even when they close their eyes for eight or ten seconds at full draw.

Closed Stance Moving your release-side foot away from the line to the target will point your chest slightly away from the target or close it relative to the target. Your toes would touch a line that is pointed about ten-degrees to the right of the target.

What's correct for you when shooting a compound bow? Determining the presentation angle that is most effective for you is vital to your success. The upper body must be calm, steady and stable over the top of the hips and feet if aiming is to be high quality and if you are going to execute back tension effectively. You should not be working against your natural upper-body position over your hips. Instead, find it, embrace it and put it to work for you.

There are many techniques for finding one's natural upper body over-the-feet position. One simple method is raise, draw, and aim your bow at a target. While aiming, close your eyes and after a count of eight open them. Note any left/right drift away from the target - up or down is not important. A closed-eye right-drift (right-handed archer) indicates the need to open your stance slightly while a left-drift indicates a need to close your stance a little.

When the correction is made in your stance then open-eye aiming can be maintained without fighting against any natural drift. Less fight against unseen forces will help make aiming steadier. Note that I didn't say "dead still" because that's not always possible and may be an unrealistic expectation that elevates muscle tension instead of reducing it.

For more advanced shooters I have another test. Place five indoor target spots in a horizontal row across the target butt at 20 yards. Spread them so that they are about 18 inches from the far left to the far right spot. Set your stance position for the center spot and begin shooting from twenty yards.

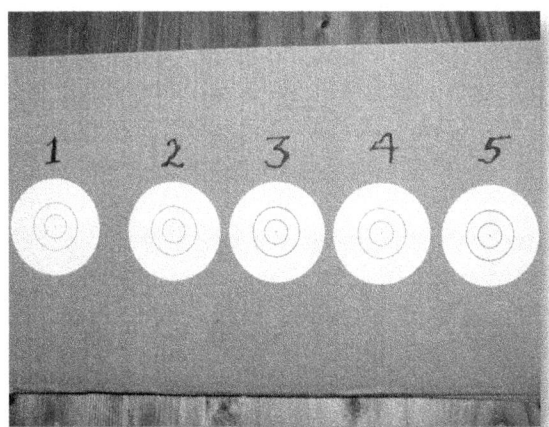

Five Spot Test *Place five aiming spots in a horizontal line as shown. Using an even stance, shoot some practice ends each day for four or five days. Shoot left-to-right sometimes and right-to-left other times. Notice if you shoot any particular spot or spots better than others. I found that I shot the right-most spot better, which indicated that I was shooting best when my hips were more open to the target.*

Shoot some ends left-to-right, others right-to-left and some in random order. Save the target and repeat this test for two or three days and then examine the target to find which spot of the five you are shooting the best. After my shoulder surgery a few years ago this test showed me that I needed a more open stance because the spot on the far right showed the best grouping in the X-ring. If you shoot one of the end spots best, try adding another spot at that end and retest yourself. Maybe that spot is even better.

Feature 3 **Left/Right Weight Distribution**

I recommend distributing your body weight equally on each foot whenever possible. That means in your proper full-draw-position you will support 50% of your body weight on each foot unless physical challenges dictate otherwise.

Standing with one foot on each of two scales will verify your weight distribution. You can also have a friend tell you if you are standing with good vertical alignment and distributing your weight equally. Have your friend take a picture showing your back and, therefore, your vertical alignment.

Feature 4 **Toe/Heel Weight Distribution**

The final stance consideration is your forward weight distribution onto the "balls" of your feet. I am most challenged shooting field targets with my toes pointed uphill. It's the most uncomfortable feeling for me as my body wants to fall over backward constantly when I'm at full draw. To compensate I wear hiking shoes which have a slightly higher heel than my cross-training shoes placing 55-60% of my weight forward on my feet and only 40-45% on my heels.

Weight-forward is more stable as your toes are on that end of your feet and help you maintain your balance. Pitching your upper body slightly forward will help you keep your back straighter so it's not arched. Experimenting with different heeled shoes will lead you to a good heel height for your body type and enable you to place your center of gravity between the balls of your feet and not between your heels.

Set and Maintain
Humans learn at different rates as we all know but, in general, it takes us about three to six weeks to learn a new habit. It takes only a short time for our subconscious to establish the necessary brain function but our muscles take a little longer to be conditioned. Therefore, practice time with our new stance will have to be allotted before it is fully an automatic, subconscious-controlled activity.

During this training and while you are shooting an end of arrows you must learn to maintain your stance. That is, you must learn to set your stance for the first arrow of the end and then not move your feet again until the end is complete. If you are setting it correctly on the first try, you should not need or want to change your foot positions for the remaining shots.

At any tournament or at any local league shoot I see many of the archers draw their bow, establish their full-draw-position and then shuffle their feet. Immediately I know that they will never be able to repeat that shot – their stance will be different every time they shoot an arrow. Set your stance correctly as your first step of form and don't change it. If it feels bad when you get to full draw then let down, reset your feet and start over. Build it correctly from the start.

Shuffling your feet during an end of arrows introduces unwanted and unnecessary tension and nervousness. Maintaining one's stance can be used to help reduce tension and nervousness. Trusting your stance is a big first step to elevating and maintaining your self-confidence.

There is an exception to this. When shooting the NFAA indoor five-spot target face I often find myself wanting to shift my stance a little to shoot the two right-side spots. The five-spot target is rather wide from side to side so you may prefer to set your stance for the left-side spots and then shift it slightly to accommodate the center and two right-side spots. Just never shift your stance while at full draw.

On-Course Adaptations To Stance
To this point we have been focused on "model form." That's important because you must first build the model you need when conditions are ideal and then, and only then, is it prudent to build form for those conditions that are not ideal. You will always be comparing your altered form to what form works best and if you don't have that model in mind you're just guessing blindly at what to do.

When you shoot field archery courses the terrain forces you to compromise. That's what field archery is, a game of compromise. Most uphill shots, for instance, have an uneven place to stand since the ground at the shooting stake is usually uphill also. The recommendation I can make is to keep your heels close together so they are nearly the same height and, therefore, can hold nearly equal amounts of your body weight. We understand that this makes us a little more likely to teeter back and forth but conditions are not perfect and this, for most, will be the best compromise.

With heels together and weight distributed equally on your feet you can at least maintain your upper body integrity; you can keep you "power unit" together and use back tension effectively. Keep your "back tension" objective in mind as you make compromises to model form and you will be able to get consistent results. Understand also that you may not get as good a result as you do under ideal conditions but you can at least be consistent with a disciplined stance.

Downhill shots are not nearly as difficult for me but I still put my heels together if the ground is uneven. I'm sure that with my heels together I can bend easier at the waist and that helps get my upper body in good position relative to the target.

Side hill shots offer a different set of conditions. Usually your toes are either pointed uphill or downhill and your body is either leaning into the hill or falling away from it. Before you raise your bow prepare yourself by leaning slightly into the hill. Lean beyond vertical so that by the time you get to full draw you will be vertical. If your toes are uphill then put more weight forward on your feet. If your toes are downhill then keep more weight on your heels so the slope doesn't pull your upper body downhill while you are raising, drawing and aiming.

As a right-handed shooter my toughest shot, then, is an uphill target that is sloped down to the left. This puts my toes uphill and my heels together. I have to aim while wobbling and falling over backwards – it isn't easy but that's why we love field archery.

The only way to get good at this is to practice shooting on difficult terrain. Find a location that offers an uphill practice lane so you can prepare for this difficult shot. Place a target butt at the top and another at the bottom of the hill so you can shoot one end uphill and then the next end downhill.

Summary

An archer's stance is the first element of an interrelated system of shooting form steps. Every step that follows depends on the stability that is created by that stance so your students need to get it right from the beginning to maximize their success. Pay close attention to the stance features of spread, angle to a line to the target, left-right weight distribution and forward-rear weight distribution. Connect yourself securely to the ground and reap the benefits of a solid launch pad.

Chapter 10
The Bow Hand

We humans are controlling animals, aren't we? All day long we try to control our tools, our surroundings and the people around us to make them suit our needs. We control our car by steering it with our hands and use our feet to make it go as fast or as slow as we want. Control, control, control! That's what we do.

But an archery bow offers us a big contradiction; the more we try to control a bow with our hands, the less we succeed in doing so! If we try to "make" an arrow go into the X-ring, we fail to get the job done with any reasonable level of consistency.

The bow, then, becomes a very good teacher for us. The bow teaches us that we can succeed at a higher rate if we "blend" with it in order to "allow" it to shoot the arrow into the target middle. This is like the Zen teachings that tell us to "become one with the bow and arrow," acting as a complement to it. In this way we can create the best conditions for getting the results we want. We just have to give up that absolute control; we have to blend as an equal partner with the bow through our bow hand.

Archery in this regard is a humbling and a good teacher. Know anyone who could use a little of this philosophy in their life?

The Beginning and the End
My mentor coach, Bud Fowkes, stressed to me that the bow hand is the first body part to touch the bow as you setup for the shot (that's Step 3 in my Core Archery form steps) and it's the last body part touching the bow as the arrow crosses the arrow rest on its way to the target (that's Step 10). This makes bow hand placement on the bow's grip section extremely important.

"The shot begins and ends with bow hand placement." Bud Fowkes

Placing the bow hand has to be done at the right time as well. Waiting until you're at full draw is not the time to reset your bow hand. You just can't repeat that action. Set it immediately after you nock your arrow. Set it correctly and don't change it until after the arrow has been released.

Most of my students, 99% of them, don't or don't know how to place their bow hand on the bow correctly. They grip the handle in some way or they stiffen their fingers and thumb in an effort to get consistency. They are doing exactly what they do all day with their hands: control, feel, manipulate, bend, push, squeeze, or pound.

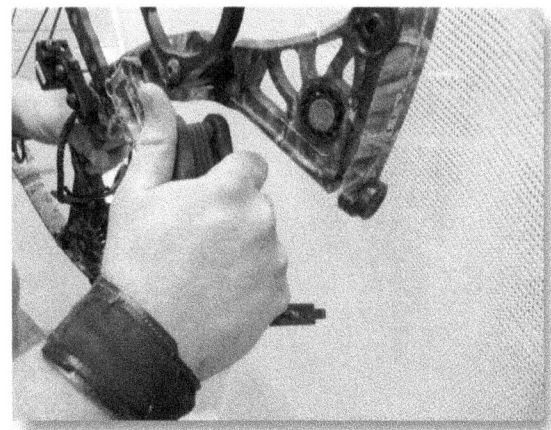

Hands On *We use our hands all day long to control tools, computers and steering wheels. Teaching your hand to relax when touching it your bow takes weeks of blank bale training with your eyes closed.*

They have not separated archery from their daily life because they haven't been taught that they need to.

Placing your bow hand on your bow is counterintuitive. In other words, it's the opposite of what you are used to doing and that makes it difficult to learn. Learning to "refuse to control" is the opposite of everything we do all day long but that is exactly what we must do in order to get consistent and accurate archery results.

Purpose

So what exactly is the purpose of the bow hand? What are we supposed to do with our hand when we put it on the bow's grip section? The answer is simple: we place the hand on the bow in a manner that allows the arm bones to resist the forces of the drawn bow.

And you thought it was all about the hand, didn't you? Well, it's not about the hand; it's about the arm bones. Just like most of the form elements I teach, bow hand placement is about the skeleton, the body's core, and how to use it effectively.

The bones of the lower and upper arm must be in line so they can resist the bow's draw force. Liken this to how you use your leg bones all day when you're on your feet. You use enough muscle – and it's not much – to keep your leg bones in line between your butt and the floor. You use your leg bones like sticks to keep your butt off the floor so, therefore, use your bow arm in the same way.

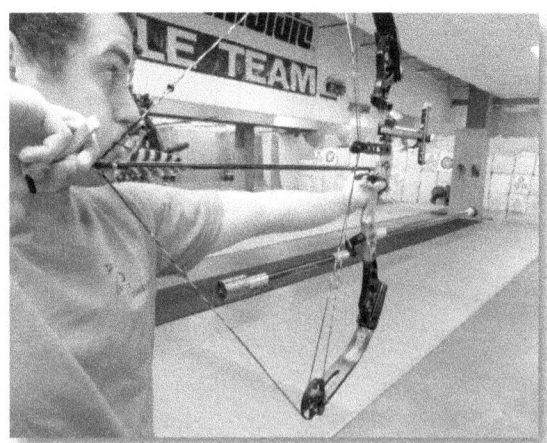

Straight Arm *The straight bow arm lines up the bones of the lower and upper arm so that they – and not your arm muscles - resist the force of the drawn bow. A straight arm uses very few muscles to hold its position.*

Bow Handle Physics

When the string is released it and the arrow move toward the target, the bow handle moves away from the target according to the law of physics that states: for every action there is an opposite and equal reaction. During the fifteen-thousandths of a second (0.015 sec.) that the bowstring is moving toward the target the bow handle is pressed into your bow hand and, therefore, a relaxed bow hand supported by in-line arm bones is the most consistent way to resist this initial action of the bow handle. (Later, after the string leaves, there is no force offsetting the force into the hand and the bow rebounds off of that surface.)

Bending your arm at the elbow recruits a far greater number of muscle groups than does keeping it straight. Try standing with your knees bent for five minutes to feel how many more muscle groups become active and, of course, how much these muscles fatigue. Your bow arm undergoes the same fatigue if you use lots of muscle to keep it bent while at full draw. Keep your arm efficient by keeping the lower and upper arm bones in line while at full draw and place a relaxed bow hand between them and the handle.

The Touch Pad

The lifeline that runs down the palm of your hand separates your hand into two regions for the purpose of archery, the "in-bounds" and the "out-of-bounds." The thumb pad is the in-bounds portion while the other pad on the little-finger side of the lifeline is the out-of-bounds region. The thumb pad and only this pad should be placed on the grip area of the bow handle. If any other part touches the handle then side torque will occur. This torque, or twisting force, will cause the handle to move while the arrow is still on the bowstring (as it is leaving) giving larger groups.

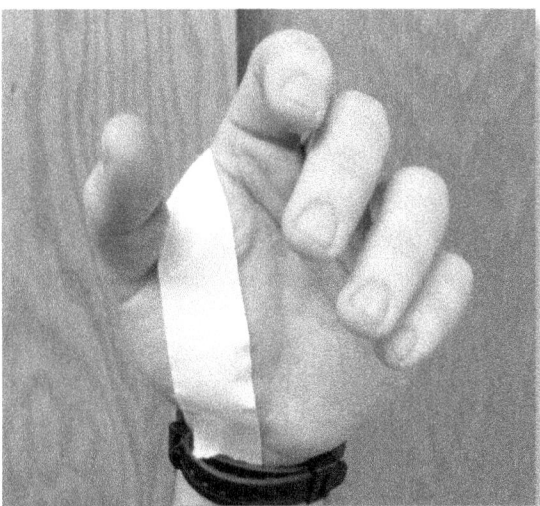

Hand Diagram I place a strip of tape on my student's bow hand to help them actually "feel" the thumb pad. They then need to place this strip, and only this strip, on the bow grip section and learn to feel it on the bow. By learning this feeling they can better repeat it while shooting.

The tape strip shown in the illustration is all that should be placed on the bow grip section. This strip must be vertical when the bow is drawn so that it parallels the vertical attitude of the bow handle. It should be obvious that this requires the bow hand to be rotated so the large knuckles are seen by the archer to be at a forty-five degree angle to vertical.

Larry Wise on Coaching Archery

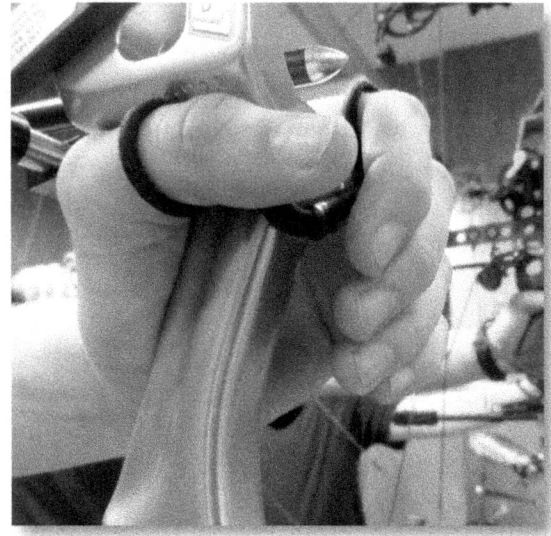

Relaxed Fingers and Thumb *Letting all of the tension out of your fingers is top priority for my Penn State Archers. Eliminate tension in the thumb and it will point toward the target (foreground). In the background you see a hand with lots of tension which can't be repeated and affects the shot negatively.*

Once your bow hand is properly set there remains only to relax your fingers and thumb. These appendages must be relaxed before the bow hand touches the bow grip. No exceptions! If they're tense when you touch them to the handle they will most likely stay tense through the entire shot.

You do not need your fingers and thumb to hold the bow. You should be holding the weight of the bow with your release hand since you've already hooked the release to the bowstring. This allows you to keep your bow hand fingers and thumb relaxed at first touch, through the bow raise, during the draw, and through the aiming steps of your form sequence.

Never allowing the fingers to build muscle tension is the best way to have no tension in them at full draw. If you allow tension to build while you raise and draw your bow then you must take extra time at full draw to eliminate it – a step that is nearly impossible to repeat at a time when we have a more important issue to focus on.

The wrist should be held in a medium-bent position. This, I feel, minimizes the amount of muscle needed to support the wrist in the optimum angle for presentation to the bow grip. Remember that we're trying to position the in-line arm bones between the bow and our shoulder but the hand is in the way of this. Therefore, we must place the thumb pad center directly onto the bow grip because that is the point on the hand directly in front of the radius bone of the forearm.

By now you should have gathered that this bow hand placement business is all about how to eliminate the hand and its effects on our archery form. This whole chapter is really about getting the arm bones in the correct position.

The Forearm Bones

The forearm has two bones, the shorter radius and the longer ulna. They lay side-by-side at the lower end to form the wrist joint. At this end the radius is located on the thumb side and forms the main part of the wrist joint. At the upper end these two bones join to the humerus of the upper arm at the elbow joint.

When the radius is lined up with the humerus they form a rigid resistance to the bow. If the bow shoulder is kept "down" then this resistance is anchored in the shoulder unit. Raise the shoulder and more muscle has to be recruited to resist the bow and that's not good.

When the knuckles are in a forty-five degree angle to the vertical they allow the forearm to be rolled out of the way of the bowstring. The elbow crease will be at a forty-five degree angle to vertical. This doesn't happen when you hold your knuckles in a vertical line; the forearm doesn't roll at all resulting in all those black and blue marks we see on beginner's arms. Get the bow hand angled correctly and the forearm can do its job and do it pain-free.

Teaching Bow Hand Position

I teach archers to make a "stop" sign with their bow hand so they learn how to present it properly to the bow handle. When you try this be sure your knuckles are at a forty-five degree angle to vertical. Next, keep your wrist bent but relax your fingers and thumb.

Bow Hand Placement Routine Here's a set of steps for getting the bow hand placed correctly:
1. Pen-mark the lower inch of the lifeline in the bow hand as a touch-point reference.
2. Touch the pen-mark to the left edge (for right-handers) of the bow grip section.
3. Relax all fingers and the thumb so they are limp.
4. Slide the bow hand upward until the index knuckle and thumb lightly touch the arrow shelf.
5. Allow the thumb pad to lightly roll onto the bow grip.
6. Do not pressure the bow hand onto the grip.
7. Pull lightly with your release hand to hold the bow in the bow hand.
8. Hold the bow hand in the proper position throughout the raising of the bow to the target level.
9. During the draw, the bow will pressure into the bow hand at the target and aiming level yielding optimum bow hand consistency.

Learning and following this routine is vital for establishing correct bow hand position. Without a set routine to follow, placing the bow hand becomes a lottery event – sometimes it hits and sometimes it doesn't.

Bow Hand Practice Routine Practice with a purpose is far better than just plain practice. Practice with the specific objective of improving your bow hand using the preceding routine is the only way to make it better for the long term. So the question becomes, "How do I practice?" or "What do I do during a practice session?"

During practice is the time for you to use your conscious mind to guide your learning of a new skill. Since your conscious can only have a single thought at any given time you must work on only one skill at a time and for now that skill is "bow hand placement." Through this kind of guided practice your subconscious will gradually take over the running of the bow hand routine; it becomes automatic after several weeks.

To ensure that your conscious mind can remain focused on the bow hand you'll want to practice close to a target butt. Close means four or five yards and this is better with no target face on the butt. Its best if you close your eyes so your conscious mind is not distracted from guiding the bow hand. It can focus on how the bow hand "feels" as it first touches the grip, during the raise and during the draw. At full draw you can best "feel" if your fingers are relaxed by flexing them a little to be sure they are limp and then finish the shot through the release to the followthrough.

Every practice session should begin with thirty shots at the blank bale – eyes closed. There can be no exceptions to this for weeks to come. If I were coaching basketball, the first twenty sessions would start with every one at the foul line blindfolded, learning to "feel" their shot. Do the same with your archery.

If shooting at other distances is part of a practice session then the bow hand must be checked during each shot. If you are shooting a scoring round then, yes, your score may be compromised because you are constantly checking your bow hand. Gradually you will be able to effectively transfer your bow hand skill to the scoring situation and your scores will be higher.

At the close of the session return to the blank bale to shoot at least ten more closed-eye shots focusing on the feel of the bow hand. Always start and end your practice sessions by working on a single objective for the practice session.

Since it takes humans several weeks to learn a new habit you are looking at practicing bow hand placement every day for three weeks. Remember, Rome wasn't built in a day. Practice, practice, practice! And practice with a purpose!

Chapter 11
Full-Draw-Position

Just one day ago from writing this I watched the best and most accurate archers in the world compete at the Lancaster Archery Classic. The men and women professionals who competed demonstrated the highest level of shooting skill and coolest performance under head-to-head shoot-off conditions. Many shot over 50 Xs in their 60-arrow qualifying rounds and 12 out of 12 Xs in the shoot off rounds. They were all fantastic. I was most impressed.

And the best part was I got to see them all up close – I was the official line judge. It was my honor to see all of this superior skill from a distance of three yards behind the shooting line. Shooting 11-for-12 or 12-for-12 X-rings in head-to-head competition is extremely difficult – and they did it on a regular basis.

The top shooters used bows with all the different cam designs: hybrid, single, and binary. They also used different release aids: 38% thumb, 9% index trigger, 53% back tension/triggerless, and one pinky release (he finished third). What is most important to those who want to improve their skill level is that all of these professionals who made the top sixteen – men and women – had something in common regarding their shooting form. They've all figured out how to stand properly at full draw in order to get optimum performance out of their bodies. They all demonstrated how to stand in proper full-draw-position. You must know what that is so you can improve your own and your student's games.

Having a standard model for full draw posture is absolutely essential to your success as an archer or as someone wh coaches archers. Knowing how to stand at full draw and why you need to do so will get you started on the best and shortest path to shooting higher scores. It's as simple as seeing the blueprint of the house you plan to build before you build it – you'll do a better job of building if you know what the final product should look like!

Two Important Definitions

Shooting form is a set of precise movements, like a ballet, each of which must relate to our overall objective. Have you defined that objective for every archery shot you make? If not, then how do you evaluate the effectiveness of each of your form steps?

Most of my students answer this question by saying that their objective is to "hit the X" or "spot." Let's look at that. If you are at full draw and aiming, isn't the arrow hitting the X a future event? Of course it is, because you are aiming in the present and have control only over the present.

Further, we also do not want to be consciously engaged in managing specific shooting skills – we transferred that work to our subconscious mind during practice. To achieve elite athletic performance you must be consciously engaged in the present and in a process-oriented goal. Present process thinking is required – your conscious mind will be thinking something so put it to work thinking the right things.

Because of this, your archery shooting form objective must be about how you intend to execute your shot. For me this is easy:

> **Objective** Complete this archery shot using the appropriately timed execution of back tension.

This objective focuses on a "process" and not a "result." There are thousands of ways to execute an archery shot – we've all seen most of them – but transferring the "holding" of the bow into the back is the most consistent method over the longest period of time by far. If you or your students invest the time to learn it you will reap the rewards.

Back Tension

So, what is back tension? We start to build good form by defining it. Being able to see our target is essential to hitting it and, therefore, knowing and understanding the definition of back tension is essential to achieving it.

> **Definition** *Back Tension is the isometric contraction of the dominant or drawing-side rhomboid muscles, levator scapulae muscle, aided by the trapezius causing a micro sliding-rotation of the scapula toward the spine.*

Further, this motion of the scapula and shoulder unit places a rotational force on the holding elbow causing it to rotate in a plane tilted about thirty-degrees from horizontal (downward and around toward your back). This rotation can be used to dis-

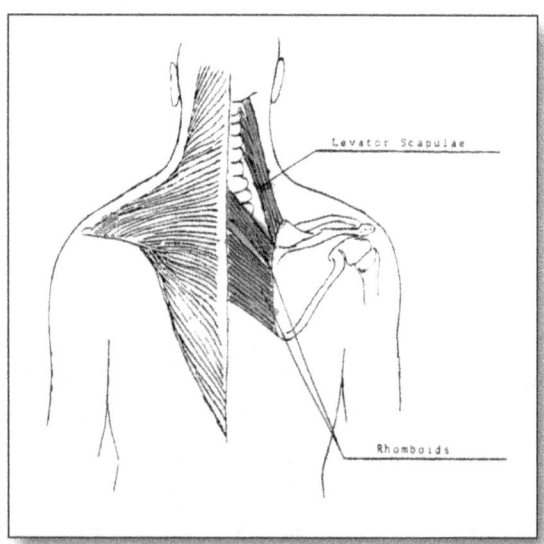

Back Muscles *At full draw, the rhomboid, levator scapulae and trapezius muscles on the drawing side (right-side in this illustration) should do the holding of the bow. Contracting these muscles places a rotational force on the holding elbow which can be used to discharge the release aid.*

charge a mechanical release aid.

The more you know about your objective, the better you can achieve it. The accompanying illustration shows the rhomboid and levator scapulae muscles that must be contracted to move the shoulder blade and shoulder unit toward the spine. At the same time the trapezius contracts, keeping the shoulder blade close to the rib cage and linking the shoulder to the shoulder blade (scapula).

Full-Draw-Position

If you adopt the back tension shooting objective then what has to happen immediately before you can do so? You must place your body in the proper physical position to effectively employ the required muscles and that position is as follows.

> **Definition** *Full-Draw-Position is the skeletal alignment that places the drawing-side scapula near the spine so as to allow for consistent and efficient back tension execution. Further, the drawing hand and forearm will be in line with the arrow shaft and string with the elbow elevated at least as high as the arrow nock.*

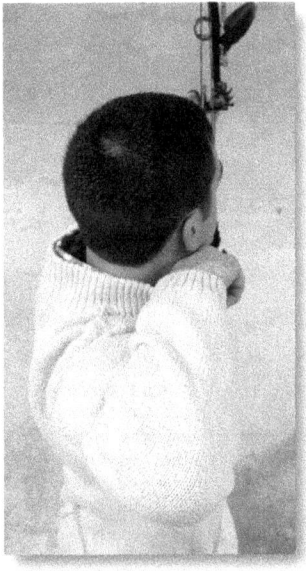

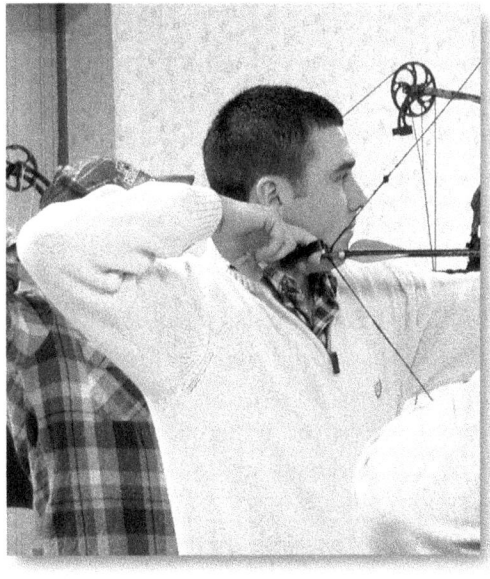

Front View *Full-Draw-Position seen from the front shows the drawing and holding elbow the same height as or elevated slightly above the line of the arrow. The amount of elevation depends on the skeletal build of the archer.*

Top View *Full-Draw-Position viewed from the top shows how the drawing forearm and elbow should line up with the arrow. Once this position is reached the holding force can be transferred into the back muscles allowing you to relax your arm muscles and execute a short and natural followthrough.*

Full-draw-position is, by definition, the prerequisite for back tension and set up by each and every preceding form step. Keeping both of these definitions in mind will be important to your understanding of each and every form step, as well as the sequence of the steps. If you skimp on any form step then the house you build will not be stable; your full-draw-position will rely on excess muscle use and falter under pressure.

This full-draw-position, as defined previously, depends on your shoulder and shoulder blade and not on where your draw hand touches a certain place on your face, neck or jaw. It is not related to your nose touching the bowstring although the peep sight must appear in front of your eye. When your shoulders are at equal height and your drawing arm is in line with the arrow (from a top view) then, and only then, are you prepared to most efficiently execute back tension. Only then have you reached full-draw-position.

The significance of the drawing forearm position has to do with physics. Your drawing arm is a simple lever and only when it lines up behind the arrow and string (elbow slightly elevated) can you transfer the holding of the bow into your back muscles. If the elbow is rotated short of this line then you are still holding the bowstring with your arm muscles leading to muscle fatigue, poor followthrough and inconsistent performance.

If you rotate your holding elbow too far beyond this line then you are pushing your scapula too close to your spine and rendering your rhomboids ineffective in creating a rotational force on your holding elbow.

Your bow side shoulder has been kept in its downward position from the beginning of the draw and it remains there throughout the holding and aiming. The bones of the bow arm must be held in line so that the force load of the bow is most consistently transferred through them and into your back. If the bow shoulder is raised or bow arm bent, then muscle must hold that position and both consistency and stamina are in jeopardy.

In full-draw-position the draw hand wrist is straight and relaxed, as are the forearm and biceps muscles. The draw-side elbow is held level or slightly higher than the arrow in preparation for final back tension execution and a "touch" is established between the draw hand and some part of your face, jaw or neck. This touch is secondary to the establishment of proper shoulder and shoulder blade position and should not be overemphasized; the shoulder and back are more important.

Our strategy throughout all of our form steps and also in full-draw-position is to minimize muscle and maximize skeleton. Bones don't fatigue but muscles do.

Full-Draw-Position Illustrated

1. *Proper Full-Draw-Position* From behind your holding elbow anyone can see if your drawing forearm is in line with the arrow. In this position you can make the transfer of holding force into your back muscles. Put yourself into this position without your bow and then make the bow fit you! Adjust the draw length until the bow fits your body position.

    Most of my students confess that they bought their bow and fit themselves into it only because they didn't know what their true draw length was supposed to be. They really didn't have any standard for deciding on their draw length. They didn't know about their body position and so they went by a friend's advice or on nothing at all.

2. *Short-Draw-Position* Again, from behind the archer's holding elbow you can easily see that a short draw length setting does not allow this archer to rotate his holding elbow in line with the arrow. This forces him to hold the bowstring with arm mus-

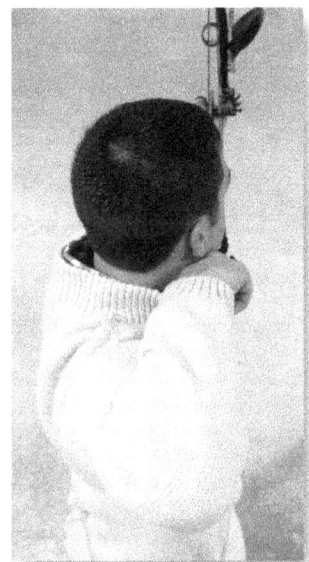  

Elbow View *Full-draw-position seen from the draw-side shows the holding elbow directly in line behind the arrow and bowstring. In this position the holding force can and should be transferred into the back where it can be used to implement a proper release.*

Short Draw *This bow is set too short for the archer and causes his holding arm and elbow to position short of the arrow line. In this position the draw force must be held in the upper and lower arm muscles resulting in inconsistent releases and the hand swinging out to the right during followthrough.*

Long Draw *A draw setting that is too long for the archer requires his drawing arm to rotate beyond the arrow line (shown here) or downward below the arrow line thus decreasing the effectiveness of the back muscles. In this position many archers improperly use hand and finger action to help discharge the release aid.*

cles. From this position you can see how the followthrough will usually be out to the right side – and different for every shot. If we lengthen the draw setting on this bow he will use less muscle at full draw; finesse trumps macho!

3. *Long-Draw-Position* In this illustration you can see that this archer's elbow has rotated beyond the line of the arrow leaving little or no space for the back muscles to rotate the holding arm and elbow. Without this capability the archer is left to execute the shot through some other means like finger or wrist manipulation of the release aid. Shorten the draw length setting of this bow and he'll be better able to execute back tension properly.

Summary

Everyone wants to shoot better and to that end we try a host of techniques . . . I've seen about all of them. Most of these techniques are home-spun ideas that seemed to work for a short time but will leave you or your students floundering and wanting more. With the well-defined terms laid out here and the illustrations provided, you can begin putting yourself into a biomechanically efficient position that helps you reduce the use of muscle by relying more on your skeleton.

Build a proper full-draw-position and make the bow fit you. Do this and you'll take a big step toward reaching your full shooting potential.

Chapter 12
The Ten Minute Coach

Coaches don't always have as much time to spend with students as the students need. Sometimes you need to work a little quicker than you'd like to to accommodate this. The following plans and tips are designed for that purpose.

I've put together some "lesson plans" for you. Adapt them to your situation so your students get the attention they need when time is an issue. You'll be teaching them the correct shooting technique and practice routines to develop them into effective shooters in the field.

Teaching Objectives

Before I retired from teaching in the public school system, every Friday during the school year my school principal required that all of his teachers submit their lesson plans for the next week. That way when he reviewed them he had an idea of what activities and subject matter were being taught, what pace was being kept and whether we were meeting school district-wide objectives. In short, he kept an eye on us to be sure we were doing our job. That was fine with me because I planned effectively and relied on those plans to keep me and my students on task and on track. The better I planned the better my classes went.

Any effective education program begins with lesson plans but you probably don't have any plans for your archery teaching so that's where I come in – I've got plans for you. Just like every lesson plan for every one of the 38,000 math lessons I taught over 35 years my plans for teaching archery begin with an objective. So here's your overall course objective for the set of simple ten-minute lessons that follow:

Course Objective

The student will learn three basic form elements of posture, back loading and release holding, to allow him/her to shoot at and hit a paper plate at 25 yards with a success rate of 9 out of 10 hits.

I hope you agree with me that this is the basic skill level needed to be a good bowhunter or a beginning target archer. 90% at 25-yards is a fair standard to expect and one that I've advocated for 30 years. We really want to hit our target 100% of the time but at the beginning of a student's learning 90% is realistic.

Section 1—Creating Full Draw Position and Execution

Lesson One Archer's "T" Position

Objective The student will learn the Archer's "T" position in order to establish proper full-draw-position and incorporate "back loading" into his form/execution.

This may sound like a lot to do in ten minutes and when you first teach it you'll need more than ten minutes but it is effective and easy to do. Getting your students started with efficient posture is the foundation to successful shooting

Step 1 **The Archer's "T"** Begin by having your student stand with his/her feet spread to hip width and arms outstretched to his side to form the letter "T". Their head should be directly over their spine with their chin level.

T Complete *Starting from a "T" position you can build proper full-draw-position by bending your release arm at the elbow and bringing your index knuckle along side of the neck. When correct the forearm is in line with the arrow allowing the archer to transfer the "holding" into his/her back muscles. You must hold your chin level while aligning the bones of your bow arm so they can resist the force of the bow.*

Step 2 **Rotate Head** Instruct the student to rotate their head toward and establish eye contact with the target. Their chin must be kept level with their head resting over top of their spin.

Step 3 **Stop Sign** Have your student make a "Stop-sign" toward the target with their bow hand and relax the fingers and thumb. Be sure to have the student keep their bow-shoulder in the down and back position.

Step 4 **Release Hand and Forearm** The student should now bend their release arm at the elbow so that the release hand index finger is positioned along the side of their neck under their jaw bone. Check to be sure that their release forearm is in line with the arrow and that their elbow is slightly raised above the arrow level.

Step 5 Repeat this process five times counting the steps "1- 2- 3- 4" each time.

Step 6 Have the student repeat this process while holding and drawing their bow. If they cannot establish the recommended full-draw-position then adjust the draw length and/or draw weight of their bow so that they can. Most of my students have draw length settings that are too short for them which does not allow their release forearm to get fully in line behind and with the arrow. These adjustments may take a few minutes extra but the proper position will serve your student's needs.

Step 7 Have your student make five shots at five yards (no target face) while you gauge their position correctness and give instruction. At this point they must learn to transfer the holding out of their draw arm and into their back muscles. This back-holding must be maintained throughout the release process. You can gauge correctness by watching (from behind their drawing elbow) their release elbow to be sure it does not move to the right (right-handers) during the entire aiming and releasing process. Their elbow must rotate to the right – toward their back – and slightly downward.

Step 8 Send them home to practice this technique for one or two weeks. I recommend that they shoot 20 to 30 shots per day at a blank bale and then return to you for lesson two.

Lesson Two Proper Release Holding

Objective The student will learn to hold the release aid with proper finger positioning and correct tightening procedure.

Step 1 Review the full-draw-position and back holding established in Lesson One to be sure the student is doing them both correctly. Have them make any necessary corrections and make five good shots at a blank bale.

Step 2 **Index Finger** I assume here that most of your students will be using an index-trigger release so instruct the student to hold the index-trigger release with the second-joint of the index finger completely around the trigger. The index finger should also be touching the side or barrel of the release aid. Adjust the length of the release shank or strap so that the archer can hold it in this manner. Use a rope loop instead of a bow as shown. Adjust the release trigger sensitivity to medium or medium-heavy

Step 3 **Close All Fingers** Practice holding and releasing five shots with the release aid hooked onto a rope loop, not a bow, making sure that, first, the student is in proper full-draw-position and holding and tightening with their back muscles. Secondly, they must also be closing and tightening all release fingers, not just the index finger. (This must not be done with a "death" grip but only a gentle finger closing).

Finger Around the Trigger My friend Scott shows how to properly place the hand and fingers on an index finger triggered release aid. The index finger should completely surround the trigger so that the second crease is on the trigger. This method does not allow the most sensitive index fingertip to be involved with the shooting process which often distracts the conscious mind away from aiming and onto the trigger causing release dysfunctions.

Step 4 The student should now draw and hold the bow with the release hand in the proper position. (Be sure to nock an arrow to prevent dry-fires.) Check the archer's full-draw-position as the new release hand position may require an adjustment to the bow's draw length. Typically when the release hand moves closer to the release jaws (and bowstring) the bow's draw length must be lengthened to place the release forearm back in line with the arrow. Without this proper alignment the archer cannot load the back muscles properly or effectively.

Step 5 With the release hand in the proper position and back-holding initiated instruct the student to execute the shot. Be sure that he/she tightens and holds with the back muscles first, and then simultaneously tightens all release fingers until the arrow is launched to the blank bale. Repeat five more times being sure that each is done correctly – correct them if they are not.

Step 6 Send the student home for one or two weeks of practice. Recommend 20 to 30 shots per day at the blank bale focusing on:
#1 = Establishing and continuing back holding and
#2 = Tightening all release fingers.
The order here is vitally important to proper followthrough and long-term shooting success – using some other order will lead to no followthrough and promote faulty technique that can lead to bad habits such as "snap" shooting or other forms of target panic. If the student focuses on the shooting "process" and not the results then he/she will learn to shoot properly.

Lesson Three Paper Plate Shooting

Objective The student will apply his/her full-draw-position, back holding and release technique to shooting at and hitting a paper plate at 15 yards.

Step 1 Review the previously learned skills of full-draw-position, back holding and release finger tightening. Be sure to correct the student's performance if needed so that he/she can correctly execute five shots.

Step 2 **Paper Plate Target** Place a nine-inch paper plate on the target butt at any distance from five to fifteen yards and instruct the student to shoot one arrow at the target. This incorporates the act of aiming into the shooting process so the student's performance must be monitored to be sure that the skills of correct posture, back holding and release finger tightening are all maintained as previously learned. Verbally remind the student to transfer his/her learning to this more complicated process. Starting close keeps the shooter's anxiety level low and aids him/her in performing correctly. Talk him/her through the shot process until the student performs one shot correctly and praise him for doing so.

Step 3 **Guided Practice** Have the student repeat the shot process three times while you use these verbal prompts:
Establish "T" posture
Raise the bow
Draw to full-draw-position

Bring the sight into line with your aiming eye
Transfer the holding into your back
Tighten all release fingers
Allow the sight to float near the center of the plate.

Continue tightening fingers while maintaining back holding until the release aid discharges. Trying to aim "perfect" is detrimental to archery success so stress that the sight should "float" near the center and not sit still at the center. In other words, the process is more important than the aiming. You'll have to remind your student over and over that good and flowing process gets far better results than trying to aim each arrow dead-center.

Step 4 **Corrected Practice** Next, require the student to execute three shots without your verbal prompting. Critique the student's performance immediately after each shot – encourage where possible but correct when necessary.

Step 5 **Self Practice** Have the student execute three shots without any prompting from you. Evaluate after the shots have been completed. Correct the weak skills and praise the good.

Step 6 The student is now ready for more practice at home. He/she should practice at no more than 15 yards at the paper plate. Five-inch spots are also acceptable but nothing smaller.

Step 7 **Follow-Up Evaluations** Have your student bring you a sample target after a week or two. This gives you a quick and easy way to evaluate his/her performance and learn of any difficulties. You also get to know if they have any equipment needs or repairs.

If their success is satisfactory then instruct them to begin shooting at longer distances – most of them probably have done this already. Twenty and twenty-five yards is the logical move for beginners, longer for the more skilled. Have them bring in another paper plate target with 30 shots in it so you can evaluate their progress and give any advice for future practice.

At this point you can tell them that they can purchase additional instruction time for another three lessons or single lessons if that suits your schedule better.

Section 2—Broadhead Shooting

The next step for your student is broadhead shooting. If your student has a facility for doing this all the better. If not, then the student is on his own for this work. Give him the following printed instructions.

Broadhead Shooting

Objective The student will establish his broadhead sighting pattern and grouping characteristics at a distance of 25 yards.

Step 1 **Sight-In Pattern** Broadheads may not have the same impact points as field points. There is no reason to expect that they should since field points don't have wings on them. Mechanical broadheads have a better chance but they, too, may not impact the same. Shooting a broadhead-equipped arrow at 15 yards is the starting point and the only way to know for sure. Where it hits relative to your field points should be noted.

Broadhead Impact *There is no reason why broadhead arrows should fly the same as or impact the same as field point arrows. Broadheads have wings – even mechanical heads have some protrusions – and will most often impact the target differently from field points. I typically find that my broadheads impact about four inches low-left from my field points so I tune for groups and then just sight-in with my broadheads.*

Next, shoot a broadhead at 25 yards and note its impact point. Over the next few shots adjust the sight pin to achieve a near center impact location. Your student's shooting ability has to be considered here as you may need more practice in order to be consistent at this distance.

Step 2 **Grouping Characteristics** It is best to shoot three practice broadheads at a three-spot target to determine if your setup is shooting reasonable groups. Three paper plates at 25 yards is a good goal. Shoot one broadhead arrow at each plate to determine if all three have the same relative impact point. If so, then adjust the sight so that all three are hitting the middle and your bow system is ready for the hunt.

Three-Spot Target *When it's time to shoot broadheads I use a three spot target and three broadhead equipped arrows. I number the arrows and shoot them at the separate dots in numerical order. Each arrow should impact its spot at the same relative position, if not then the system is not grouping and corrections must be made. When it's time to go hunting I put new blades on those same three trusty arrows and use them as my starting lineup.*

If the three impact points are different or some erratic arrow flight is visible then you and/or your system needs some work. The areas that may need adjusting are nocking point location, centershot/arrow rest adjustment, draw weight adjustment, arrow size selection and shooting form correction and/or practices.

Once you have established that your system is shooting at a satisfactory level then install new blades/broadheads on the arrows you plan to use for the hunt. Keep at least one practice broadhead-arrow so you can take a few shots every other day to check your system accuracy. Take other practice shots using field points on a regular schedule so you keep your shooting skills sharp.

Future Lessons
Since you have already established the basics of proper full-draw-position, back holding, and release holding your first three or four lessons would reinforce those skills. Lesson One would be all review with no target. Lesson Two would be a short review and then some spot shooting to improve consistency and have a record of performance. Lesson Three would have more spot shooting and score recording to gauge improvement.

Future lessons would enable you to give instruction on bow hand position. I would prefer to work on this first but it takes most archers a long time to get their hand placed on the bow correctly. It takes them even more time to get it relaxed so this skill doesn't fit into the "Ten-Minute" theme so well. Remember to use no target when developing a new shooting skill – focus on the new process rather than a score.

Range Time
Giving them shooting assignments at various distances can give you a quick way to check their skill level. I like to see my students shoot 30 arrows at a five-inch spot at 25 yards. You don't have to watch them shoot, just have them bring you the target face to read. From that you can learn if their misses are left, right, high or low. From that you can make recommendations or assist them with shooting form changes or bow tuning issues.

When they are shooting at a satisfactory level at 25 yards then have them move back to 30 or 35 yards and repeat the 30 arrow scoring round. Eventually they will build their skill level at 40 yards and be able to compete in the 3-D animal rounds at the local, regional or state level.

Encourage your students to save their target faces and scores. Make sure they write the date and distance on them as well. Seeing their improvement on each new target face will keep them interested and quickly uncover any problem that needs attention. And, you don't have to invest much time, just a minute to read the target face and four or five minutes to help them make a correction.

Summary
Making the most of your time – but not spending too much time – with new or old shooters is important to managing your coaching time. Being organized by having specific objectives keeps you focused on exactly what they need instead of getting side tracked by shooting stories or other unimportant issues. It's important to always "plan your work" and then "work your plan" and now you have that plan for teaching good form to the beginning target archers and bowhunters.

When practiced and maintained the *Ten Minute Coaching Techniques* will enable anyone to shoot effectively in all situations for years – not just in practice for a few weeks. And you need to convey that confidence to your students while optimizing your time with them.

Chapter 13
How to Properly Shoot and Train with a Release Aid

One week after the first bow was invented that first archer had sore fingers and began searching for a better way to release the bowstring. That's why the first release aid was invented. Maybe it was a smooth curved stick, a strap of raw hide or a bone ring of some sort but the first archer found a device to hook onto, draw, and release the bowstring. And his fingers felt better.

However, the release aid didn't solve all of his problems. It only opened the door to a different set of shooting problems. So, with the increase in accuracy that the release aid can give comes the possibility that you or someone you know will develop some form of snapshooting, trigger punching or freezing off of the target spot aiming. These are all forms of release-aid dysfunction or "target panic." All of them produce high levels of frustration and can drive people out of archery . . . forever. Worst of all, they can cause bowhunters to miss or wound game animals.

There's a way archers/bowhunters can get through this problem, especially the problem of "punching" the trigger. It takes some work but I've helped many archers, both target shooters and bowhunters, to better control their release process and hold steadier also. Following is a method that you will be able to implement for yourself or with students who have less than ideal release aid management skills.

Examining The Index Finger Triggered Release Aid
We all know that the index-finger trigger release is the most popular release on the market. Just look around at the next local 3-D tournament or at your local indoor club. There're about all I see when I go bowhunting or watch bowhunting shows on television.

It's easy to understand why they are so popular – it's easy to use. The trigger feels like the trigger on a gun and the release straps onto your wrist so you can draw the bow without using your fingers to hold anything. You can wear a glove on your release hand if you want and, besides, everyone else is using one so they must be good . . . and they are good. Saying they are bad because people can get target panic with them would be like saying that spoons and forks give people eating disorders. It's not the device that's in question here; it's how the device is managed that's the issue.

The Release Hand

The brain manages the release aid through the hand that holds it. That's quite simple; we all know that. What most people don't know is how to properly use the hand. In other words, they don't know how to hold the release aid in order to get the best long-term results so that's where any program to improve release technique must start.

We use our hands all day long to hold, grip, manipulate and touch nearly everything we contact. That's what our hands are designed to do, feel things and control them so we can get our work done, but in archery that type of control leads us to less than ideal results. We have to alter our thinking about "control."

Our bow hand is a good example of the contradiction that archery presents: controlling the bow with our gripping bow hand actually produces poorer results. The more we control the bow the less likely we will produce "repeatable" performance and the less likely we will hit the target. So, we must learn to relax our bow hand fingers and thumb to allow the bow to freely repeat its mechanical action. A tight bow hand transfers torque to the bow handle during the power stroke of the bowstring and that, we learn through time, must be avoided. Relax the hand and we get that desired tight grouping of arrows in the target-center; the relaxed bow hand allows the bow to be more consistent.

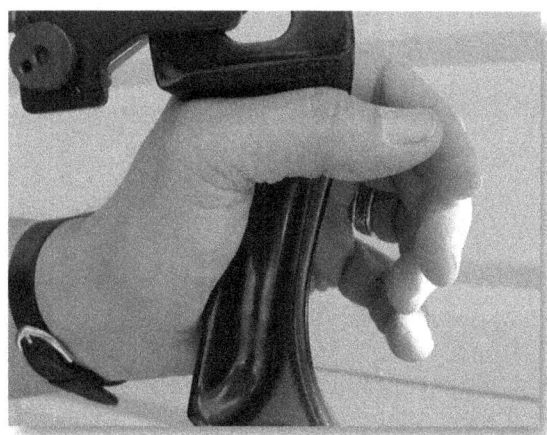

Bow Hand Using the bow hand correctly means that it is relaxed, knuckles at a forty-five degree angle and the thumb pointed to the target. Tightening the fingers and gripping are what we do with tools but not the bow handle. If we let it, the bow will consistently repeat its action so relax the bow hand.

Just as the bow hand must be used differently than you would first think so the release hand must be used differently. Most archers/bowhunters I know want to hold their mechanical trigger release so that only their index fingertip or thumb tip touches the trigger. After all, this is how they learned to shoot a gun. What they don't realize is that by using their finger or thumb tip the way they do with the tools of their trade or profession they are setting themselves up for some degree of failure. A different approach has to be taken.

The fingertips have a high density of tactile receptors in the dermis, which is the layer under the epidermis (outer skin layer). These receptors are linked by nerve fibers to the brain where sensory impulses are processed making our fingertips highly sensitive and sophisticated, much more so than the remaining parts of the finger or hand.

When the fingertip or thumb tip is placed on a trigger the conscious brain is made aware of this "touching" sensation—more aware than if some other part of the finger or hand was touching the trigger. This high degree of awareness can become a problem. This "noticed" touching could distract the archer from focusing on a more important part of the shot process; it makes the "trigger" far more important than it should be. And for some unlucky souls the "trigger thought" becomes consuming until that's all they can think about. Believe me, as a coach this is not a fun thing to watch and it's even worse to experience.

Finger Around Trigger Surrounding the trigger with the index finger will place a much less sensitive part of the finger on the trigger. In this position the conscious mind will be less likely interrupted from process or aiming thoughts and better shooting will result. From this position all fingers can be tightened, along with the back muscles, to set off the release aid.

One way to avoid falling into this "release dysfunction" is to avoid placing your fingertip or thumb tip on the trigger. Instead of using the most sensitive part of your finger or thumb on the trigger use a less sensitive part instead. For the index trigger use the second joint (middle crease) of the index finger curled around the trigger. For a thumb trigger, extend the trigger length so that it rides against the base of the thumb and not the tip.

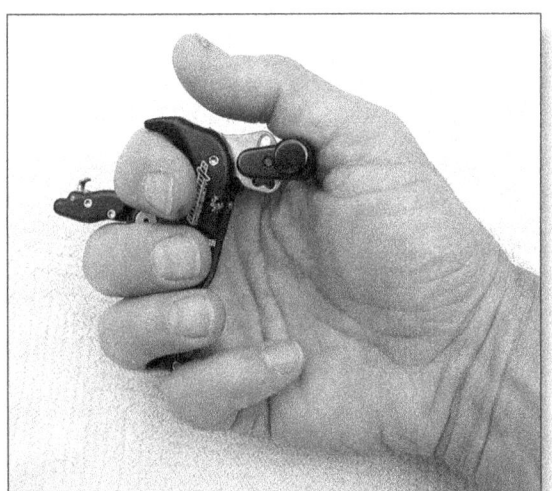

Thumb Trigger The trigger on a thumb-triggered release aid should be extended so that the trigger reaches the base of the thumb. In this position the release can be rotated into the thumb-base instead of pushed by the thumb tip. The rotation into the thumb base can be driven by back tension and the resulting elbow rotation.

Set the trigger tension to medium-heavy and surround it with finger or thumb and you'll be better able to avoid the problems that lead to target panic. When you create a medium amount of contact and pressure between your finger and the trigger then you won't be afraid to touch it. Most who set it lighter become more afraid to touch it! Besides, while you are hunting an unwanted light bump on the trigger could set off the release aid.

The Bow Arm

The bow arm can be another problem source for shot execution. Many bend their arm at the elbow and recruit all of the arm muscles to hold the bow at full draw and thereby expose themselves to a muscle fatigue problem. Extend your arm so the bones are in line to resist the force of the bow and relax much of your arm muscle to be more efficient.

When you engage more muscle than necessary to complete a task then your ability to complete that task again and again is greatly compromised; it's more difficult to repeat an action when you use excess muscle. In the case of holding a bow at full draw the fatigued bent-arm begins to collapse at the instant of release. That's okay as long as the collapse occurs after the arrow has been discharged but when it occurs while the arrow is in the act of being launched then accuracy is compromised.

I've seen many cases where the archer both bends the bow arm at full draw and touches the trigger with only the fingertip. This combination is a recipe for failure because it marries two potential problems. The fingertip alerts the conscious brain that the trigger is about to be activated and since the bow arm is not isolated from this conscious thinking it collapses at the same time or before the trigger is squeezed – or before the trigger is "punched" in the worst cases.

The best bow arm is the one that is extended so the lower arm bones are inline with the upper arm bone. It only takes a few small muscles to keep them in line and once in line the bones will resist the force of the bow without fatiguing or collapsing. Your leg bones do this all day long as they keep your butt off the floor so put the same technique to work in your bow arm.

Learning Consistent Shot Execution

This is what everyone wants to do – shoot consistently. But not everyone is willing to pay the price to make it happen because making yourself better requires practice. But not just any practice, you must practice the right technique.

Shooting more arrows only reinforces the bad habits you already have so a change must occur and I know what that change has to be – you must learn how to transfer the "holding" of the bow into your back muscles before and during the execution of the release. Holding with your back muscles allows you to relax your drawing arm during the "hold and release" phase. After the release your release hand and arm will have a smooth followthrough directly away from behind the arrow nock. Your hand won't fly out to the side away from your face, drop down or move toward the target. Your straight and relaxed release wrist and arm will perform consistently and your followthrough will be correct.

Now for the hard part: learning how to shoot archery by holding your bow with your back muscles. To do this effectively you have to use a back tension/triggerless release aid. You can't learn to swim by watching from the riverbank; you have to get into the water. And to learn how to use your back muscles you have to draw and hold the bow with a back tension release aid in your hand.

Yeah, I know, this is hard work and many archers resist this sort of thing. So how do you get them to try it? How do you get them to try it just for practice? All you have to do is point to the best shooters in the world because lots of them are training with back tension release aids and many are shooting them all the time and "winning".

Shooting perfect indoor scores back-to-back-to-back at the Las Vegas Shoot requires a correct shooting process and the ultimate in consistency. Shooting a back tension/triggerless release aid promotes that correct process by teaching you or your students how to use back muscles to hold the bow; a new process is developed without the trigger.

Once you learn it, you can transfer this correct process to another release for hunting. The tough part for many archers is making the commitment to learning the process and then relearning how to hold their old release with the proper bow arm and release hand, transferring the hold into their back, maintaining that hold and then, and only then, executing the release. Yeah, I know it's not easy like other methods but no other method is more consistent and consistent is what you need when bow hunting – you gotta make that one shot when the stakes are high!

Proper Full-Draw-Position . . . Again

As mentioned already, your release hand position and your bow arm are most effective when you hold them in their most biomechanically efficient position. That is to say, you must stand with the proper full-draw-position. I've defined full-draw-position before and written about it several times already because it's that important. If you don't stand with the correct posture to shoot archery you can practice until your arms fall off and you won't reach your full potential.

So when is a person correctly at full draw? What are the visual clues to full-draw-position? To answer these questions you just have to know the standard model that defines full-draw-position.

> ***Full-draw-position*** *is that position to which you draw the bowstring in order to place your shoulder blade and back muscles in the most effective location for executing back tension.*

Full-Draw-Position Learning how to stand at full draw is essential to executing the archery shot with back tension. Upright posture, level chin and shoulders, extended bow arm and a release forearm that is in line with the arrow shaft are the main features of this position. Only after the drawing arm is in line with the arrow shaft can the "holding" load be transferred into the back muscles creating the best chance for consistent shot execution.

This photo is a good example. What you should notice most about the archer in the picture is his drawing forearm. Where is it? You should see that, from a top view, his drawing forearm is in direct line with the arrow shaft. This tells you and me that his drawing shoulder is positioned so that his right-side back muscles – the rhomboid muscles – can have maximum leverage on his scapula (shoulder blade). In short, in this position he can transfer his holding power into his back muscles and is able to relax most of his arm muscles. In this position he can aim steadier, execute the shot more consistently and have proper followthrough.

The full draw front view should show his drawing arm either level with the arrow shaft or his elbow slightly elevated. His drawing arm should never be below the shaft, as this would push his scapula too close to his spine and significantly reduce the ability of the back muscles to hold and to complete the shot process. It's all about leverage in the back muscles.

From behind the shooter, you should see his drawing elbow lineup directly behind the arrow shaft. If it is wrapped too far around then he has drawn too far and the draw length of the bow is too long. If his elbow has not rotated far enough to get directly behind the arrow then the draw length of his bow may need to be set longer. Reset the draw length of his bow until the shooter can stand correctly in full-draw-position and align his drawing forearm with the arrow shaft.

A holding lever is most efficient when lined up in direct opposition to the force being held.

Getting your drawing forearm directly behind the arrow shaft is a major step toward making a consistent release. It is from this position that your release hand can escape cleanly and directly away from behind the arrow nock when the release aid activates. From other positions behind the nock your hand and arm may impart pressure and torque to the release and bowstring. This, in turn, will cause each arrow to impact differently in the target.

Shooting archery well is all about body position. It's all about maximizing the use of your skeleton and minimizing muscle use. It's about relaxing as much muscle as possible and that happens when the force you need to draw the bow is transferred into your back and out of your arms.

Using A Back Tension/Triggerless Release Aid

Once the "hold" has been transferred into the back muscles (the rhomboids) finishing the shot requires a subtle increase in your holding tension or muscle tightness. This tightening in your back muscles causes the release elbow to rotate about the shoulder joint – the elbow does not move directly away from the target as many try to do. The elbow rotates a microscopic amount in a slightly tilted plane (tilted about 30° to the horizontal) and this rotational force is what causes your back tension release aid to discharge the bowstring.

You can pull directly away from the target all you want but the release won't discharge until the handle has a rotational force applied to it; that's the way they work. Most of my first-time students work really hard at pulling the back tension/triggerless release directly away form the target as though they are pulling more arrow across the

Elbow Rotation An archer's followthrough indicates proper back-muscle tightening between the spine and shoulder blade. Prior to release activation the force on the holding elbow is trying to rotate it about the shoulder joint. This rotation occurs while the arrow remains stationary on the arrow rest. The elbow is actually moving perpendicular to the arrow in a plane that is tilted about 30 degrees from the horizontal as shown by the followthrough. Pulling the bowstring away from the target does not make the back tension release discharge the bowstring – the rotation does.

rest and, so, they have to learn that there is an easier way that takes finesse instead of brute force. Once they learn to rotate their holding elbow about the shoulder joint, their execution process gets easier and their groups tighter.

Practice Regimen For Back Tension

Step 1 **Learning Without a Bow** The first step to practicing with a back tension release aid is learning how to operate it. I teach beginners how to do this without the bow. Instead of a bow I have them use either a rope loop or a practice device. To further remove the fear element from the learning process I recommend that your students use a release aid with a safety on it.

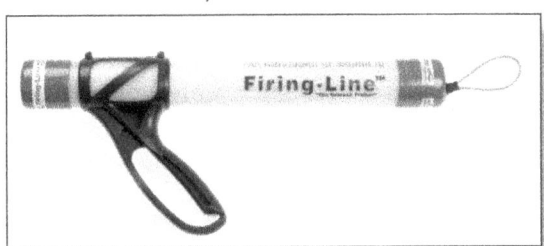

Practice Aids A simple rope-loop made of any kind of non-stretching cord can be used as a portable practice bow. Other more sophisticated devices can be used like the Saunders Firing-Line. These devices can be used any time and anywhere to get in a little practice without being at the archery range.

Step 2 **Practice Often** Use the practice device often. By often I mean three or four times a day. Short, frequent learning sessions will bring you a higher retention level for the skill you're learning. The rope loop and the release aid can be carried with you during the day and when you get a break you can make three or four practice shots. You don't have to make many practice shots but the ones you do make have to be done correctly – emphasize quality, not quantity. Remember, you're trying to build a conscious thought process as well as the physical action needed to shoot consistently with your back muscles. You're trying to tighten back muscles in order to hold the bowstring and to cause a rotation of the holding elbow that will, in turn, cause the release aid to discharge.

Step 3 **Blank Bale With a Bow** After three weeks of using the practice apparatus you can begin using your bow at the blank bale. Stand close, say five yards, to the bale. Remove any target face from the bale. In fact, it's best to close your eyes for this practice so that your conscious thinking can be totally focused on controlling the back-muscle action needed to set-off the release aid.

Most people don't listen to me and keep their eyes open instead. As I watch them shoot I can see them aiming their second arrow at the first arrow they shot and instantly I know that their conscious mind is focused on aiming and not on building a new muscle action. Keeping your eyes closed and your mind focused on the back-muscle action is the quickest way to getting results.

Continue the Step 2 daily practice with your training device. Don't stop this important practice, ever! It's important to reinforce your proper back-muscle action in order to overcome previous dysfunctions and maintain proper execution. Remember, some of those problems took you years to create and it will take you months to overcome them.

Step 4 After three weeks of shooting both the training aid and your bow you can begin shooting a few shots at a target face. First shoot ten shots at the blank bale then shoot ten shots at a target face at ten yards. Then go back to the blank bale for more practice. Always begin and end at the blank bale where you can consciously focus on and reinforce your muscle process.

Step 5 After five practice sessions repeat Step 4 but move back to fifteen yards and fifteen shots. Always begin and end at the blank bale. After five successful practices move back to 20 yards and 20 shots at the target face. After that you can move to varied distances from the target face but always begin and end at the blank bale in order to reinforce your proper back-muscle action.

Release Aid Availability

Most of the release aid manufacturers make at least one model of a back tension/triggerless release. Some make several different models so they are not hard to find. I find that the Tru Ball *Sweet Spot II* release with a safety button is an easy way to start a newcomer on a back tension release. The safety takes the fear out of the process and it can be used for hunting if the shooter is not ready or able to switch back to an index finger trigger. Learning back tension and continuing to practice it as part of a regular routine is smart archery for those willing to put in a little extra time to do it right.

Summary

There are lots of back tension/triggerless release aids on the market that will help you build the skills necessary to shoot a mechanical release aid properly. Learning to transfer the "hold" into the back muscles is essential to developing the best technique for shooting archery so choose a release aid that will help you do that. The biggest problem for a coach is getting our students to commit to learning that technique because it seems that they just don't want to give up their old "trigger" in order to get better at shooting.

As a coach you can plant the seeds for learning back tension in your student's minds and hope they take the idea seriously. Unfortunately, most wait until their release aid dysfunction is so bad that they are ashamed to admit it, quit archery, or finally give in to the inevitable and ask someone like you what they should do to fix the problem. The ones that come to you for help can follow what I've outlined in this chapter and get better at shooting—it will be a start!

It's the ones that don't come in for help that really hurt archery because they just "quit" and we never see them again. Regardless, we have to keep getting the word out that there is a way to deal with release aid dysfunctions called "target panic" and learn to shoot accurately for lots of years.

Chapter 14
How To Cope With Target Panic / Release Aid Management Skills

The huge Alaskan Brown angled across the tundra just forty yards out. After hours of stalking and with a little luck it would cross at twenty yards from Ron Murphy and his guide, Mike, and that would be perfect for a shot. What a great opportunity, a dream come true for Ron if he could make the shot. But making the shot was not in his thinking because he knew he would make the shot, he'd trained for it for two years. He had every confidence that it would happen automatically so his biggest concern was aiming at the right spot just behind the shoulder in the lung area.

Bear *Ron Murphy killed this huge Alaska Brown at a distance of eleven paces. That's not a time for release aid skills to fail and his didn't! Learn the proper skills and you'll have them for life.*

As the great bruin passed behind a small alder bush Ron drew his bow. The bear passed into the clear but needed to be a little closer. Then, as it usually does, the unexpected happened; the bear looked their way and saw them. Curious, it turned and walked straight at them.

Shooting a nine hundred-pound bear in the chest was not an option so Ron had to wait it out at full draw. The bear continued walking toward them and stopped at eleven paces.

Yes, eleven paces!

It swung its head back and forth for what seemed like minutes, but in reality was only six or seven seconds, before it turned to its left to continue on its way. Had it taken another step toward them the guide would have had to shoot, but luck was with them and Ron had the shot of a lifetime.

Ron saw his arrow pass through the lung area of the biggest bear he'll ever shoot.

In fact only a few bowhunters have ever shot one bigger as this bear will rank in the top twenty ever killed with a bow.

For this accomplishment Ron gets my *Core Archery Student-of-the-Year Award*. Why? Ron has target panic!

That's the bad news. The good news is Ron also has R.A.M. Skills! That's Release Aid Management Skills and after two years of continuous training he can manage his hunting release aid through the most tension-filled and exciting moment of his forty-five year hunting career. As Ron puts it "I have no recollection of the release aid in my hand, only waiting, aiming where I was supposed to be aiming and the arrow hitting its mark."

So how could a bowhunter who, just two years ago, could not get to full draw without "whacking" the release trigger build the skills needed to harvest this magnificent Alaskan Brown? As Ron will tell you "it wasn't easy" and at times "I fell back into old habits and had to start over" but, in the end, "I learned to manage." I'm really proud of Ron for his determined persistence and sticking with the Core Archery R.A.M. Program that I will outline in this chapter.

Ron will always have target panic lurking in the background but with the right training he can manage his shooting skills properly and accomplish his goals. The same is true for you or your students who have have target panic. With the right training steps learned in the right order you can learn to manage TP and – I really like this part the most – you will enjoy archery again.

What is Target Panic?

The dreaded dysfunction of target panic is mental. Conditions surrounding the activation of a release aid trigger can, through time, build unwanted responses into any archer. Mostly, but not always, the act of touching or preparing to touch the release aid trigger gets associated with a conscious thought. This conscious thought comes at the most inopportune time, at full draw, and distracts you from the more important task of consciously focusing on your shot process. Then, because you are consciously aware of the trigger, you make another conscious decision to activate it and do so.

It sounds so natural and harmless doesn't it? The problem is, you see, the rest of your body is not isolated from this "conscious" triggering process. The aiming and execution process falls away or you anticipate the trigger activation moment and react prematurely to it. Thus, an association is created between a body action and a conscious mental thought. And that promotes poor archery timing and accuracy. And, through continued practice of this habit the association is strengthened until it consumes all you do when the bow is in your hand.

In the worst cases this thought gets associated with the visual image of the target and as soon as the target comes into view you activate your release aid trigger. Through time this process gets shortened and the sight of the target activates your trigger finger. And your archery game is now officially "in the toilet." It's out of control, spiraling downward. At this point you either stop practicing or quit archery altogether. Or you look for a coach to help you out of this hole.

Conclusion: Release Aid Dysfunction is Mental Dysfunction.

Two Common Types Of Release Dysfunction

Type 1 The visual sighting of the target initiates release aid triggering. The preceding description summarizes this kind of dysfunction. This is what most archers mean when they say they have "target panic."

Type 2 The visual sighting of the target and the sight pin promotes "freezing." In other words, the sight pin freezes or locks up somewhere other than on the target middle. This dysfunction is also mental but instead of leading to an uncontrolled action it leads to inaction. Your conscious thinking is consumed with how difficult it is to put the pin and spot together while the release aid is in your hand. Most can aim well when they don't have a trigger in their hand. But, introduce the trigger and your sight freezes off the middle.

Some archers describe it as though the target spot was a magnet repelling another like-polarity magnet, the sight pin. No matter how you approach the target with the sight pin, it won't go into the middle. And so, you shoot on the move (we call this "drive-by" shooting), or you compensate by sighting-in with your sight pin under the spot.

I'm sure there are more types of target panic but these are the two main types that I deal with as a coach. The mental-physical associations that develop in both types are very strong and can consume and destroy archers. However, being mental they can be dealt with by reprogramming your mind through a series of practice steps that I call *Release Aid Management Skills*, ot R.A.M. Skills for short.

You're Never Cured

Have you ridden a bicycle lately? You say it's been years since you rode a bike? Even so, if you got on a bike today you'd have no trouble getting it going and staying on it for twenty yards. You'd be shaky but you'd be able to ride. The mental/physical associations you made years ago when you learned to ride a bike are still there and that's the way it is with the release aid trigger – whenever you go back to the trigger you will most likely get the same response you used to have with it, good or bad. So, if you continue to use the same release aid with which you have "panic" then you cannot expect different results.

What you have to learn, then, is a new set of release aid management skills. It's also necessary to have a different kind of release aid, one that can't be triggered. Combining the new skills with a new and different release aid will give you the best chance for rebuilding good and lasting release technique. Once you create new and proper mental/physical associations you may be able to cope with a trigger release for brief periods of time. But, first, you must retrain your brain.

The R.A.M. Skills Program

The following steps are written as instructions for a coach. If you are the coach then you must first learn how to operate a back tension release aid with some degree of proficiency. Until you do, you can't effectively understand or instruct these steps. My book **Core Archery** and matching DVD **Core Archery Back Tension** will assist you in this effort.

Step 1 The mental dysfunction that occurs in most target panic situations involves an excess of inappropriate conscious thoughts. These thoughts occur at the time when you should be consciously engaged in your shot-making process and not in the interaction between your finger and a trigger mechanism. You need to recognize and accept this problem before going further.

Step 2 Eliminating the symptoms of target panic means eliminating the cause of those unwanted and unneeded thoughts. Take the big step and eliminate the trigger. Now, that alone won't cure anyone of TP but it's the best way to long-term management success.

Removing the trigger from the equation begins the process of rebuilding the sequence of conscious mental thoughts associated with releasing the arrow. Using a release without a trigger puts the archer's fingers around and fully engaged with the triggerless release aid handle and that removes the thought about having "to touch" a trigger to cause the release.

Index Trigger The proper method for holding an index finger trigger is by surrounding the trigger with your finger and curling all fingers. Using the sensitive fingertip draws your conscious attention to the trigger when your conscious should be engaged with your back muscle holding action, so do not use it.

This finger employment is necessary so that your highly sensitive fingertips are not involved in and have no control over the release of the arrow. Most importantly, they don't send any "touch" signals to your brain while your conscious thinking is immersed in your "shot-making" process.

This means – and you must understand this clearly – that once your sight has joined your aiming and you have fully transferred your holding effort into your back muscles your thoughts no longer involve your fingers, a trigger or the release of the arrow. Instead, your conscious mind must focus on further contracting your rhomboid muscles to cause your drawing elbow to rotate around a hinge point in your shoulder; focus on back tension. You will not be pulling the arrow further across the rest; the arrow will be still. The release will occur when the release aid handle rotates one or two degrees causing the two metal parts of the release to separate.

In the beginning use no sight, no target, no bow and no arrow. Use only the release aid, a piece of rope or a training aid and your mind. So, in the beginning, you must rebuild your thinking pattern, your body position and your physical action connected to your thinking.

Step 3 Selecting a release aid for the R.A.M. Skills program is easy; choose any back-tension/triggerless release aid on the market. You can't pick one that is advertised to "shoot like" a back tension release aid; you have to have the real deal.

I recommend a release with a safety like the TRU Ball Sweet Spot. I also recommend that you use either two fingers or three but not four. Keep your pinky off the release aid handle so your wrist remains relaxed on that side.

Holding it properly is important. Surrounding it with your whole hand is not necessary. You need to hold it with the first two segments of your fingers only. This position will enable you to flatten your knuckles, and keep your wrist straight. This, in turn, is the best way to get your forearm relaxed so the release activation can come from your back muscles. In athletics, we perform better with muscles relaxed than when we're over-tensed.

Straight Wrist *Keeping your wrist straight while holding your release aid promotes a relaxed forearm. At full draw you then have the best chance to transfer the holding of the bow into your back muscles increasing your ability to execute a consistent release.*

Set the release aid tension so that a medium to medium-heavy force is needed to make it discharge. A light force will be counterproductive and only teach bad habits. You need to work hard from the start. If you struggle too much then lighten the tension setting a little.

Step 4 Rebuild your thought sequence. You have to do this now, before you do any shooting, to make the correct first impression in your mind!

First, hold the release aid with two or three fingers engaged correctly around it.

Second, learn to keep your wrist and forearm relaxed during the process.

Third, at full draw keep your drawing forearm in line with the arrow shaft so that your scapula is correctly positioned.

Fourth, under tension similar to the bow's holding weight you must further contract your rhomboid muscles so your draw-side elbow rotates about a hinge point in your shoulder.

Fifth, this force on your elbow will, through time, cause a rotation of the release handle and the release of the arrow.

Sixth, you must be patient.

Step 5 Demonstrate how to hold the release aid, attach it, raise, draw and release an arrow from a bow. It's always helpful for your student to see the final objective of his retraining program. Show them the accompanying photo so they get the release hand correct.

Next, instruct your student to hold the release aid while you attach and hold a loop of string to it. You must act as the bow and provide the force for your student to pull against while he establishes proper full-draw-position. Getting his or her release-hand position correct is important from the outset.

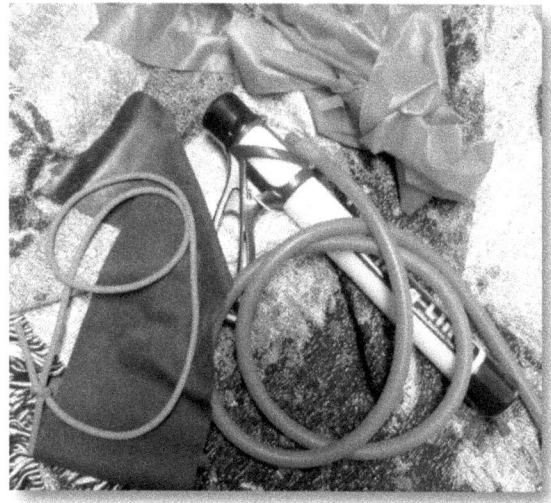

Practice Aids Stretch bands, stretch tubes and the Firing Line training device by Saunders provide great ways to learn and practice proper release aid technique. It all begins, however, by learning how to use a back tension release aid correctly from a qualified coach.

Be sure also to position his drawing forearm so that it is in line with an imaginary arrow shaft. Getting the forearm correctly lined up puts the shoulder blade in the best position for the rhomboid muscles to do their work. You must instruct correct form any time you get the chance and this is a really good chance. This person is really ready to listen to you because he or she wants rid of this terrible dysfunction called target panic.

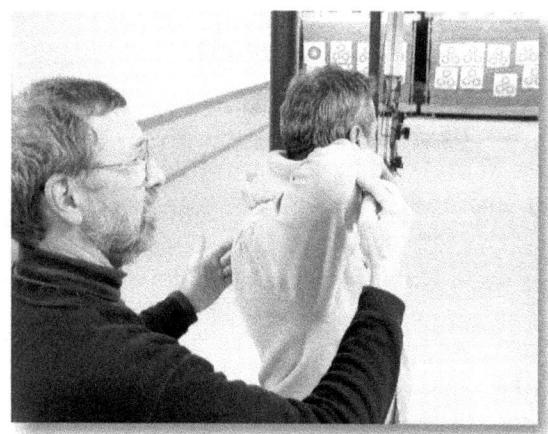

Full-Draw-Position Adjusting the draw length of the bow so your student can align their holding arm in the same plane with the arrow is essential to learning good technique. From this position you can transfer holding effort into your back muscles, further contract those muscles and use the resulting rotational force on the elbow to discharge the back tension release aid.

Once they have attained the correct position and you are applying some pulling force to mimic the bow, instruct your student to tighten their rhomboid muscles. Remind them where to tighten by touching their rhomboid area. (Use a pen instead of your finger if you're concerned about the "touching" issue.) In most cases, my students try to pull more arrow across the rest and I have to remind them that they must cause a rotation of their elbow about a point in their shoulder. The force from their back muscles rotates their elbow about their shoulder joint; their elbow does not move in line away from the target. Your student is practicing body position and correct muscle use for right now.

Next, have your student release the safety mechanism and repeat the muscle-tightening process. Hopefully, with some moderate amount of rotational effort, the release aid will discharge. Continue this process until you're sure your student is getting it correct. You'll have to remind them over and over about tightening their rhomboids and rotating their elbow about their shoulder. Eventually with your guidance they will get a feel for it – they must feel it!

Remember that first impressions are lasting ones so make your student perform correctly at this point.

Step 6 Allow them to hold the short string-loop as they assume full-draw-position and execute a correct release discharge. From behind their elbow you can again remind them which muscles to contract and how the elbow should rotate. This micro rotation operates in a plane that is tilted about 30 degrees from horizontal as that plane is where the shoulder operates most easily. Make sure they are holding the release correctly (two or three fingers only) at each step of this process.

Have them practice ten of these release actions with their eyes closed. You can stand behind their draw side elbow and help guide them through the rhomboid contraction and elbow rotation process. Remind them over and over to cause a rotation of their elbow about a hinge point in their shoulder.

Step 7 Now build a "string bow" for them with the long piece of release rope they have been using. Or, you may use a training device like the Saunders Firing Line instead. This mock bow will be their training aid for the next few months, and maybe for years to come. They can take the string loop with them everywhere they go, pull it out of their pocket, and take a few quick practice shots. They may get some strange stares but remind them that doing this several times daily is how they can reprogram their conscious mind – physical action association. You don't need a bow and arrow to practice archery technique – your mind won't know the difference if you keep your eyes closed!

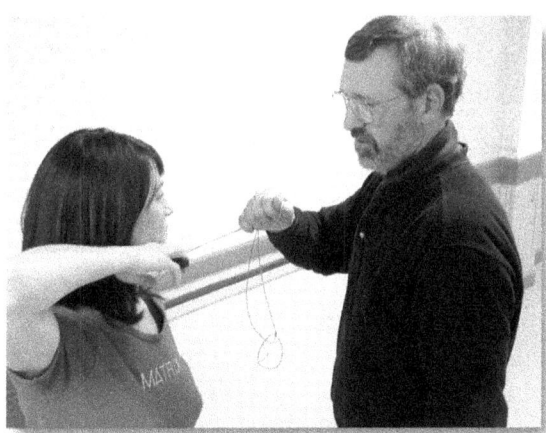

Using A Loop *I require my beginning students to use a rope loop instead of their bow. This allows them to focus on just the holding position and their back muscle action and not on what the bow or arrow are going to do. Learning to use your back is all about "feeling" the required muscles and the elbow rotation action.*

The string bow you build them must be the correct draw length so they can be in the correct full-draw-position at all times. Their real bow must be adjusted to match this same position. Correct position gives them the best chance for optimum rhomboid muscle use. Proper body position yields proper muscle use which in turn yields proper release technique.

You may have to demonstrate how to use the release aid with the string bow and how the string will be launched forward several feet when the release discharges. Most of my students have difficulty getting the string to go anywhere; it usually just hangs around their hand after their first few efforts. Remind them that they have to mimic the 15# to 18# holding force of the bow during their setup and back tension execution – many forget to do this.

Stand behind their elbow in order to guide them correctly through several executions. Touch their rhomboid muscle area and push their elbow to assist their rotation effort. Get them going in the correct direction. They need to do this ten or more times while you assist to be sure they are doing it correctly.

Send them home to practice for a few days. Or for a few weeks. Ten to twenty shots during each of four daily practice sessions is a great way to retrain the brain and the body. Tell them not to do all eighty shots during one session, as they will learn far more from the first few shots of each session and not from the last sixty of one long session.

They should not shoot their bow until they come back for the second lesson. You want to be with them as they shoot the first shot out of their bow using the back tension/triggerless release aid. The first shot has to be done from the correct position and under your guidance so that they get it done correctly. Remember, this archer is mentally damaged and cannot be trusted at this point. I mean that sincerely with no malice toward your student. They have a serious problem and to solve it they must follow the program in detail – don't let them take short cuts.

If your student seems too impatient, remind them that their impatience with their old release aid is what got them into this situation. It took them months to get into their predicament and it will take months to work out of it. Make them write, "Patience is a virtue" one thousand times! Okay, I'm joking here. Do what you can to keep them patient.

Step 8 Lesson two should begin with a review of the string bow operation. At this point they should be in control of the release aid and launching the string bow several feet on each shot but have them demonstrate ten shots anyway to be sure. If they need some assistance to get it correct then help them.

At this point switch them to their real bow and arrows. They should find this to be easy if they have followed their practice schedule. The large majority of my students tell me that operating the real bow is easier than operating the string bow – I agree. The real bow supplies a force that they must naturally resist instead of artificially supplying that force with the string bow.

Correct full-draw-position is an absolute must. If the draw length of their bow does not enable them to attain this position then adjust the bow to fit. I find that a full 70% of the archers I work with or see at tournaments have bows that are too short for them and, so, they are not able to adequately transfer the holding force of the bow into their back muscles and operate with poor efficiency and faulty posture.

Now assist them with their first shot using their real bow. Get up close to the practice butt, remove any target faces and remove the sight from their bow. In fact, it's best if their eyes are closed so they can focus on their back muscles throughout these first shots - they need to focus on the process and not the results. Remember, focus on results was a leading cause of their mental dysfunction in the first place.

Stress these steps:
1. Set hands correctly
2. Raise
3. Draw
4. Set full-draw-position and continue holding transfer.
5. Relax drawing wrist but keep fingers equally tight.
6. Transfer holding from forearm to back muscles.
7. Further contract rhomboids.
8. Slowly rotate elbow.

Retouch their rhomboid area and direct their elbow so that it rotates correctly about their shoulder joint. Get them thinking about rotating their elbow through back muscle contraction.

Twenty shots under your direction should enable them to be self-sufficient. If not, guide them some more until they become self-sufficient. Walk away so they are alone for another twenty shots.

When you come back to them, check their shot execution for another few shots. When you're sure they are executing correctly, send them home to do some eyes-closed close-range practice.

Step 9 *A home blank-bale practice session should be done from a distance of 3 - 5* yards and have the following exercises in it
String bow practice = 10 shots, eyes closed.
Real bow practice = 20 shots, eyes closed.
Real bow practice = 5 shots, eyes open.
Real bow practice = 10 shots, eyes closed.

Continued daily practice with their string bow is a must for months to come. In fact, they may have to do this forever in order to maintain the correct mental/physical associations.

Step X Through time your students will move to shooting target faces during practice and their routine will be the following:
String bow = 5 shots, eyes closed.
Real bow = 5 shots, eyes closed.
Real bow = 5 shots, eyes open.
Real bow = 10 to 20 shots, on target @ 10 yds.
Real bow = 5 shots, eyes closed.
String bow = continue 3 – 6 times daily.

When they come back to you for a check-up, watch them at 10 to 20 yards on a target face. If they try to "rip" the release aid through the rotation sequence it will show up here. Ripping is a sign of either a "quick" setting on the release aid or continued impatience by your student.

Set the release aid to a heavier force setting so more rotation is needed to set it off. Make them work harder and slower. If they are just impatient then put them back on the "eyes closed" practice routine and no target. It takes some people weeks and weeks to overcome the impatience they have engrained into their target-shooting routine – this is where the string bow or training device is really helpful, used several times daily.

Eventually your students will incorporate long-distance shooting at a variety of target types into their practice routine. All of this must be done with the back tension/triggerless release aid! Every shooting session must begin with "closed eye" practice so as to constantly rebuild the proper mental/physical associations needed for shot execution.

Step 11 My student, Ron, worked from November through the following July before we entertained the idea of trying a release more suited to hunting. There was no way I was going to put him back on the very release style he used previously. He needed a release aid that would feel the same in his hand as the back tension/triggerless release he was using . . . Ron needed a "pinky-trigger" release.

The little-finger release would put the finger with the least amount of dexterity on the trigger. This keeps all of your "smarter" fingers engaged around the release handle during the draw and also during the aim and back tension process. At that point, tightening back muscles followed by tightening all fingers will discharge the release aid. Tightening the bigger fingers will cause the little finger to tighten as well.

It's important that your students follow the process set forth in Step 8 of this program. They must continue to use the same shot sequence with the pinky release as they do with the back tension/triggerless release. They must also follow the "closed eye" shooting practice schedule with the new release.

Never put the back tension/triggerless release aid away. The back tension/triggerless release should remain an integral part of every practice session in order to keep your student mentally loyal to the back tension process. Any hunting release should be used for that purpose only with most practice being conducted using the back tension/triggerless release. Failure to heed this warning will result in a relapse of the target panic syndrome and the student's work must start all over.

Summary

Dealing with the mental dysfunction of target panic is never easy – it took your student months to acquire target panic and it will take months to learn to manage it. The R.A.M. Skills program presented in this chapter works, so the biggest challenge for the archer who has target panic is the big question facing all athletes: Are you willing to give up what you are so you can become what you can be! That being said, the underlying issue involves putting in the time it takes to accomplish the task and with target panic it will take some time. Your job as coach is to keep you and your student motivated and directed with the R.A.M. Skills program . . . because it works.

Chapter 15
Matching the Bow to the Archer: Selecting a Correct Length Bow

Speed (and I mean arrow speed) can be an advantage! We all know that and that fact has been driving bow design for the last twenty years. It is a great thing to be able to misjudge the distance by a few yards and still hit reasonably close to where you're aiming, but . . . (you knew this was coming, didn't you?) a fast miss is still a miss!

Let me clarify that a little for you. If your student's skill level isn't high enough to consistently make the shot then even 400 ft per sec. isn't going to help them put the arrow in the middle.

Or how about this issue: if your bow doesn't properly fit then your student's chances of making that one, all-important shot at that all-important time are poor at best. A bow that is not the correct draw length will not allow your archer to use his body to its best advantage and therefore shoot consistently. Instead it will promote poor and ineffective use of muscles resulting in missed shots when the risk/reward is highest. In other words, they'll miss that big buck when he finally steps into that open shooting lane. Or they'll miss that last shot in the tournament allowing their competitor to win, all because their bow doesn't fit them properly.

I've been on both sides of all of these situations and, yes, the mental game has a lot to do with hitting or missing. Sometimes we just miss. We're only human and missing is part of archery, but having a bow that does not fit properly is totally avoidable and shouldn't be the reason that we miss. The sad truth of this matter is that I see far too many archers who are using bows that don't fit. This chapter addresses ways you can help them get "fit" for archery.

So much of the new bow marketing focuses on speed and it is not that arrow speed is unimportant, there is just a higher priority – getting a bow that fits your body size! I like speedy arrows just like everyone else but the top priority when buying a bow must be how it fits the shooter's needs. Your student's height, strength, and full-draw body position must come ahead of all else.

You recurve coaches know that recurve bows are measured from limb tip groove/notch to limb tip groove/notch. Compound bows are measured from axle-to-axle. Recently quite short axle-to-axle lengths (27″–33″) have been popular with the manufacturers, but there are more bows in the 34-inch to 38-inch length being produced in recent years. These bows fit the taller guys that need the 32″, 33″ and 34″

draw lengths. I also see lots of bows made to fit youth archers who need draw lengths in the range of 16″–26″. So, here are some tips about fitting axle-to-axle lengths of bows to archers of all sizes.

Measuring Draw Length

Measuring your draw length is easy but getting it measured correctly requires a knowledge of proper full-draw-position. Your student can stand in many different positions when he draws his bow but only one position uses his back muscles most efficiently to hold and release the bowstring.

Proper full-draw-position requires that the archer stand erect, shoulders level, the bow arm extended (no bent elbow) and the drawing arm/elbow in line with and behind the arrow. This is easy to check from behind the archer's elbow as shown in the illustration. If the elbow is not rotated behind and in line with the arrow then the holding of the bowstring must be done with the arm muscles but holding with back muscles is far more consistent. Holding with arm muscles promotes inconsistent releases with the release hand pulling out to the side instead of straight away behind the arrow.

Full-Draw-Position *Matching any archer to a bow must begin with their body posture in the optimum position for shooting consistently. That position should have them standing erect; chin level, bow arm bones aligned and the drawing forearm and elbow in line with the arrow. This alignment will place their draw-side shoulder and shoulder blade in the best position to, first, hold the bow and, second, to tighten back muscles in order to consistently execute the release of the arrow.*

The elbow can be rotated too far around. In this over-rotated position the back muscles are compressed and far less efficient in providing that necessary and consistent rotational force on the elbow.

Place your student in the correct position shown – release arm in line with the arrow – then use a measuring arrow to determine the distance from the nock to the pivot point in his grip. This distance matches the arrow rest-mounting hole in most compound bows. This distance is defined as the archer's True Draw Length.

The ATA Standard Draw Length is calculated by adding 1¾″ (1.75″) to the True Draw Length. This measurement takes into account the width of the riser between the pivot point and the back of bow (target side) and is how bows must be ordered from the factory. The ATA standard must be used so that arrows are long enough to avoid pulling them off the arrow rest. Short arrows are just too dangerous so we must avoid

Short (left) Many archers draw short of the proper full-draw-position. Here the draw side elbow is not rotated behind and in line with the arrow resulting in the archer's holding the bow with his/her arm instead of the back muscles. In this position the drawing arm never gets to relax and releasing the arrow is inconsistent at best – it fails under pressure!

Long (right) Some archers overdraw the bow. In this position, the drawing elbow is rotated beyond the line of the arrow so that the back muscles needed to hold and execute the shot are compressed and not fully useful. Once again, shooting with this posture produces inconsistent results.

any confusion on the issue and order our bows using the longer ATA standard.

Most of the archers I coach, about 70%, do not have the correct draw length setting when they arrive at my door. Most have their bow set too short for them because they are not postured correctly at full draw as defined above. As they learn and understand what is required from the back muscles and skeleton they quickly align their drawing arm correctly and feel the difference in consistency. Loading their back muscles and skeleton properly allows them to achieve accuracy dividends and that's what we are all seeking. Obviously if the bow's draw length is set too short, you cannot measure their actual draw length until it is adjusted. If the archer's bow has run out of adjustment room, then another bow needs to be used to find his True and ATA Draw Lengths.

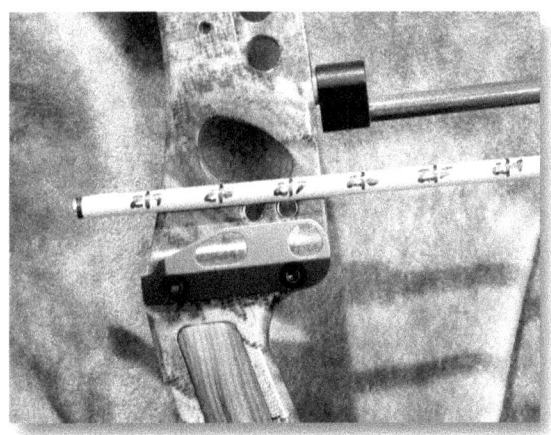

True Draw Length Measure Measuring an archer's true draw length is easy with a marked arrow. Have the archer draw the measuring arrow to full-draw-position as defined earlier. Read the measure from the nock to the grip pressure point or to the arrow rest-mounting hole (they usually match). This measurement is the true draw length and can be used to determine the ATA Standard by adding 1¾" (1.75"). The illustration shows a true draw of 27.5" to the grip pressure or pivot point. The ATA draw length would be 27.5 + 1.75 = 29.25".

Let the archer's body position determine the draw length that they need. I could give you several mathematical formulas to determine draw length but none of them take into account all of the anatomy and release aid variables encountered. We need to rely on our body to tell us what draw length bow each of us needs. We need to buy our bows the same way we buy our shoes – by how they fit our body.

Building & Designing Different Draw Lengths
I'm six-foot-two. Well, I used to be that tall (I think I'm 6´-1˝ now) so the years have taken their toll although I still shoot a 31˝ draw length bow. That can be a reference for you to use with all the tall guys that want to shoot archery. If they're over six-feet tall they will need at least a 30˝ draw length bow. If they're 6´-3˝ to 6´-4˝ then you should be thinking about a 32˝ draw length bow. If they're even taller then you'll need to special order a bow that is 33˝ or 34˝ in draw length.

Many archery shops don't stock many bows that give 32˝ draw-lengths or more. All those short 32˝ axle-to-axle compounds probably won't fit taller archers so you'll have to think longer axle-to-axle. Our primary focus should be getting each archer properly outfitted so he/she can shoot with accurate and proper form.

Longer Axle-To-Axle Distance There are several bow-design concepts that create more draw length. I'm sure, you're aware of most. First on the list of lengthening features is the longer axle-to-axle distance. A bow that is 36˝ to 38˝ long has the potential to significantly increase draw length over the 32˝ bow provided that they have the same brace height and same wheel diameter. An increase of four inches in axle-to-axle length increases draw length about one inch if all else is held constant.

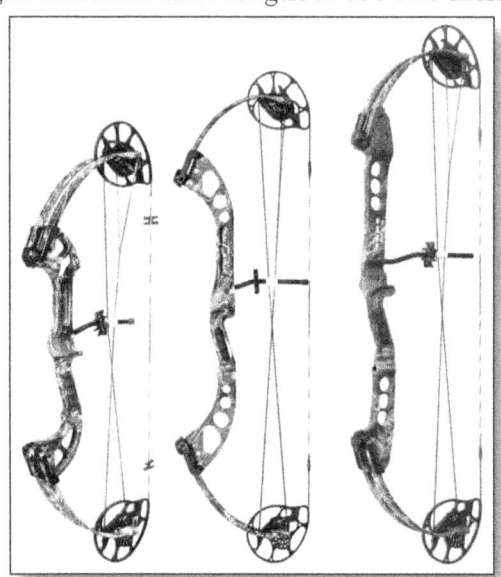

X-Force Standard, Long and Short The PSE X-Force is a good example of what can be done with a bow to achieve different draw lengths using different handle designs. The standard reflex handle gives a brace height of 6˝ while the long draw handle is reflexed less to give an 8.5˝ brace height and draw lengths up to 33˝. The X-Force Super Short uses a handle that shortens the bow from 33˝ axle-to-axle to 26⅝˝ axle-to-axle. This allows this model to provide draw lengths as short as 26˝.

Cam Size A second design feature that increases draw length potential is cam diameter. Greater cam diameter, and therefore circumference, requires more bowstring to wrap around it. This in turn means that the string must be drawn a longer distance in order to unwrap itself from the cam and get the bow to full draw.

Brace Height One of the more obvious draw-lengthening features is brace height.

If the handle riser has a deflex design (the handle grip section curves away from the archer) and therefore a higher brace height then, if all other factors are held constant, the bow has a longer draw length by the amount of deflex. Deflex risers have anywhere from ¼" to 1" more draw length over a straight-line design and over two-inches more than a reflex designed riser. Typical numbers to look for here are 9" to 9.5" deflex brace heights versus 6.5" to 7.5" for reflex risers.

Longer Risers and Limbs There are several other methods for making a bow longer axle-to-axle. First is the actual length of the riser. Longer risers will make the axle-to-axle length longer if all other features are held constant. A second method having the same effect utilizes longer limbs; having 14" limbs versus 12" limbs will make a bow two to three inches longer depending on the mounting angle between the limbs and the riser.

Delfex and Reflex Risers Many bow manufacturers incorporate handles/risers with different amounts of reflex to alter the brace height. The base-model PSE X-Force has a reflex handle with a brace height of 6" while the X-Force Long Draw has a more straight-line handle with a brace height of 8½" thus allowing the LD model to produce draw lengths of 30" to 33" with the same limbs and cam.

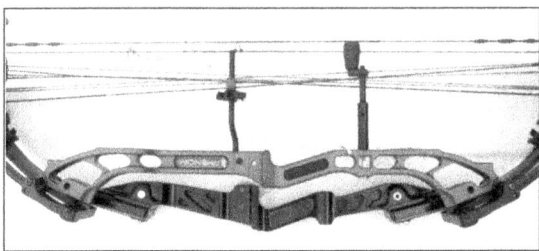

Deflex VS Reflex *The deflex riser design locates the grip pressure point further from the bowstring while the reflex riser locates it closer to the bowstring. The lower brace height of the reflex riser design promotes a longer draw stroke and more arrow speed.*

Long-Draw Guide

So here's the guide for your tall students. If he's over 6 feet tall and wants to shoot with proper form he'll need a bow that is 36" long or longer, big cams and a brace height of 7½" or more. If he insists on a shorter bow then he'll need hellishly large wheels – make sure he knows that. Most of these guys want the advertised speed of the short bows not realizing that they may not get a draw length long enough to suit their needs. Many of them also don't realize that with their longer draw length they can get that speed with a longer axle-to-axle bow by storing more energy over a longer distance – and the bow will fit them.

Guide
6′ Archer → 30″ ATA Bows

People of heights over 6′-4″ will need to combine several of the features mentioned above. A 38″ axle-to-axle (ATA) bow is a must in order to build a 33″ to 34″ draw length bow – chances are even better with a 40 – 43″ bow.

A good candidate for the long draw would be the Hoyt *Protec* I have hanging on my wall. With the longer 3000 limbs and the biggest *Cam & ½* cams this bow will make 34″ of draw length with an axle-to-axle length of 41″ and brace height of 8¾″. My Mathews *Apex* is another good candidate at 42½″ axle-to-axle and an 8″ brace height.

Medium-Draw Guide

This is easy! Most of the bows made today are for the average "Jack & Jill." That means most bows are made to fit guys and gals having draw lengths in the range of 27″ to 30″. Adjustment ranges on cam systems that are made to fit multiple draw lengths often cover this four-inch span since about 70% of archers fit it – just check any bow manufacturer catalog.

Guide
5′-9″ Archer → 28″ ATA Bows

This is a piece of cake! Most bows will fit these archers.

Short-Draw Guide

This category includes youths and women as well as shorter men. Draw lengths under 27″ are almost as difficult to fit as the long-draws because of product availability but the good news these days is that there are more short-draw bows available than in the past. And they are adjustable to fit that growing youth.

My friend Josh is about 5′ 6″ tall and a very good shot. You can use him as a good example of a 26″ draw length. Properly postured with his draw arm in line with the arrow he needs a twenty-six inch draw length bow using the ATA Standard. That includes a D-loop, release aid and the standard removed grip on the riser.

Guide
5′-6″ Archer → 26″ ATA Bows

This 26″ draw length then will require some design considerations. To fit this draw length you will need a 32″ axle-to-axle bow adjusted to the shortest draw setting. Some 33″ long bows may adjust to 26″ but you'll find that bows similar to the PSE *X-Force Short Draw* will put 26″ in the middle of it's 24″ – 27″ draw length adjustment range. However, the Bear *Truth 2* in its standard 33″ form uses modules to fit lengths from 24 to 30 inches.

Guide
5′-2″ Archer → 24″ ATA Bows

Short draw length bows require design features like shorter handles, smaller cams, and more reflex risers (lower brace height) or a combination of these features. So, for draw lengths less than 27″ you'll have to consider a bow that is not one of the standard models.

The design most likely to give the greater speed will utilize a reflexed handle. The lower brace height of this bow will translate into a longer power stroke for the shorter archer and that, as you know, can produce as much as 10 fps more speed per inch of draw stroke increase. The down side is the increase in string slap against the archer's forearm. Since the low brace height bowstring starts closer to the shooter's bow arm it can produce more arm contact after the bowstring release.

System Adjustability Features

Getting anyone properly fit with a bow depends on more than just its axle-to-axle length – it also depends on the draw length adjustability features of the bow. We have to do more than just get your draw length "close;" we have to get it correct within ⅛″. A bow that is a half-inch short for you will leave you struggling with your draw-arm out of position; you'll be holding the bow with your arm muscles instead of transferring the hold into your back muscles. A half-inch too long will also put you out of proper position, a position you may not be able to reach when drawing on an uphill or downhill target.

Modules I like the adjustable module system as a means of adjusting draw length on a bow. Just remove two or three screws, rotate or change the module and replace the screws. In most cases a bow press is not needed so it's really simple to get your bow properly fit.

String Anchor Posts Many of the bow manufacturers are designing extra string anchor posts into their cams. This second or third anchor post allows you to alter the draw length of the bow by attaching one end of the bowstring onto a different anchor post. In many cases the two posts are labeled with a zero (0) for standard and a minus (−) for the shorter draw post. If there are three posts they may be labeled with letters, A, B, and C for the longest, middle and shortest settings.

By moving the bowstring from the standard post to the short-draw post you are removing string from between the two wheels/cams and effectively making the string shorter. This rotates the cam into the draw stroke slightly thus reducing the distance the cam needs to be drawn to reach full draw. The result is a slightly higher brace height and a ⅓″ to ½″ shorter draw. This is simple and very effective but does usually require a bow press of some sort.

If there are extra anchor posts on both sides of the cam you do not have to adjust both string ends at the same time. It's easier if you do because the nocking point will not be affected. If you adjust one side only then you will have to relocate the nocking point and peep to their proper height relative to the arrow rest. It's a good idea, however, to check the nocking point location any time you adjust draw length no matter what method you use.

Wheel/Cam Size Changes Adding or deleting twists from the power or "buss" cable can alter compounds with a dedicated (single length) draw length cam. You can make these small adjustments using a bow press. Be careful to maintain the cam within its optimal rotation range indicated by markings on most cams.

If you have to rotate the cam out of its optimal range then you need a different cam size. This is why many shops have a few extra cams available for customer trade-ins. You may have to order the cam size you need.

D-Loops You always have the D-loop to help you adjust draw length a small amount. I often have to lengthen my students' bows by this method. The primary focus of my shooting schools is to get archers standing with the proper posture and that requires that their bow be correctly adjusted to match their needs. If they need a ¼″ more draw length then the D-loop is the easiest way to get it because you have to change nothing else in the system . . . and it's cheap! I always have a spool of BCY release rope with me for this purpose.

In radical cases where the bow is several inches too short for you, tie on a new D-loop that is two or three inches long. This will suffice until you get the right module or the correct cam size. It's no different from cutting the toe-end out of a pair of sneakers that are too small for your feet; it feels great until you get the correct size.

Release Heads *Different release aids and different length release heads must be figured into matching bows to shooters of differing heights. Switching to the longer release head will dictate shortening the D-loop or the bow's draw length in order for the system to remain the same length. Adjusting the D-loop length is an easy and cheap way to change draw length.*

Release-Head Length Many bowhunters, as well as target shooters I know, switch release aids as often as they change shirts. Most of these shooters don't realize it but they're changing the draw length of their bow/D-loop/release system because the release heads are all different lengths. That means that when they switch from a caliper release to a thumb model their drawing arm and hand are either a little further from the bow or a little closer.

If you or your student switchs release aids, your full-draw-position is affected and may be out of the optimum range for using your back muscles. If your drawing arm is not rotated in line with and behind the arrow then you will have to hold and activate your release aid with arm muscles and, as mentioned before, this is a highly inconsistent method of shooting.

It's simple to deal with the differing release aid head lengths by compensating with the D-loop length. If your new release head is longer, shorten the D-loop, etc. The primary concern is for the entire bow/loop/release system to be of sufficient length to allow you to establish and maintain proper body alignment.

Bow Grip Shape and Style Lots of bows have removable grips and, of course, archers do remove them and shoot right off of the handle. When you do this please remember that you have effectively increased your bow's draw length. The amount of change is equal to the thickness of the removable grip at the bow-hand center of pressure point; this is usually about ¼″ to ½″. If the increased draw length puts your body in correct alignment then all is well. If not then the D-loop needs to be shortened, the module needs to be changed or some other compensation has to be made to match your proper full-draw-position.

Summary

Regardless of what type of archery you plan to shoot, you need a bow that, first, fits your draw length. And, that, as you know, often dictates a certain range of axle-to-axle lengths. So, if the bow you or your student wants is not a good match for your draw length and will prevent you from shooting effectively then you must change your thinking. You have to get a bow that is matched to your height and that may be a different axle-to-axle length bow than what you think you need. Don't ignore body size and its needs when selecting a bow. Use proper full-draw-position and select the bow that fits.

Section 5
Parts of the Mental Game: Thinking in the Present and Thinking About Goals

Serious archery students need goals. You as their coach must lead your younger students in this department until such a time that they can help with and then take over the goal-setting job.

As a coach or as your own self-coach you must understand that skills are built through process-type goals and only later can you undertake setting goals that relate to personal best scores or finishing on the podium. Knowing this difference and using your goal-setting skills properly will get you where you want to go.

In this section read and learn first about process and then about goal types and some examples of each. Then put your knowledge to use with your students.

Chapter 16
Shooting Better with Brain Power

Have you ever heard: "I shoot well in practice but when I go to a tournament I always fall apart!" or " I shoot well in tournaments except for two or three targets or two or three ends." These are common comments I hear when I talk with people at tournaments or when they call me for help. There are lots of people who can win "World Championships" in their back yard but when they get to unfamiliar surroundings they do not perform at a level high enough to finish well.

I understand them because I've been there. I've been lots of places with my shooting. I've been up, down, and all around with winning, losing, shooting well, shooting poorly, winning long shoot-offs and losing them. I've had my bow stolen and bows break in the middle of tournaments but somehow I kept coming back and winning again. And so, the up-and-coming shooters or the old timers having problems call me and want to know what my secret is. They all want to know how to handle their "mental" game so they can compete and win.

There is no secret! That's the secret! Two things have to happen to manufacture a competent mental game – the same two that have to happen to manufacture competent shooting form. To perform well in practice and in tournaments you must first make a plan, a written plan, and then you must fully implement that plan. You must adopt the adage: Plan your work and then work your plan! If you don't, then every shooting venture away from home is a lottery – you don't know what you're going to get other than a high probability of losing.

I will bet my life's fortune that 99.99% of all tournament archers competing today have no written plan for the mental thought sequence they are going to use for the next tournament. In fact, most don't have a written plan for their shooting form. Do you think Tiger Woods has a specific set of conscious thoughts he disciplines himself to use for every shot? You bet he does! And he sticks to them knowing that implementing his plan yields his best chance to perform well. No, he doesn't always win but having a plan puts the odds in his favor. Going without a plan is not an option! Going without a plan puts you in that lottery situation with winning – maybe you'll win but probably you won't.

Part One: A Physical Form Practice Plan
In practice, you use your conscious mind to micro-manage your body while you are learning specific form elements. Since your conscious mind can hold only one thought

at a time you and your students should work on one form element at a time and that requires a plan. Without a written plan you won't build the best form you're capable of building.

> **CORE ARCHERY**
> *WIN WITH BACK TENSION*
>
> **STEP-BY-STEP SHOOTING FORM**
> 1. STANCE
> 2. NOCK
> 3. BOW HAND POSITION
> 4. RELEASE HAND POSITION
> 5. POSTURE SET
> 6. RAISE
> 7. DRAW
> 8. FULL-DRAW POSITION
> 9. AIM/CONTRACT/AIM
> 10. RELEASE
> 11. FOLLOWTHROUGH
> 12. SYSTEM RESET
>
> larry@larrywise.com
> 717-436-9168

Twelve Steps If you are serious about shooting and winning you will have a step-by-step plan for your physical form. You may choose to label and count them differently than I do but teach your students to approach their form in a systematic manner so they can make notes, incorporate changes and eliminate bad habits. They need to plan their work and then work their plan.

I've written about "Practice With A Purpose" before. Shooting lots of arrows by itself will not build good shooting form or a good mental game – it will build endurance however. To learn good shooting form a practice session must have at least three parts to it: First, blank bale shooting at close range; second, a scoring round of some kind; and last, finish with more practice at blank bale.

A good practice session will also be logged. You have to keep a small notebook if your practice sessions are going to have their greatest level of usefulness. If you don't write them down in a notebook you'll forget what you did during those sessions and have to waste time repeating those corrections or bow tuning changes.

Blank Bale and Conscious Control

You and your students must shoot at a blank bale in order to practice a specific shooting element. An example here would be practicing proper bow hand placement. 99% of my students do not have proper relaxed bow hand placement so they must spend time learning it. Do it up close to the bale, no target face and keep your eyes closed.

So, logging a written objective about your bow hand placement guides you to one specific task. Learning this one skill is done most efficiently when you micro-manage it with your conscious mind and to do that you need to close your eyes. If your conscious mind is undistracted by visual input then it is better able to focus on the bow hand and keep it properly placed and relaxed during the entire shot process.

Twenty shots for twenty days or, better yet, thirty shots for thirty days will establish this new hand position as a habit. In other words, after this kind of intense blank bale practice this hand position will be run by the subconscious part of the brain – neural links will be established in the brain to control this action and your conscious will no longer have to micro-manage it. This happened for all of the skills that you have learned over the years like "riding a bicycle" or "brushing your teeth."

Making blank bale shooting the beginning and ending of every practice session is essential to learning each specific form element and building an overall good form. You can skip this essential activity but you will pay the price down the road when you get to that next tournament.

Shooting the same scoring round as part of your practice sessions on a regular basis will help you gauge your progress. These recorded scores will tell you if your skills are improving or not improving. You and your students need to know that. So, sandwich a scoring round between two sets of blank bale arrows several times a week.

Completing Form Building

As outlined above, you and your students must work on one form element at a time because the conscious mind can micro-manage only one thing at a time. So, after several weeks of blank bale work on one element move on to the next flaw that needs attention. After another twenty days of retraining that element you can move to the next and so on. It takes time but in this manner you can rebuild your own or your student's entire shooting form and watch his or her scores get higher and more consistent. Remember, there is no overnight fix to your shooting form problems.

Part Two: Making A Mental Game Plan

Let's say that with your guidance your student works hard for six months to build a very consistent shooting form that relies on proper posture and use of back tension. Let's also say that his/her scores have improved - scoring 298 or 299 every time on the Vegas Round - and they head to a tournament to test their ability. What do you think will happen? How will they score at the tournament? Are they really ready? Will their blank bale practice pay off?

The answer to these questions is "doubtful" at best. I'm not trying to submarine someone's dreams by saying this, not at all. I've spent my entire teaching career – 40 years now – helping people build skills so they can accomplish their dreams. But I have to be honest here and tell you that they are only half ready. Even if they have great confidence in their ability they are not fully prepared because they have not built and practiced a mental game plan!

So far in their training they have used their conscious mind to micro-manage individual form elements like the bow hand, the release hand, head position, etc. That's what you do in practice so that the subconscious mind can take over the operation of those individual skills and the conscious no longer has to manage them. We do this because the subconscious can control many operations at the same time – the conscious cannot. The conscious, as mentioned earlier, can process one and only one thought or "picture" at a time.

So, once all of the form elements are in place and functioning like a well-oiled machine what is the conscious to do? When we are shooting an official scoring round what should we think? If we try to micro-manage any one form element our shooting process will stall because our body will tighten and this produces poor results.

If we think about "shooting a ten" then again our body will tighten because while we are aiming, the arrow landing in the ten-ring is a future result. If you think about results then you can't be mentally engaged in the process of shooting and your form will falter.

Several things are clear at this point: one, we can't engage in micro-managing thoughts while shooting an official scoring round; and two, we must not think about results, past or future, while executing any shot.

So what must we do? To perform at your highest potential you must engage in present process thinking! We must channel our conscious thoughts so you involve only the present time, the here and now! And you must involve the shooting process in general terms not in specific terms.

This kind of thinking requires first a plan and then the discipline to execute the plan. Yep, just like with our physical form we must plan the work and work the plan when it comes to the mental game. So if you go to a tournament without this plan you are taking part in a lottery . . . and the odds are against you.

The Recipe

What are the ingredients for a good mental plan for the time you are shooting a scoring round? There are other plans for the off-season, pre-tournament and post-tournament but for now we need to build a plan for that time when you are actually standing at the shooting line shooting arrows for score.

I find the following conscious thought sequence very helpful:
1. Affirmation of my shot objective
2. Relaxation breath
3. Visually acquire target and "see" the arrow impact it
4. Feel transfer at my full-draw-position
5. Tighten
6. Evaluate and breathe.

Others use some different ingredients or they use these same ingredients in a different order. Each shooter has to decide what works for him/her and build the most effective plan.

It must be a written plan. It must be logged so that its effectiveness can be evaluated and modifications made as needed to improve it. If you do not write it down, keep notes about it and make changes to it you are not *committed* to archery, you are only *involved* in archery.

Let me explain the difference between "being involved" and "being committed". To grasp the difference think of the "bacon and egg" breakfast. Yes, the simple breakfast of America's farmers. In making the ingredients for this meal the chicken was "involved" but the pig, aahh the pig, he was "committed!"

Committed archers write a plan and then work to implement it. They practice it

Breakfast *Are your students involved in archery or committed to it? The difference is explained in the simple bacon and egg breakfast. The chicken is involved in making the bacon and egg breakfast because she laid the egg. Then she went on her merry way to lay another. The pig, on the other hand, was committed to making the breakfast because he gave everything he had!*

during official-like scoring rounds where they try to maintain their focus on it during each and every shot. They practice their plan during every league shoot and at every local tournament. And they revise their plan as they feel necessary.

Explanation of the Ingredients
One: Affirming Your Shot Objective This, of course, implies that you first have a shot objective – many do not. To be an effective athlete you must focus on the process of you sport-action, not the result that you want to achieve. I watched the NASCAR race the other night at the Chicago Land Speedway where Mark Martin, the old veteran, was in third place for the restart with just a few laps to go. The two guys in front of him were more focused on "beating" the other guys and began banging fenders and took themselves out of the race (testosterone may have played a role there). Mark stayed cool and focused on the driving process that would get his car safely around the track – and won!

Do not let your desire to hit the "10" or the "X" get in the way of making a process-oriented objective. "Tens" and "X's" are results and, as you are at full draw, they are "future" events and have nothing to do with the present shooting process. So if you focus on results you will allow your shooting process to be unattended and your success rate will be much lower than it should be.

The objective I like to have is to "execute this shot with back tension." If I focus on that process then I will set up the best scenario for the arrow going into the target center. This must not be a micromanaging thought but a general thought about shoulder position or back muscle contraction. Micromanaging individual form elements will slow your shooting and tense muscles so don't do it while shooting for score; instead stay focused on the general process.

If you want to see some good examples of both just watch golf on a Sunday afternoon late in the round. Those who are process thinking will manage their bodies properly and make the critical putts while those who focus on results will tighten and miss them. Some athletes are what we call "gamers" and some are not. I suggest to you that the gamers are the ones focused on their process while the others get side-tracked into thinking about results.

Many coaches talk about a concept called "commit to the shot." Well, this is it. Affirming your objective is shot commitment. The only thing on your mind is completing this shot, completing your objective. You must be committed to it when you nock that arrow on your bowstring.

Two: Relaxation Breath We have to breathe, right? So why not put it to work for yourself by using it as a relaxation technique. Properly placed in your mental game sequence it will help you relax your muscles so that you can perform your shot sequence better.

Muscles require oxygen in order to function well. If you fail to give them enough of it then your aiming is shaky, your staying power is lessened and your ability to execute is in doubt. Consciously reminding yourself to breathe not only helps your muscles it helps your mind stay "in the present" with a thought that helps your process and blocks out other non-productive thoughts.

Three: Visually Acquire The Aiming Spot This is something that you also have to do at some point in your shot sequence anyway so put it to good use in your mental game plan. For me, this occurs after I've nocked the arrow and set my hands properly. That's when I have to set my posture upright, head over top my spine and turn my head toward the target.

As I first see the "gold" or "spot" I begin aiming. Not with the bow sight but physically my eyes, my head and my entire body become oriented toward that one point in space.

It is at this time that I prefer to run a little video in my brain. This mental visualization is always the same for me and consists of seeing my arrow being aimed, launched toward the target and actually hitting the middle. This "rehearsal shot" gives your mind and body the best preparation you can get for actually making the real shot.

Four: Feel Transfer at Full-Draw-Position As I'm drawing my bow I can feel the holding and control of the shot being transferred into my drawing shoulder and back muscles. This feeling of power and control is how I will fulfill my objective. This feeling is affirming that I am in charge – that I am in complete control. I know that I will complete this shot correctly because I am putting myself in the best physical position to do so . . . and I can "feel" it.

This always gives me the sense of going home. Have you ever been away from home on a long trip? And when you finally get close to home and pull up your driveway it's a great feeling. You're comfortable again. You're in complete charge again. That's the way you need to feel at this point in your mental shot routine – in charge physically and mentally.

Five: Tighten After you've established your full-draw control position then your conscious thought moves to feeling your back muscles tighten. Your eyes, head, and body are doing the aiming. When I was shooting my very best I was able to do this effortlessly – it just happened. In other words, I was in the "zone" that athletes talk about. The only image in my conscious was "back control" and my focused eye line was on the target center.

I never made a conscious decision (and I don't think anyone can) to just suddenly "go into the zone." I did make conscious decisions to establish the best conditions (my mental game plan) for it to happen. And sometimes it happened and sometimes it eluded me. When it happened I shot my very best ever.

Six: Evaluate and Breathe Because you've been looking at the target center when the bowstring and arrow are released you will see the arrow hit the target. The natural thing to do is to check the impact point with your binoculars or with your spotter if you have one.

Once you've learned the impact point you must then use discipline to evaluate it. You dare not get too high on praise for a good landing or too low on criticism for a bad one. You must have the discipline to carry yourself as near to neutral as possible because over the top emotions very often carry over to the next shot with adverse effects.

You must evaluate the "shooting performance" more than the landing and make a quick note about how well you met your execution objective and how to make the next one closer to your model form. If you made a good performance then you must affirm that you will do it again on the very next shot.

And now the really difficult part. You must forget the shot . . . completely!

This part is the downfall of many shooters because they can't let go of the emotions surrounding a shot arrow in a highly meaningful situation. By that I mean a "high pressure" shot when you're tense and you expect a lot from yourself. This is the situation where you can't clear your mind of the emotion and it interferes with your focus on shooting the next shot. In other words, you can't run your mental program cleanly and efficiently without interruption.

Thinking about future results or about past results can prevent any shooter from precisely running their mental program. Therefore, to be successful you must recognize that your mind is cluttered and stop all shooting action, allow your mind to clear (yep, this takes practice and could be a complete article by itself) and then get on with the next shot using only the thoughts that you've programmed into your mental plan.

What's Not In The Plan Is Also Important

It is important to note here that there's a lot that is not in the plan. There is no room in your plan for negative thinking. There's no time in your plan for thoughts about "winning" either because if you're thinking about either of those then you are not thinking about what's important for making this shot right now, in the present moment.

Likewise, there's no time to think about your day job, your spouse or kids, how your friends are shooting, or whether your car will start when the tournament is over. Although these are important things in your life, none of them contribute to getting "this arrow" into the target center so you must eliminate them from your mind before running your mental program.

The important concept to remember here is that you must "choose" what you consciously think. You can choose to think about the present task and allow other non-present thoughts to pass out of your mind. It takes practice, yes, but you can learn to do it – you can learn "tunnel" vision for your mental plan. And once you learn it your game will get better when it's "crunch" time.

The biggest asset you have for getting your mind back into the present is breathing. When interfering thoughts disrupt your plan then take a few deep relaxation breaths and think about them while doing it. You'll soon find yourself back in the present and ready to start you mental plan.

Trust

Many archers and other athletes work hard at both their physical game and their mental game but don't reap any rewards for their efforts. They don't get results because they don't trust what they've built. They don't believe in themselves or see themselves as winners. In short, they lack a good self-image.

Belief in yourself, of course, has to be there before the tournament starts or you're destined to fail. And so, we get to another part of the mental game; pre-tournament preparation. That is where you build your self-image. And if you are committed to doing that properly you'll "write it down."

Summary

It didn't take me long after starting my first year as a public school math teacher to discover that when I didn't plan well for an eighth-grade math lesson it went poorly. In fact, some of them were disastrous. The same is true for archery tournaments – plan well and your efforts will reap rewards. Take a plan with you to a tournament and you'll have a better chance of shooting the scores you do at home.

So, your job as a coach is to impress upon your students that they must plan both their physical and mental form. And they must practice both if they want to create their best chance to win.

Once again, there is no secret to being ready for success, all you have to do is plan for it and then practice your plan. For many years I had a sign over the door in my classroom:

Success is preparation meeting opportunity!

Preparing always comes first – it's true for learning math and for learning archery . . . and for winning!

Chapter 17
Present Process Thinking

Hour by hour, day by day, we are bombarded with advertising. Our radios, televisions, newspapers, magazines, billboards, computers and now our cell phones tell us how we can become the most beautiful, the handsomest, the most attractive human being on the planet if we only buy and use this one, special product. You can't avoid it, you can't hide from it and you can't get it out of your head. It's everywhere! That's the way our culture is now.

If you look closely at all of this advertising you'll soon realize that most of it focuses on what you can become in the future. It is all telling you how you can become "perfect" or nearly so just by purchasing a specific product. Buy this suit (and get one free) and everyone, including yourself, will like the way you look – you'll be perfect! In the future!

Of course the underlying and unmentioned flip-side of these ad statements is the conclusion that if you don't buy this particular brand of beer you are a hopeless jerk! A nerd! You are worthless! A failure!

It's easy to fall into this kind of thinking when it comes streaming at you all day, every day. It's easy for humans to fall into this "result-oriented" kind of thinking. We're suckers for it. Our eyes and ears find it easy to overrule our mind when it comes to making decisions regarding what we need. We far too often make decisions based on what we want and what we want is influenced by the advertizing that surrounds us. We and our society are focused on results.

Archery and archers are no different. We pick up a bow and we want results. We want arrows in the middle of the target and points on the score card. We want the best release aid, the best arrows, the best bow and we want them now! We have to have them because, we think, they will make us score higher and get us closer to that "elite archer" status that the advertizing tells us we can be.

Elite performance, however, is very elusive when you focus on results. Our culture tells us that the arrow in the target has to be the most important thing in archery. We are judged by our score. We judge ourselves by our score. That's what our society does.

But the arrow in the target cannot be the most important thing in archery. The arrow in the target does not get there on its own. Something happened prior to the arrow striking the target to cause it to go there. A human act occurred at some point in time before the arrow impact. Shouldn't that act be the most important thing about archery?

I, and I assume you do this too, shoot archery to measure my own ability to repeat a human action with precision. Doing it once is great but I'm in this game to repeat my action over and over and over. I'm in this game to see two, three or more arrows in the center of the target when the smoke clears. Elite performance then can't focus on the target, it has to focus on the human act of shooting because if the action doesn't duplicate itself then the arrows will be scattered; arrows can never on their own find the middle.

So, when you are standing on the shooting line, at full draw in the midst of aiming a scoring arrow you cannot, you dare not, focus on the arrow impacting the 10-ring. You see, that event is in the future. Yes, it's only a few seconds in the future, but nevertheless, it is in the future. Your body must shoot the arrow in the present and, if you want to create your best chance to "repeat," your conscious mind must be there with your body's action as it acts. If your mind and body are separated in time and/or in point of focus, then your physical efficiency and effectiveness will be less than optimal.

To achieve elite performance your mind's thoughts and your body's actions must both be in the same time zone. That is why I teach that your mind must be engaged in present process thinking while your body engages in that physical process. Do this and you create the best conditions to propel the first arrow into the ten-ring and have the second arrow impact beside it.

The Question

To open discussions on this most vital concept I ask all of my students the same question, "When you are at full draw, standing on the shooting line aiming a scoring arrow, what is your objective?" What really is your shot objective?

It is important that you understand the significance of this being a scoring arrow and not a practice arrow. When we shoot practice arrows we are most often focused on correcting/improving a particular form element. If we use the bow hand as an example then we maintain conscious mental focus on the feeling of the bow hand throughout the entire execution of the practice shot. We use no target and for best results keep our eyes closed. Score plays no role whatsoever and our mind is focused only on proper bow hand feeling.

So what answers do I usually get to this leading question? What answer did you come up with as you read the question? The most popular answer (by far) is "Hitting the X" or "scoring a ten." Others say "making a good shot" while some say "getting to my anchor."

Of course, the first two are thoughts about the future and not in a present time frame. The third answer is not very well defined and more like a wish. The fourth is focused on a form element that they incorrectly believe is the most important part of their form. None of these answers is good enough to get your students to the top of their game.

If your conscious thoughts are on any of the above then they are not on the physical process that makes a good shot. If you are consciously focused on the arrow hitting the 10-ring or the sight being centered on the middle of the target face or on the feel of your hand under your jaw then the more important physical process that actually makes the shot happen is left unattended. You are allowing that all-important process to happen at random . . . and you get random results.

What Is The Process?

So, if we are to engage in "present process thinking" then, what process should we use? What process with our compound bows and release aids should we use to shoot our arrows?

The answer for me is simple. It is what I learned to do many years ago and used to shoot my highest scores and win at the highest level. I use back tension. And I use a true and simple back tension/triggerless release aid that relies on a hinged seer design which activates when the release aid handle rotates a fraction of a degree. I generate contraction in my back muscles that produces a rotational force on my holding elbow which transmits to the release aid handle in my hand. It all comes from my back and not by changing pressure in my fingers to manipulate the release aid or some trigger device.

The official definition is as follows:

> **Back Tension** *is the contraction of the dominant side rhomboid and levator scapulae muscles aided by the trapezius which causes the scapula to slide and rotate a micro amount toward the spine.*

In turn this action places a rotational force on the dominant side elbow, forearm, and hand which can be harnessed for the purpose of releasing a bowstring through the use of a mechanical release aid.

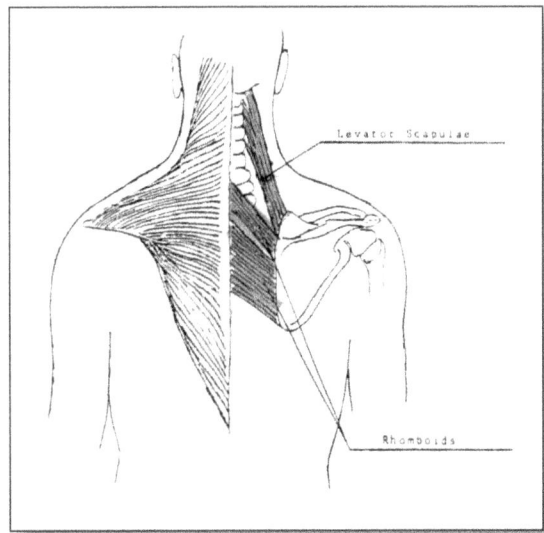

Muscle Diagram *The rhomboid muscle group and the levator scapula muscle are essential for shooting good archery. These muscles and the overlaying trapezius muscle can hold the bow at full draw if the holding arm is lined up (top view) with the arrow. Further contraction of these muscles places a rotational force on the holding elbow which can be harnessed to discharge a mechanical release aid.*

Now, do you need to know the names of these muscles? No, but you better know where they are in your back and you better learn what they feel like when you place a bow-holding load on them. And you better know how this rotational force operates so you can be efficient at producing it.

For right-handers it works as follows. When you contract your dominant right-side back muscles (*rhomboids* & *levator scapulae*) those shortening muscles pull your holding elbow around your shoulder joint. In short, your elbow rotates about the shoulder joint a micro amount, maybe half of a degree.

Study the shoulder joint a bit and you'll notice that when raised your upper arm rotates easily about your shoulder joint in a plane tilted about thirty-degrees from horizontal. Rotating your elbow in the horizontal plane is very difficult if not impossible because of the nature of the acromio-clavicluar joint at the end of your clavicle (collar bone). I always suggest that you should do what your body does most efficiently if you want to repeat your action. Understand this rotational movement, learn it, and apply it to your form to shoot your best. Same goes for your students.

Existing Preconditions

You don't get this rotational force from just any anatomical position. You must place your skeleton – and thereby your muscles – in the optimum position for efficiency and effectiveness. To consciously choose to do otherwise is making the choice to ignore the laws of physics and thereby ignore good biomechanics. To do otherwise is to impose a limit on your or your student's performance!

While drawing your bow is not necessarily easy, holding it at full draw is. It's easy to hold if you apply the physics of the lever to your holding arm and rotate it so that your forearm is in line (top view) with the arrow at full draw. From a front view your arm should be at least as high as the arrow and perhaps slightly higher.

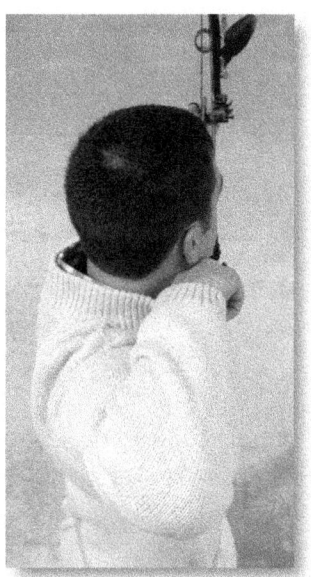

Full-Draw-Position *When you settle into proper full-draw-position then, and only then, can you transfer the holding force into your back muscles. Adjusting the bow's draw length to allow you to get into this position is essential for reaching your highest efficiency level.*

What you are doing is placing the holding arm so that it directly opposes the force it is resisting. In this position the bow-holding force can be transferred to the back muscles. To hold the draw arm short of this position means that you cannot fully or efficiently transfer the bow-holding force into your back muscles. Instead you continue to hold most of the force in your arm and not directly in line behind the arrow thus determining that you are less efficient and that your followthrough will not be directly away from and behind the arrow. By choice, your poor full-draw-position dictates left and right errors in arrow impact.

If you over-rotate your holding arm position then you compact your back muscles into a less efficient position. You also allow no operating rotational space for your elbow so, if you set up long or short you cannot execute with your optimum efficiency and thereby limit your ability to repeat.

By my counting at tournaments and assessing student records I find that 70% of archers are short of proper full-draw-position and are limiting their performance. About 10% are set up too long leaving only 20% of archers who are correctly positioned to be efficient. Is it any wonder a few archers win most of the tournaments? We coaches have a lot of work to do!

Conclusions
First Body position is critical to your archery shot execution. Your holding forearm must be in line with that arrow in order to achieve an optimal performance level.

Second Once you achieve your optimal full-draw-position you must transfer the holding force into your back muscles as named in the definition of back tension.

Third Once transfer is complete and the sight has joined your visual contact with the target center you must further contract you back muscles. This action results in a slight elbow rotation which affects the release aid handle and results in the bowstring release.

Fourth To achieve your highest level of performance you must have the mental discipline to consciously focus on this back tension process in the same moment that it is happening physically in your back. This focus is not a micro-managing your thoughts but is a more general thought of power and control that emanates from your back muscles. I feel as though I am establishing my "home control base" when I finish my draw stroke and transfer holding into my back. I feel my body "in charge" of the shot process and I like that feeling.

The Power of Present Process Thinking Just think, if your process is your goal on every scoring shot you make, then you get to celebrate on almost every shot. You get to celebrate while most everyone else around you isn't celebrating anything. They only get to celebrate when they finally achieve that elusive "high score" they set as their goal and have in their mind, or they only get to enjoy archery when they finish on the podium or win the tournament. In other words, they don't celebrate very often and maybe never. Unfortunately in our culture when you don't get "results" you can fall into the trap of seeing yourself as a "failure" when you are not.

You, on the other hand, are celebrating on almost every shot you make. You are operating in a much more positive frame of mind and, therefore, enhance your chances of achieving that podium finish or getting that "win". You, by choosing to operate in the "present," are functioning in the "positive" realm. You are the happy archer - by choice! You are successful – by choice! By your own choice!

You perform at your highest level when you control your mind to be in the present with the process that makes a good shot happen. If you take care of the process then the bow will take care of the arrow!

This will work for you. This will work for your students.

Chapter 18
Thinking About Goals:
Much Ado About Something

Goal 1 The reader of this chapter will be able to write each of two types of goals with 100% accuracy following five practice writings of each type.

Goal 2 The reader will be able to write goals for the short, medium, and long terms with 100% accuracy.

With these two goals well defined you now know what you should be able to do when you complete your reading of this chapter and your practice writing of some goals. Do you set out goals for your archery students that are this clear? Are you writing these goals? Are your students writing these goals in their log book? If not then read on and learn what types of goals your students need and learn how to help them set, write, evaluate and reset those goals for their training plans.

Two Types Of Goals

In most of the reading that you may do about goals you will find what I consider to two basic types: process-based and outcome (result) based. Each type has its place in an athlete's training plan depending on the needs of the student in a given time frame.

Our "Western" culture points us towards result-oriented thinking so much so that we easily overlook the more important "process" goals that we must use to build our shooting form so read on. Learn the difference, along with "when" and "how" to apply each, so your students get the greatest benefit from their effort.

Process Goals

A process goal focuses on how to improve a certain skill that has been identified as a weakness in one's shooting form. Continued student practice leads to skill mastering and skill mastering leads to improved performance and greater results. In short, process goals are the building blocks for getting "results." Without an effective "process" no one will reach any other type of goal they set.

Examples:
1. For each practice for the next month I will begin by shooting 30 shots blank bale focusing only upon my bowhand being relaxed.
2. By the end of the next three months I will execute every shot using proper "transfer of holding" into my back muscles.

Outcome Goals

Outcome goals are results oriented. In some of the archery literature you will read about Performance Goals as a separate category even though they are score- or results-based, hence just another kind of outcome goal. Regardless of the names you use for them these goals depend on how and where you finish at tournaments. They are based on the score you earn at a tournament.

From the outset here you must realize that you don't have full control over your place of finish because there are always other archers shooting at the same tournament and their performance may exceed yours.

Outcome goals point to where you want to go but alone they don't connect you in any way with how to get there. The outcomes grow out of process-based goals which must be appropriately applied on an individual basis.

Some of your students may need goals that are related to "personal best" scores instead of their place of finish. Regardless, they can only happen after a set of process-type goals have been achieved.

Examples:
1. I will score higher than my 70-meter average at the state target championship.
2. I will shoot a personal best score at the USA Archery Target Championships.
3. I will score above 400 at the State 3-D Championship.
4. I will win the State Target Championships.
5. I will qualify for a place on the US World Team.
6. I will qualify for the final shoot-down round at the ASA Classic.

The Characteristics of Effective Goals

Goals that are effective have several common characteristics. They are all specific, measurable, attainable, relevant, and time-based, **SMART** goals for short. I'm sure you can think of several other attributes to mention here but these are the five really important ones that I use in every goal or objective I write.

Specific Just saying "I want to shoot better" is not a goal. It's too general in nature; it covers a very wide spectrum of skills that have to be improved. An effective goal will begin by saying "I want to improve my bow hand placement." It will name one specific issue that needs to be remediated in order to enhance your skill level.

Example I will improve my bow hand placement.

Measurable You manage your goal by measuring it. The goal statement is a measure for the project; if the goal is accomplished, the project is a success. Choose a goal with measurable progress so you can see the change. "I will increase my average score by one point per scoring end" shows the measure of the goal. "I want to shoot better scores" is a weak goal because it is not measurable. And, if you can't measure it, how will you know whether you have met that goal?

Establish concrete criteria for measuring progress toward the attainment of each goal you set. When you measure your progress (and record it), you stay on track, meet your target dates, and experience the positive reward of achievement on a regular basis and that motivates you to continue exerting the effort required to reach your end goals.

Example I will correctly place my bow hand on each of 30 blank-bale practice shots from a distance of three yards.

Attainable If the goal being set for a given student is not attainable or realistic then it is worthless. A beginner, for instance, has no business thinking about winning anything. A beginner should be thinking about building a single skill or gaining enough body awareness to manipulate the arrow and bow while pointing it down range. A student who has not yet established a firm value for his 70-meter average has no business setting a goal for a podium finish or making a national team.

You as a coach must assist your student in determining what is attainable and what is not. Your job as the coach is to define the steps by which your student will eventually get to the podium. Team work here is important so that the student does not become disappointed too early, too often or too easily. In the example goal, four weeks is a much more appropriate time frame for learning proper bow hand placement and makes this goal attainable and more realistic.

Example I will correctly place my bow hand on each of 30 blank-bale practice shots from a distance of three yards at the beginning of each practice session for the next four weeks.

Relevant If the goals you write don't get you or your student to where you want to go, they are irrelevant. To succeed at making an Olympic team, your focus must be on shooting the 70m Olympic distance. You could set goals for 18m indoor tournaments, but they are irrelevant to making an Olympic team.

Example I will tune my bow and arrows until all of my competition arrows go into the 10-ring at 70m using a shooting machine.

Time-Based Everyone has dreams. Dreams are great and we can use them to help us achieve small and/or great things. To be useful dreams must be converted to goals and we do that by the simple operation of assigning a date to them. A goal is a dream with a date attached!

I can remember thinking to myself one fall, "I want to win a state championship." It was a dream I had. Sometime during that following winter that dream changed because I started saying to myself "I want to win the state indoor championship on April 4th."

Assigning that date to my dream changed everything. I now felt a sense of urgency that I didn't have before. I now had to plan backward from that April 4th date so that my training would condition me for that specific tournament. Writing that goal on paper made it far more real to me and I could begin seeing myself receiving the state championship medal. My brain was now fully engaged and my motivation elevated. A fire began to burn inside of me just because of a date!

Example I will correctly place my bow hand on each of 30 blank-bale practice shots from a distance of three yards at the beginning of each practice session for the next week.

When you incorporate all five of these elements into a goal then, and only then, do you have an effective goal. This goal is useful. Skip any of these five attributes and your goal is far less effective and may lead to student and/or coach frustration. If you are going to take the time to write a goal then be certain to include all of its parts and make it effective.

Time Frames and Goals
Another dimension of a goal is the time it takes to accomplish it. Some goals may take only a few weeks to accomplish while others may take four years or more. Choosing the appropriate time frame for your students' and your own goals is critical to achieving them. The wrong time frame can, by itself, lead to student frustration and anxiety.

In coaching we consider three basic time frames for setting goals: short-, intermediate- and long-range.

1. *Short-Range Goals*
Most consider short-range goals as those usually attainable in less than a year. Short Range Goals may be goals that lead to medium and longer-range goals. Many short-range goals are subsets of intermediate- or long-range goals.
2. *Intermediate-Range Goals*
Intermediate-range goals are normally attainable in a year or two. These goals consist of many short-range goals and will, obviously, take some time to accomplish. Achieving intermediate range goals may be dependent on the archer's growing maturity level or increasing skill, as well as, his desire.
3. *Long-Range Goals*
Long-range goals are attainable in three to five years. These goals are formed by combinations of intermediate range goals and are sometimes "career oriented". Certainly making the Olympic Team is a long range goal for any JOAD archer while winning a national field championship is long range for someone shooting their first field round.

Collaborative Goal Setting
I never had a coach so any goals that I set were done completely on my own. I learned that doing that is not always a good thing. I made far too many mistakes along the way and wasted great amounts of time and energy. Had I consulted a coach (there were no compound coaches then) I could have made much better decisions; two heads are better than one.

A coach provides a wealth of experience and a broader view of the archer's situation and skill level. The archer needs a coach to provide that perspective to him when he sets goals. So the coach's role is vital to the goal-setting process.

For inexperienced student-archers the coach may do all of the goal setting but as the student grows he/she must assume a larger role in the process. As soon as the student is able to participate in the decision-making process with the coach he should do so.

Reviewing and Resetting Goals
Coaches should foster their student's involvement in the goal-setting process as soon as possible. The student may begin by setting the number of arrows to be shot during each practice session for the coming week. After the week is complete the coach and student should review the student's log and decide how that work load met the student's needs and adjust the load for the next week accordingly.

This should be done together in the beginning until the coach is convinced that the student understands and can implement goal setting effectively. That occurs when the student can make realistic and honest evaluations of his own performance. That happens over a long period of time during which the coach is guiding the student.

Cooperation and trust have to be built between the two parties and that takes time. So in the beginning the coach makes most of the goal-setting decisions but as the relationship grows the student can take over more and more of the decision making. When the student becomes an elite athlete (some do, you know) then he/she will be making almost all of the decisions while the coach is used as a sounding board for the athlete's ideas or questions.

Building Ladders To Success
Goals are the rungs in the ladder to success. Skipping one or two or getting the rungs in weak order may result in a fall so the coach must be adept in not only choosing the goals but also in choosing them in the best order for the individual student.

In my beginning work with a student I base my own goal-order decision making on the twelve steps of shooting form I teach in my system of Core Archery. For instance, if a student's draw stroke is not properly executed then she will not correctly build herself into full-draw-position at the end of the stroke. Following that she is not likely to complete her back tension process easily or effectively. The earlier step of drawing the bow has to be corrected before the remaining steps can be effectively learned and performed.

Later in a student's development you can look to competition-oriented goals. Just getting to and completing a tournament while having fun is a good place to start. After your student gets a few of those under her belt then she can think about finishing in the top ten or on the podium.

As the coach you must guide these steps by choosing the appropriate goals at the appropriate time. Good luck choosing – it makes all the difference.

Section 6
The Structures of Coaching and Competing

Once you and your student have set the appropriate process goals to build adequate form and execution skills you may begin thinking and planning for those outcome goals that you have set. That means you and/or your students are going to take your game "on the road" and shoot at a tournament. To optimize your efforts in that regard you must write a training plan.

Read in this section about training cycles and the kind of structure they must have to be effective. Then learn about the kind of activities in which an archer must engage to be effective before a tournament, at a tournament and after the tournament is over.

I've also included a chapter about coach certification courses that you should be considering if you have not already done so. Earning that Level Two or Level Three certification is important to both you and your student in that both of you will then recognize that you, the coach, are training to understand both the compound and the recurve form models. A good coach should know the basics of both.

Chapter 19
Training Cycles

To make training more effective the archer and coach should divide the training schedule into manageable time units. These time units then can be organized so that the necessary form-building can be managed in the near future and tournament preparation can be optimized in later time frames.

Approaching your training in a random fashion – doing whatever you feel like at the time – is not an option if you want to reach a high level of performance. If you aim at nothing . . . you'll hit it!

Make a plan and then implement it. Try to hit something! The following will help you get a plan in place to guide all facets of your student's, and your, daily training.

Training Cycles Time Scales
There are three time frames that many coaches use to organize a complete training program. In order of increasing length they are the microcycle, the mesocycle and the macrocycle. Following are the definitions of each.
1. *Microcycle* The microcycle is usually a week to ten days long. Each microcycle varies in level of intensity and volume of training. Multiple microcycles make up a mesocycle.
2. *Mesocycle* Each mesocycle is usually four to six weeks long. Each mesocycle varies in overall intensity and level of training depending upon timing in the overall annual training plan. Multiple mesocycles make up a macrocycle.
3. *Macrocycle* A macrocycle is usually a year long. The macrocycle may be longer if necessary depending on the overall training plan. A macrocycle is a combination of mesocycles and may culminate with end-of-season events. Athletes should be at their final and highest peak of training at the end of the macrocycle.

Elements of a Training Program
Periodization of Training Training at a high level of intensity for long periods of time usually results in a slow degradation of performance. A training plan is needed as a roadmap and must include heavy, light, and rest days to allow for strengthening and recovery.

Training Load Training load is the amount of work done during a set period of time:

Training Intensity + Length of Sessions + Effort Expended = Training Load

Fatigue Fatigue is the inability to exert force with one's muscles to the degree that would be expected given the individual's general physical fitness. Fatigue is different from exhaustion which is a temporary weakness in individual muscles. Fatigue is a chronic condition that worsens over time if training loads aren't reduced.

Recovery Recovery is a muscle's ability to regain its strength. Recovery occurs quickly with minimal rest in physically fit athletes. A brief rest period, from a few hours to a few days, is usually sufficient for physical and mental recovery. Without rest periods your body won't recover.

Supercompensation Supercompensation is the body's ability to recover to a strength or ability level higher than from which it began. This is possible as a result of a proper training plan that incorporates recovery periods.

Overtraining No activity can be maintained at maximum effort over a long period of time without resulting in decreased performance and possible injury. Extended maximum-effort training periods result in fatigue, decreased performance and injury. Athletes who train at maximum effort immediately before a competition will have lower than expected results because their muscles and body will not have time to recover sufficiently before the competition. The muscles and body need time to sufficiently recover to avoid an "overtrained" condition so a training plan must include heavy, light, and rest days to allow for strengthening and recovery.

Specificity vs. Balance Along with the varying intensity of training cycles there must be variety in the training. Specificity training involves specific muscle groups performing specific activities so without this balanced strength training an athlete will experience muscle imbalances and be more prone to injury. You must work front-back, top-bottom and left-right, not at the same time, but in balance. Be smart about your training plan and you'll get your body in balance.

Maintenance Training Maintenance training keeps an athlete at an elevated level of performance for prolonged periods of time. Eventually there will be a plateau and possibly a decline in performance. At that point the training cycles must begin again. The cycle goes like this Overload-Fatigue-Recover-Supercompensate.

Training Logs

Training logs can be used effectively when planning training cycles. The empirical data from the logs can be used to show training intensity and the related results of the training. Of particular interest is the relationship between training intensity, training load, training duration and overall performance.

A practice log should include records of one's amount of sleep and general mood including feelings of anxiety, elation and depression at the time of the practice. Mood is related to performance, training intensity, and rest. This is a circular relationship of events that are keys to your overall health.

Training logs help you to evaluate the effectiveness of your training schedule and allow you to tailor training cycles to better prepare you or your students for competition. The old days of "just working hard" are being replaced with working smarter. There are plenty of resources available on the Internet to help you plan training cycles.

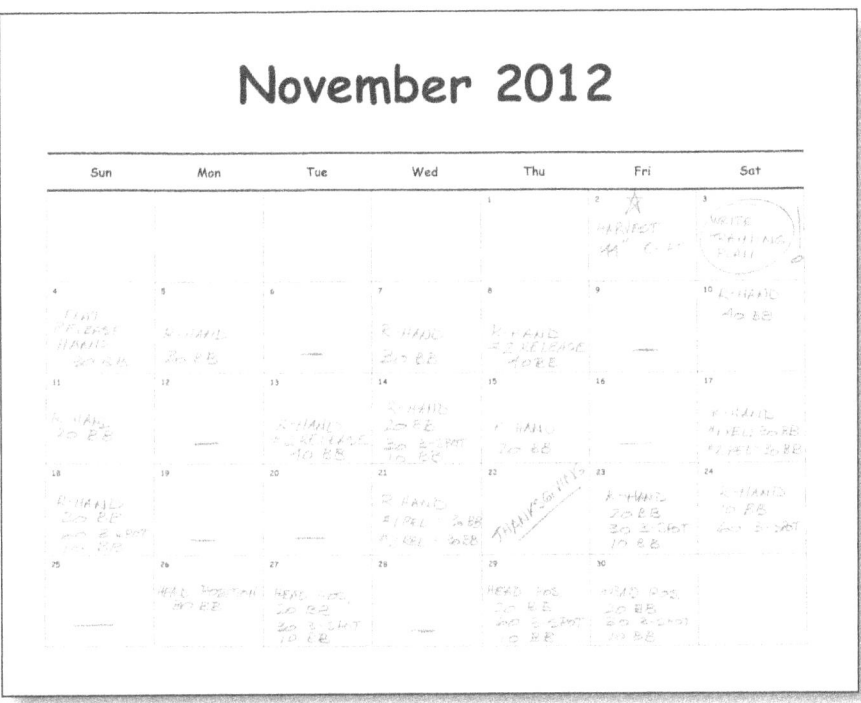

Training Plan Long before a major tournament you should begin training by correcting what you establish as form flaws. If you need to rebuild your release hand then this training plan is for you. It takes lots of blank bale with your eyes closed to establish a new habit so after three or four weeks of serious work on one issue you can move on to correcting another issue. In this example the month of December will include more blank bale training but gradually transition into more scoring rounds in preparation for the end-of-January tournament.

Chapter 20
Coaching Proper Archery Technique: Are You Certified?

Is anyone teaching archery in your local shop? Are there any coaches at your local archery club? If there are coaches, are they teaching the proper skills that are recognized and presented in the programs of the national organizations? Are new archers learning standardized safety rules and biomechanically sound skills or just flinging arrows any way possible? Are you a certified coach?

These are important questions to archers everywhere for several reasons. First, far too many of us learned archery with only the well-intended help of a few friends who passed along many home-spun tips and techniques that seemed to work, at least work well enough to make our arrows stick into a paper or rubber deer target. In my case that target was an old Tide soap box stuffed with cardboard – way too many years ago to remember.

Second, many of us (maybe all of us) have developed at least one bad habit during our years in archery and didn't, or don't, have any idea about how to change that habit for the better. Third, we've all done some things that were just not safe. I mean really not safe stuff that no one should be doing with bows and arrows; even kid's plastic bows can injure someone if not used safely – we have to be safe and teach safety.

Without a doubt we need coaches teaching archery. We need lots of coaches. Coaches, who know proper technique, know safe archery rules, and have the basic teaching skills needed to present these concepts in a way that is safe, interesting, fun and easily understood. In other words, we need coaches who have been trained and certified by our national organizations so that our sport grows through the addition of properly skilled new archers. After all, safe and skilled archers have more fun and stay in the sport longer.

National Organizations
Several years ago representatives of three of the national organizations: the USA Archery (USAA), The National Field Archery Association (NFAA), and the Archery Shooters Association (ASA) gathered together to collectively build new coach certification courses. Two courses were adopted by these organizations as part of their standardized program. The Level 1 and Level 2 courses are designed to teach basic instruction techniques for programs like summer camps and archery clubs. You

may know these two courses by their other names: Basic Instructors Course and Intermediate Instructors Course.

The Level Three/Community Coach Course

A third course, The Level Three Course or The Community Coach Course is designed to be the first level course for those who want to enter an archery coaching career and is still under development. This twenty-hour course introduces potential coaches to topics and concepts that will enable them to teach proper archery techniques in a safe and effective manner.

The essential coaching concepts presented in the Level 3 course are:
- Coaching Philosophy
- Recurve & Compound Shooting Form Models
- Goal Building & Setting
- Basic Bow Tuning
- Mental Game Building
- Tournament Preparation Skills
- Training Plan Building
- One-On-One & Group Teaching Skills
- Teaching Camp Instructors.

You can see that these concepts are designed to give a beginning coach the foundation he or she needs to begin working with individual athletes and with groups of athletes. In my mind these concepts enable a coach to do the following with an archer-athlete who wants to be coached:

Step One   Observe the Athlete
Step Two   Evaluate the Athlete Relative to a Standard Form Model
Step Three   Write a Correction Plan
Step Four   Implement Corrections

Step Five   Set Goals
Step Six   Build a Training Plan
Step Seven   Implement the Plan

One thing to note about the first four steps in this sequence is that they are a cycle for coaching. Each time the athlete comes to you for a learning session you must begin again by observing the athlete, evaluating, writing corrections and implementing them.

The last three steps get revised periodically as needed. For instance, following a tournament the coach and athlete review the goals that had been set and reset them for the next important future event. A new training plan can then be built around achieving those new goals.

There is an additional step: *Teach Others to Instruct Basic Archery Skills* that coaches have to learn as well. It will be addressed below.

Each of the seven steps in this coaching routine are supported by the information and skills taught in the Level 3/Community Coach Course. Here's how.

***Step One* Observation** Knowing where to stand when you watch an archer shoot is important. Of course, you don't stand in front of them or you'll get yourself shot! We all, at least, know that much. You also could guess that standing face-to-face with your archer/student on the shooting line will give you some very useful information about his/her shoulder position as well as their head, arms, hands and hip positions. You can also see their stance.

I find that standing behind their drawing and holding elbow is most helpful in several areas. First and foremost I can see if their bow is adjusted to the proper draw length by whether or not their forearm and elbow are in line with the arrow. An alternate position here is to stand on a step ladder or chair to see this alignment from an elevated position. Since I'm taller than most people I have this view naturally. Secondly, I get to check their vertical body alignment. And thirdly, I get to watch their followthrough.

Another good position is to stand looking at their back, again on the shooting line. Here again you get to see their head, shoulders, arms, hips and stance. I also like to see the back of their bow hand.

All three positions can also be viewed from a greater distance. Watch your student from about ten yards and you'll see how each of his form steps flows from one into another. This is important for more advanced archers and that is why I use both sill pictures and video for them so they can see the "flow" of their form sequence.

You can observe from these positions and tell your archer what you see but that can end up badly as some students will want to question the coach's eyesight. Don't go there! Get your camera and take still pictures of your full-draw student from each of these positions and simply show them. Usually you don't have to say anything – much of what you could describe is obvious. That's a big deal to me because a) then the student recognizes the problem themselves and b) he recognizes he needs your help to fix it. He needs to know how to fix it and when that happens you build trust with your student.

Front View *When taking pictures of any student I always begin with a front view so I can see stance, vertical alignment, release hand, head and shoulder position among others.*

As I mentioned already, I use video for my more advanced students. Usually their needs involve transitions from one step to another. They also need to be aware of the time certain form elements are happening – do things at the appropriate time and the shot is executed in its most repeatable manner.

Step Two Evaluation Once you have observed the archer you must begin your evaluation of his/her shooting form. Here is where good training is really important. Here is where knowing the standard form models for shooting recurve and compound bows, the National Training System (NTS), is critical to your student's success.

Knowing the models is like having a blueprint for what you want your student to be. Comparing the biomechanically sound NTS form models to your student's body positions allows you to note his/her strengths and weaknesses. Without a model for comparison you can only guess at what is good and what is not so good by using home-spun archery ideas that many times place the body in poor biomechanical positions.

Good biomechanics produces repeat performance so learn and use the NTS models. The models show archers how to most efficiently transfer the holding of the bow into their back muscles. This effort then allows the archer to relax his draw arm so that a more consistent and accurate release is attainable. We have to teach students to minimize muscle by optimizing skeleton use. This is the "Easy Button" for archery.

Step Three Write a Correction Plan Once you have evaluated your student's form – both form (body positions) and execution (action) – then and only then does it make sense to write (yes, write) a plan of correction. Writing it on paper or recording it on your laptop or smart phone is the best way to make sure you accomplish it. Recording it and continually checking your plan is how the serious archer and coach get things done.

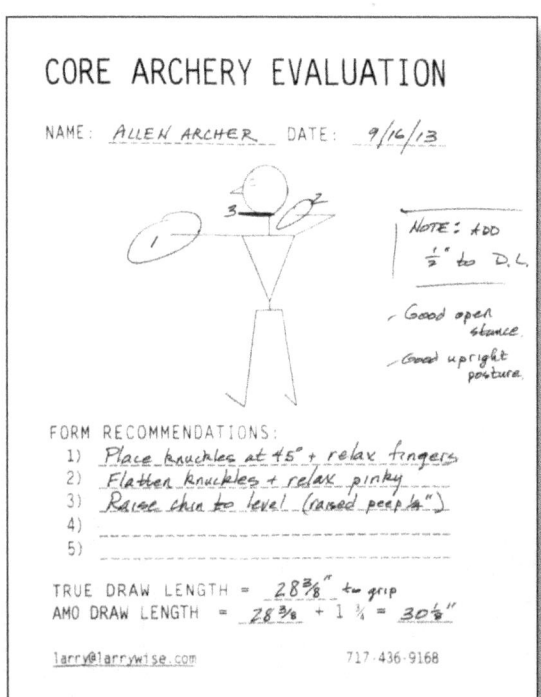

Stickman When I make my evaluation of each and every student I circle the areas that need improvement on my Stickman form. Following that I make a short note of instruction for each so my student knows exactly what needs to be done to make the correction. At the end of our first session when my student is in correct full-draw-position then, and only then, do I measure and record the true draw length of his bow should he decide to obtain another bow or rebuild this one.

My approach on plan writing is to record two or three high priority issues that need attention and begin working on those. Typically I pick those issues that occur earliest in the sequence of twelve form elements that I teach. Usually it's an archer's bow hand – 99% of my students need work on their bow hand. Even the most skilled archers that I have worked with need reminding about their bow hand. Many also need work on their release hand, fingers or release aid; a third issue may be an archer's head position.

Three issues to work on are enough for a start because it takes the average learner several weeks to learn a single new habit. The proper practice habits mixed with a good training plan will yield results on a single form issue in three weeks or so. The student can then work on the next issue in his correction plan over the next three weeks. And so on it goes until six or eight months later the learner has developed a much more reliable and repeatable form and is ready for some serious scoring rounds.

Step Four Implementing the Plan Here's where good teaching and communication skills come into play. I insist on being with my learners one-on-one to guide their every move as we begin working on, for example, their bow hand. First describing and then demonstrating are the most helpful methods to use. Then actually help the learner place their own hand correctly, keep it relaxed during the raise and draw steps, and maintain that relaxed condition through the release of the arrow.

Words create pictures in student's minds. This means that part of Level Three Course has to focus on choosing the best words for teaching a given form element. Essentially we tell students what to do and how to do it by using positive reinforcers and stay away from telling them what not to do.

Being there every second for the first few shots is essential for me to be sure the student does it right and "feels" the right method at work. Archery is a "feel" sport and you must do all you can to help your students feel correct archery form.

Using more still pictures here is also good. Once they get their bow hand correctly placed and relaxed be sure to take a picture of it for them to see. Make sure they get the pics on file so they can view it when they are practicing on their own. They can also compare new pics they take themselves with the correct pic you gave to them.

Eventually you must be sure that your student can complete the skill correctly on his/her own. They must do it without any prompting from you before they go home to practice on their own. If you do this then you can be reasonably confident that they will practice the skill properly by themselves instead of reverting to their "old ways." Practicing doing it the wrong way is worse than counterproductive.

I like my students to perform this new skill about twenty times with my assistance then take a short break. Following the break allow them to perform the skill alone but be ready to give guidance if they falter at any point. Repeat this "short break" thing several times until your student can come off the break and perform the skill correctly five or six times. When they can do this completely on their own then, and only then, are they ready to go home to practice.

I review the written correction plan with my student before I send them home and answer their last remaining questions. Then I have them shoot a few final shots to be sure they are correctly performing the skill in question.

Step Five Setting Goals Plans of correction get the job done when you as a coach have fostered a good line of communication and trust with your student. Through this process the student-archer develops a reasonable skill level and desires to compete. If you are training a bowhunter then he/she may decide to book that special hunting trip. This means it's time for the student archer to set some goals.

Goal setting is a neat exercise but if the student is left on his/her own it can turn out to be disastrous. Without some level of guidance from a coach, the student may set goals that are not realistic, not timely, or not measurable. The coach has to understand the concept of "goal setting" and so that is a major concept in the Level Three Coach Course.

In the Level 3 course we teach the concept of SMART goals. SMART is an acronym for Specific, Measurable, Attainable, Realistic and Time-based. Goals should be all of these with emphasis on choosing what's best for your student at this particular time.

Course time is spent defining two types of SMART goals: Outcome-based and Process-based. Most students want to choose an outcome goal like "winning" the next tournament but that is not appropriate for most beginners or intermediate archers so you as coach have to guide them to another type of goal.

At the heart of student learning, however, is the use of process goals. These goals focus on learning and achieving a level of success for a certain process or skill. Example "I will execute 50 out of 60 shots with correct back tension during Sunday's tournament." These kinds of goals build better archers who can, at a later time, achieve those first place kinds of goals.

Goals have to be monitored by both the coach and the student. That's why they have to be written down in a student notebook or in a computer. They have to be reviewed on a regular basis and rewritten as needed if the student is to make real and steady progress. Coaches have to be willing to do this and have the skills needed to communicate it to their students.

Step Six Writing a Training Plan Once you set goals then a schedule of when and how they are to be reached must be written. That means a Training Plan must be built to meet the needs of the athlete.

For the purpose of training it is convenient to think of your time in small, medium and long blocks. The terms used here are microcycles of 6-10 days, mesocycles of 4-6 weeks and macrocycles of about a year in length.

A good coach knows that training for next year begins now. Therefore, the coach must work with the athlete to choose those few really important tournaments in next year's schedule for which the athlete has goals set. Planning for those is then broken into smaller time units, mesocycles, beginning at the tournament date and working backward toward the present.

We work backwards because we always know what training has to take place in the last few days and weeks leading up to the tournament date. Usually that involves shooting many official practice rounds and working on your mental game plan.

As our planning gets further back from the tournament and closer to the present training must be different. Training in the next few months, for instance, must consist of form improvement and equipment tuning. Mapping this out in a week-to-week format and making it fit the athlete's schedule is vital to success next year.

Good coaches learn that training must vary in load (number of arrows, intensity and time) and activity. Shooting five hundred arrows a day for several weeks only succeeds in breaking down an athlete; one has to work smarter than that. Two days off each week is a must to my way of thinking; you have to give the body time to recover and become stronger.

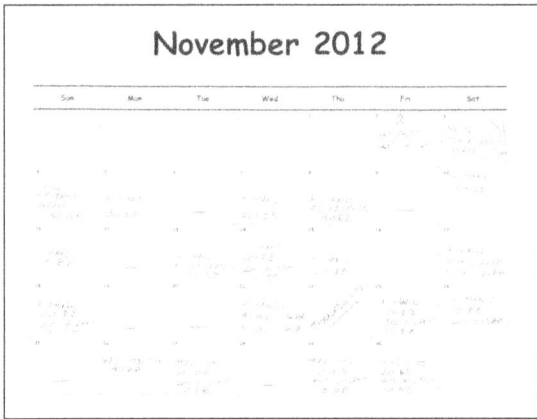

Sample Plan A good training plan requires an objective for each training session. It also includes blank bale shooting to establish new form elements and days of rest so your body can recover and grow in strength. As a tournament draws closer more and more emphasis is placed on official scoring round practice.

Level 3 coaches learn the basics of planning. Learning how to listen to athletes and work with them to build their own unique plan takes time and experience.

Step Seven Implementing the Training Plan Much of the training plan must be implemented by the athlete while working alone. The coach must be the taskmaster or monitor checking on the athlete regularly to be sure he/she is actually doing what is written in the plan.

I guess you could say that you have to "mother" them a bit to be sure they are working hard and smart. Helping them keep their attitude in balance is important; never let them get too up or too down. Monitoring their motivation is part of that.

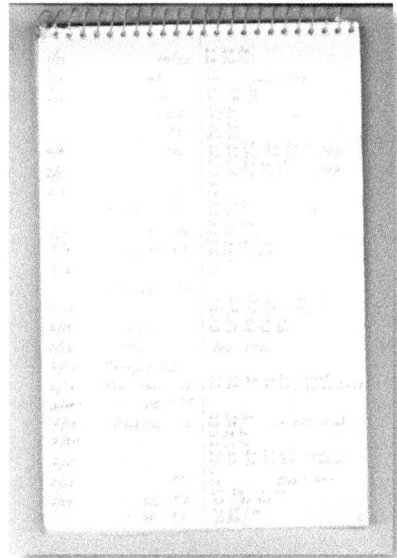

Log Book A log book can be simple as shown. Date, objective, number of arrows shot, and a few notes is enough information to make your future practices efficient – you will avoid duplicating effort on non-essential issues.

Larry Wise on Coaching Archery

When your student comes for a one-on-one session you must be thorough in implementing the first four steps of the coaching cycle. Their future success depends on your efforts in observing, evaluating, writing a correction plan and implementing that plan. Be sure to do it every time they come so that they progress within their long-term training plan and meet the goals of that plan.

Teaching The Level One And Two Courses
The Level 3 coach must also learn to teach the Level 1 *Basic Instructor* and the Level 2 *Intermediate Instructor* courses. Teaching others is how we can reach the maximum number of archers and pass along to them proper safety and shooting techniques. These are simple courses to teach but they must be taught effectively and thoroughly.

A few of the simple teaching techniques learned are:
- setting an objective for each lesson
- writing a time-period lesson plan
- incorporating drills that teach the skills needed
- learning to teach the Archer's "T" position
- listening to the student
- observation positions
- camera use
- positive language skills
- writing correction plans
- goal setting
- writing long-term training plans

The Level 1 Basic Instructor Course Anyone wanting to coach in a short-term youth archery program should have the Basic Certificate earned through completion of the Level 1 Instructor course. This certificate and the others described here are all available through the USAA, NFAA, and ASA national organizations and attest to the training needed to manage and instruct youth with little or no experience in archery.

Level 1 instructors must be at least age 15 (18 for NFAA). However, at least one instructor of age 18 or older must be present when any archery program is in progress. The certificate is good for three years and is issued directly by the Level 1 Course Instructor upon completion of the eight to ten hours of instruction.

The main areas of learning in this course are:
- range safety
- range set-up
- basic equipment setup and repair
- how to teach the basic steps of shooting
- learning to shoot a bow
- learning how to teach archery

To facilitate the learning in these three areas the following course content has been established:
- safety orientation
- archery range setup

- steps of shooting a bow
- teaching new archers
- developing archery skills
- equipment management
- archery program development
- archery history
- archery vocabulary terms

At the conclusion of the course the instructor-candidates must take and pass a short test on the above topics.

The Level 2 Intermediate Instructor Course The Intermediate Course is designed to prepare instructors to teach both beginning and intermediate level archers and to also teach the Level 1 Instructor course. The course is 12 to 16 hours long including a session-ending test. Teaching techniques for both recurve and compound shooting form is stressed in Level 2 as is the teaching and certification of Level One Instructors.

The Level 2 Course content is as follows:
- introduction to the sport of archery and its organizations and games
- review the basic instructor course
- review steps of shooting form for both recurve and compound bows
- methods of instruction
- archery class formats and lesson building
- class drills and skills
- teaching the Level 1 course.

Once certified as a Level 2 instructor you are able to teach and sign the certificates for Level 1 instructors. So, if you are a camp director you can certify your archery instructors for each camp season and eliminate the hassle of finding someone else to do it each year. Likewise, a shop owner can certify instructors as needed for each youth or beginner league season.

Hosting A Level Two Instructor Course

I write for *Arrow Trade* magazine which is exclusively for archery show owners and managers. So to those folks I say when you get serious enough about selling archery goods and services that you open your own shop then I assume you intend to do it for the long term. Or, I assume that if you take a job at an archery retailer then the store owner intends to stay in business for lots of years. In either case the "long-term" concept requires that you deal with those who have little or no experience in archery and, therefore, need a bit of coaching to get them going in the proper direction. It's tending to the needs of these folks that garner that "repeat" business keeping your shop doors open for the long term.

With that in mind then, why not invest a little time into learning the basics of coaching and teach your new archers the proper way to shoot and practice? Helping the new customers benefits you as shop owner because these new archers will come back for more. They will come back knowing that you provide certified proper and standardized archery instruction. Before long they will be your old "reliable" customers upon which you can build a successful business.

If you have a few shooting lanes or a local club nearby then you can host a coach certification class for yourself and those archers interested in doing a little teaching. It doesn't take much space to teach archery; just a target butt and few yards distance is all that is needed. I like to say that "to learn good archery skills you don't need practice walking, you need practice shooting" and two or three yards is distance enough to do that.

If you and the others in your group have some archery experience then you need only contact USA Archery to find an instructor in your area who can present the course you need. Most experienced archers would start with the Level 2 Intermediate Instructors' Course. As mentioned above the time frame needed is about 12 hours. The more experienced the group, the less time it takes to develop the knowledge level and basic teaching skills needed to instruct small groups of beginners and intermediate skilled archers which is, of course, the main objective.

The cost is minimal at $25 per materials packet plus the course instructor's fee. You'll have to contact the instructor to learn his/her fee schedule and the cost of his/her expenses. Some charge on a "per student" basis while others may have a set minimum fee.

I like to have enough chairs and tables for everyone – we do lots of note taking. You would also need a large video monitor so everyone can view Powerpoint presentations or video examples of shooting form. A marker board, markers and an easel would also be helpful. In my own case I usually bring all of these with me just to be sure I have them.

You should also have available several 15#-20# recurve bows and several 40# adjustable-draw compounds. The light weight makes it easy for everyone to draw the bow to proper full-draw-position and, therefore, learn the proper technique. I always bring my own back tension release aids (TRU Ball *Sweet Spots*) with me for that training – some course instructors may use only triggered release aids.

At the conclusion of the course the instructors will be able to manage the operation of a safe and effective archery learning program. Also, they will be able to teach the Level 1 Instructor's course and issue the corresponding certificate.

What A Certified Coach Can Do!
Here's a list ten things that I think a certified coach can do to help a business or club. A certified coach can:
- organize and teach a weekend youth program
- teach adult lessons
- teach Level 2 instructors to help with youth
- teach proper body position for recurve & compound
- properly fit bows to match archers' body position
- teach proper release aid technique
- assist with bow tuning
- help organize leagues
- help minimize the effects of target panic
- prepare archers for competition.

Summary

A Level 3 coach must spend the time and money to take the twenty-hour course. He or she may have travel expenses to do so if the course offering is not close by. Further, the coach must pass the end-of-course test, submit an application with his test, and also undergo a background check. When all of this is completed and approved then, and only then, will he or she get their certificate. That's a real commitment!

We need more trained coaches and we need more of Level 2 and 3 courses to be taught and more shops and clubs to host them. If you're thinking about doing that please give the USAA, the NFAA or the ASA a call or go to their websites. The investment of your time will be well worth it to your bottom line.

My archery success came through lots of trial and error. It took a long time to do it that way but I made it happen somehow. It's easier than that if you have a certified coach. And it will take you a lot less time!

Chapter 21
Tournament Preparation

Shooting archery is fun. And I plan to have lots of fun this summer. After all, I'm able to shoot right-handed a little bit again although my bow is only set at 35#. You can assume that I'll be a bit range-challenged at 70 and 80 yards. No matter, I'll just aim high and wing it down there. If it hits for score okay and if not that's okay, too. I'm not going to let four shots out of one hundred twelve get in the way of having a good time shooting field archery. I really like shooting field archery and I've missed it over these last three years so I'm going to enjoy it this summer.

Shooting archery to win is different. Shooting to win is hard work. Shooting to win requires complete commitment and the smartest approach to practice and preparation that you can muster. After you've done all of that then you have to remind yourself that archery is still fun (and mean it) . . . and then go shoot the tournament.

Let's get back to that "smartest approach to practice and preparation" stuff. There's a lot here that we need to discuss. In another chapter I presented the mental game plan for defining and using your conscious mental thoughts while shooting a scoring arrow. The concept I presented is that your conscious mental thoughts should not be a lottery selection but rather a chosen and practiced plan.

Pre-tournament preparation is just as important for the mental game as it is for the physical game. Following are some concepts that will help you do a better job of getting mentally ready for your next tournament or for next season.

Training Cycle Organization

Organize your long-term training plan by dividing it into smaller, manageable time frames. You can build into these time frames the work you need to do on the pre-tournament physical and mental practice. This planning is a big part of the mental game.

The largest training-time unit is the "macrocycle" which is about a year long. Serious training plans will divide that year into eight to ten "mesocycles" each four to six weeks long with each mesocycle divided into seven-to-ten day "microcycles." Using this structure we can effectively manage athletic training to reach our peak performance level for those few really important tournaments we plan to win.

Backward Planning Mesocycles Begin by printing full-page calendars for each month of the coming year. With the two or three most important tournaments marked on these pages you can begin planning backwards from each major tournament.

We know that the mesocycle immediately preceding any tournament is the most important for practicing both official scoring rounds and your mental game plan. During this four- to six-week period you need to be practicing the mental thought sequence you plan to use for each and every scoring arrow as well as your physical form steps. You also need to do any pre-tournament travel planning and equipment preparation.

The mesocycle immediately preceding a tournament should be divided into four or five microcycles (time permitting), each seven to ten days long. This will enable you to regulate your practice load and mental focus levels according to a plan instead of at random. When you played high school or college sports your coaches did this for you by regulating your practice schedule, load, and type before the first game of the season and between games after that. Now you have to do it for yourself. If you're smart, you'll ask a coach to help. Leaving it to chance is like playing with fire . . . you're going to get burned.

Practice at random and you'll get random results!

Sample Microcycle 10-Day, Low-Volume, NFAA Indoor Prep
(Remember to set a form improvement objective for each session. For this example I'll use bow hand technique.)
1. 30 shots @ blank bale (BB) + 10 @ 20 yd @ five-spot target
2. 10 BB + Score 30 @ 20 yd five-spot + 10 BB
3. No shooting
4. 10 BB + Score 30 @ 20 yd @ local club
5. No shooting
6. 20 BB + Score 30 @ 20 yd @ local club
7. 30 BB
8. No shooting
9. 60 @ 20 yd @ five-spot + 10 BB
10. 10 BB + 30 @ 20 yd @ local club + 10 BB.

Every shot at the blank bale (BB) must be focused on correct execution of the bow hand. Stand close to the target butt and keep your eyes closed to get your best results.

Archers preparing for a major tournament will shoot more arrows than this but everyone must schedule rest days so their bodies can recover and grow stronger. No one can maintain a continuous high volume of shooting over a long period and expect to get better.

Every microcycle must have two or three days of rest built into it and a variety of activities, focus and duration. This variety is good for both the mind and body so that neither gets stale or over-conditioned to one specific activity. Vary your practice activities and you'll improve your adaptability.

The intensity of consecutive microcycles must be varied as well. If the sample cycle above is of greater total load (Load = intensity + length + effort) than the previous cycle then the following cycle must be of lesser intensity so the body can recover from the workload. (Subsequent alternating cycles after that may have increasingly higher loads in order to build endurance.) During this recovery a stronger and more developed body will emerge. Without alternating periods of reduced and elevated workload the body's performance will not recover and may, in fact, regress.

Review Your Mental Thought Sequence

As you near tournament time your physical form has been whipped into rather good shape. That means that you no longer need to micromanage any single action or phase of the shot sequence – they are operated by your subconscious mind. That leaves your conscious mind free to "think" about other stuff and the really neat feature of this situation is you or your students get to decide what those thoughts are and when to think them.

Here's a sample of the conscious thought sequence that I have used. You may like to arrange it differently, which is fine, just be certain to have a plan to follow. Your plan, however, must include Step 5 – you must be present process thinking at the point when your back muscles are making their final contraction which results in the release of the arrow.

Sample Thought Sequence

1. Affirmation of my shot objective.
2. Breathe to relax.
3. Visually acquire target and mentally visualize the arrow impacting it.
4. Feel transfer of holding when setting full-draw-position.
5. Engage in the process of back tension.
6. Evaluate and breathe.

The important concept to remember here is that you "choose" what you consciously think. You can choose to think about the present task and allow other non-present thoughts to pass out of your mind. It takes practice, yes, but you can learn to do it – you can learn "tunnel" vision for your eyes and "tunnel" thinking for you conscious mind. And once you learn it you will create the best circumstances for reaching your highest performance level.

What's not in the plan is also important. What's missing are negative thoughts or extraneous thoughts that take you away from the present time and process. If you learn your plan and stick to it then there is no time to be thinking about matters other than the thoughts in your plan. And so when one of these "other" thoughts barges into your desired thought sequence you have to stop, let down, allow that thought to pass and then restart your mental program at the beginning. You can learn to do this and get good at it but only if you plan it and then practice it.

The most critical part of your program is what you think as you are physically engaging in your back tension process. Your conscious mind's attention must be in the same time frame with your physical action and focused on the process that generates a good shot – back tension.

The Pre-Tournament Mesocycle

The four to six weeks prior to any tournament is a critical period in training. It is for any athlete in any sport. A very structured schedule of action, diet, and rest not only prepares one's body for the upcoming important event it also prepares the mind. That same time should also allow you to do some contingency planning for those times when something goes wrong – it's like Murphy said, "If it can go wrong, it will!"

Here's a sample training program you might use to prepare for the NFAA Indoor National Championships. That tournament uses the five-spot blue and white target face on which you must shoot one official round each of two consecutive days. The five-spot target is more difficult to shoot than the three-spot target because of shooting five arrows in the four minutes allowed. In short, it's more physically and mentally demanding.

Sample Four-Week Training Plan
(for the NFAA Indoor National Championships with 28 days to train)

Prep Week One
28. Full Practice Round #1 Bow = 10 Practice + 60 Score
27. Half Round #1 Bow = 10p + 30s, + Half Round #2 Bow = 10p + 30s
26. Bow Tuning Issues As Needed (100 Shots Max)
25. Exercise Only
24. Mental Game Practice = No Target 20 Shots, 10 Min Break, Repeat 4 Times
23. Half Round #1 Bow = 10p + 30s + Half Round #2 Bow = 10p + 30s
22. Bow Tuning If Needed = 50 shots Max

Prep Week 2
21. Mental Game Practice = No Target, 20 Shots, 10 Min Break, Repeat 4 Times
20. Full Practice Round = 10p + 60s
19. Rest
18. Mental Game Practice = 20s, Break, Repeat 4 More Times
17. Start Game Practice = 10p + 15s, Repeat Twice + 1/2 Round Practice = 30s
16. Mental Practice = 20s + Full Practice Round = 10p + 60s
15. Exercise

Prep Week 3
14. Starting Game Practice = 10 Practice Shots + 15 Scoring, 10 Minute Break. Repeat 4 Times
13. Half-Round Practice = 10p + 30s, 10 Min. Break. Repeat 3 Times.
12. Exercise + Finalize Travel Arrangements
11. Starting Game Practice = 10p + 15s, Repeat 4 Times
10. Full Practice Round = 10p + 60s + Backup Bow Practice = 10p + 60s
9. Starting Game Practice = 10p + 15s, Repeat 3 Times
8. Exercise Only

Final Prep Week
7. Full Practice Round = 10p + 60s
6. Full Practice Round = 10p + 60s + Backup Bow = 60s

5. Exercise Only
4. Full Practice Round = 10p + 60s + Backup Bow = 60s
3. Full Practice Round = 10p + 60s
2. #1 Bow = 30p + #2 Bow = 30p
1. Exercise Only + Travel

During each and every scoring shot of your prep weeks you must use your mental thought sequence as if you were in the actual tournament setting. If you or your students cheat on this you are only cheating yourselves and this leads to disappointment on tournament weekend. Learn to "see" and "feel" yourself already at the tournament for these practice rounds.

It helps to have your thought sequence printed on a 3x5 card in your quiver. Get it out and read it often. Read it before the first arrow of each end. Read it after the last arrow of the end. Read it between shots. Doing so will keep your conscious mind on the "present" task at hand and help prevent your thoughts from wandering off task.

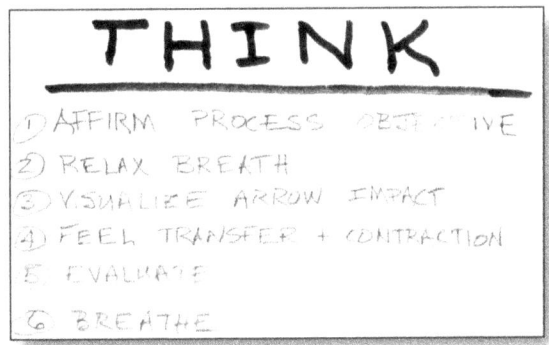

Sample 3x5 Card Writing your thought sequence on a 3x5 card and keeping it in your quiver or pocket is a great way to help you stay on track. Read it before each end or before each arrow and then stick to it during the shot execution. Plan it and then do it so you stay in the present when it counts.

During those hours when you are not shooting it may be helpful to think about your beginning game. In other words think only about the first few arrows of the tournament. See yourself shooting the two practice ends and getting smoother and settled during those ten arrows. Then see yourself shooting that first arrow for score and smoothly moving to the next and then the next, etc. This is a manageable task. Thinking about shooting the entire first round with a perfect score is a bit too much to carry in your head so don't do it – reduce the load and think about the beginning only.

KISS = Keep It Smart & Simple because simplicity repeats under pressure!

Most indoor archers I know shoot in a local league several nights a week. If you do this then your practice schedule will have to be adjusted to accommodate the league shooting load and the duration so that you do not beat yourself into the ground trying to get ready for the big tournament. Control the number of arrows shot and be certain to schedule rest days.

Setting Goals
Take out a piece of paper or find a page in your archery notebook/log and write your

goals for the next tournament for which you are training. Have your students do the writing for themselves—seeing their goals in their own handwriting gives them a sense of ownership. There are two types of goals you can make, results- or outcome-oriented goals or process-oriented goals.

Result-oriented goals are those that focus on where you finish relative to your competitors. An example would be "I want to finish in the top three" or "I want to win".

A process goal would be "I want to execute at least 50 out of 60 shots with good back tension." These types of goals are more for an archer who is still learning or someone who is rebuilding form and not ready to set results type goals.

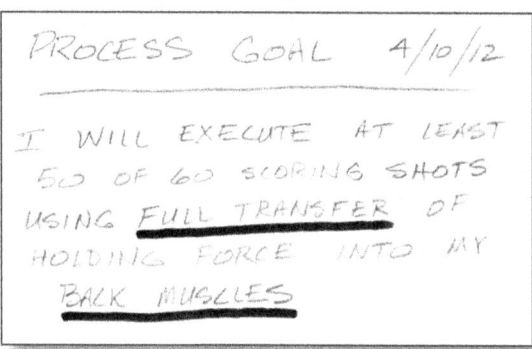

Process Goal Having a process goal is the first thing you must do if you want to get better. Writing it and reading it frequently is a strong step toward accomplishing it. Make this goal fit into your training plan and record your progress in your shooting log.

Set a goal; write it in your notebook and save it for after the tournament. A few days after the tournament is over you can review it, evaluate it, and make a new goal for the next tournament. Be sure to wait several days because your judgment is clouded the day immediately following a tournament – clearer several days later. Coaches should participate in this process as athletes do not always see things clearly, especially when winning or falling very short.

Summary

Get organized by planning your training. Stick to your plan. Be sure to also organize your mental thoughts and practice them. If you fail to organize then how will you evaluate your performance and adjust your training plan after the tournament is over? Answer: you can't. You're just rolling the dice when you go to a tournament without a plan.

Plan the Work,
then
Work the Plan!

Chapter 22
Tournament Site Practice

I always found travel days relaxing. I guess mostly because I had to prepare several days of lesson plans for my substitute teacher before I left my classroom. I also had to pack clothes and equipment, complete house and yard chores, and squeeze in a final bit of practice. So, when my butt hit the airplane seat or the car seat I could breathe a sigh of relief and think only about the tournament.

Chilling out was my main focus during travel. As I got nearer the tournament site I could begin thinking about the practice I was going to do. I could reaffirm my practice day plan and relax some more. The question is, "What is a good plan?" I have some ideas that worked for me that I'll pass along in the following paragraphs.

Tournament Site Practice
Once you get to the tournament location you and/or your student will want to practice. I recommend shooting only a half round, taking a break and then shooting another half round. Or concentrate on doing some starting game practice. After all, there is nothing you can do now to better prepare yourself.

Affixing an enormous amount of value on the score of a full practice round, I always found, was counterproductive. If I shot really well I got to thinking about shooting a complete and perfect round the next day instead of thinking about shooting a smooth beginning and letting my preparation take care of the rest. Or, if I shot a lousy score in this practice round I was in a negative frame of mind and overly anxious for the next day. If I missed a few shots that's all I thought about for hours. Instead, focus on getting smooth during the two practice ends and first few scoring ends – this has real and positive benefits for your mental attitude.

Don't shoot too much! Some archers I know always shoot as many practice arrows as they can the day before the tournament. Some of them shoot two full practice rounds or more. This dissipates that built up nervous energy but doesn't help you for the next day – it may, in fact, wear you out. Having a specific purpose for your practice is much more beneficial and gets you mentally relaxed – set your purpose and accomplish it and you'll feel mentally and physically ready for the next day.

Because you've kept a log of your practice scores during the four weeks prior to the tournament you know your "true" average. Don't expect to shoot over your average at the tournament. That's unrealistic. Do expect to shoot equal to or very near your average. That's realistic.

Your game is not going to take a big jump in skill or score just because you arrived at a new location. Yeah, you think you'll be more focused but don't forget there will be more "new" things to distract you if you let them.

Tournament Day

The first thing I always did the morning of a tournament round was to go for a short jog or a brisk walk. This was my way of getting my body into a more normal rhythm just like at home where I jog and walk as part of my exercise program. During this time I could think about how relaxed I was feeling and was going to feel when my time to shoot arrived. I could also think about those first practice and scoring ends and getting smooth during them. In other words, I prepared both my body and mind for the start of the tournament.

I guarantee that you and/or your student will be nervous – I always was and still am. Experience taught me to keep my thoughts simple and not worry what others were thinking about me or what they were doing. Experience taught me how my body was going to react and how I could best prepare "me" for the start of the round and it had nothing to do with what others were doing, saying, or thinking.

During the last thirty minutes prior to the start you will find yourself most vulnerable to "negative goblins." Expect them. Recognize them. Learn to fend them away by retreating into your learned conscious mental thought sequence and remind yourself that nobody else has prepared as well as you have and that your plan is the best for you. It just doesn't matter what anyone else does or thinks so focus on getting started just like you have in practice many times.

The Start Game

At the start of the round you need to focus on what you practiced and you practiced two ends during which you concentrated on making smoother and smoother shots. Don't worry where they hit – you have to get into your "home practice" kind of feel for each shot. You have to work on "body management" so you feel like you did in practice. When you do this the first scoring arrows will be as smooth as can be expected.

This is the time when you need to see yourself shooting in practice and try to place yourself there in your mental picture. Imagine being in practice, shooting as smoothly as you do there and then run your conscious mental sequence as you execute each shot. This is your best chance for success – it's no guarantee, only your best chance. It works most of the time and that's all you can expect since all of us are "only human."

Mid-Round Shooting

In the middle of the scoring round you'll need to remind yourself that your intensity level may fall slightly unless you protect against that happening. Pull out your 3x5 card with your mental thought sequence on it and read it. This will help you chase away those extraneous thoughts that creep in after the first few ends of scoring. It also helps you keep your physical effort elevated so you don't get lazy and let your posture slump prevent your lungs from getting full oxygen supply to your muscles.

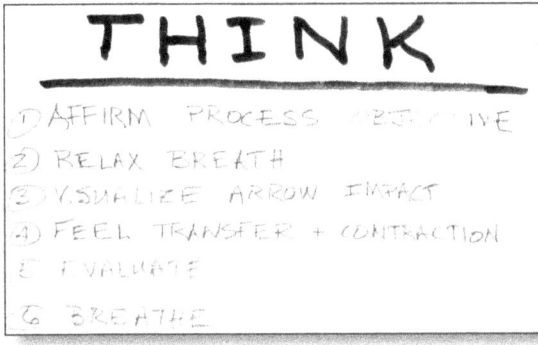

Sample 3x5 Card *Writing your thought sequence on a 3x5 card and keeping it in your quiver or pocket is a great way to help you stay on track. Read it before each end or before each arrow and then stick to it during the shot execution. Plan it and then do it so you stay in the present when it counts.*

Don't worry about what others may think of you as you frequently read your 3x5 card – they have nothing to do with your game. Read the card often, stay with your plan and make the others wish they had a plan (remember, most of them don't!).

End Game

These ends are no different from the others. They count the same as the others and require the exact same physical and mental effort, no more and no less. If it's the first of two days, remind yourself that the final few ends will get you to half-way in the tournament because there's another round to shoot tomorrow. Don't put any extra weight on the final few ends of the round. Read the 3x5 card and breathe!

If it's the last few ends of the final round then you must remind yourself that they are worth the same as the previous twenty ends. The effort you used to complete every end up to this point needs only to be repeated. Nothing special has to be done; the target will be the same size and the same distance. You have to repeat to yourself that what you have done thus far in practice and in the tournament is all you need to do at the end. Read the card, breathe, review your plan and then execute it with the confidence that you will use the form that got you to this point and are willing to take whatever it gives you at the target. In other words, shoot your form with confidence.

If you execute your final few shots with the form you practiced you will feel that inner pride that comes with a job well done. How can you do more? You can't aim harder, think harder or shoot more perfect shots. You can only shoot the same shot you've practiced over and over – that's all that is possible for you to do! So read the card, breathe and do it!

Summary

The basic ideas presented in this chapter are not new ideas, however, they are effective for those who choose to put them into practice so your job as shop owner/coach is to pass them along to your student/clients. You also have to motivate them a little so they actually try them. Yeah, I know that's not so easy – all you can do is try.

Be sure to tell them to make revisions to what I've presented if they or you think it would work better a different way. I learned a lot by trial and error without even so much as a hint of what to do so with a good starting plan you and your students will be able to make it all happen with a little less effort.

Chapter 23
Post-Tournament Evaluation

Well, the final shot was released and the tournament is now officially over. Don't evaluate it now; give it a break for a few hours at least. It's hard to be objective at this point – even if you or your student has won – so back off for a while before you draw any conclusions about the performance or place of finish. My old friend and many time National Field Champion, Dean Pridgen, used to say "Well, that's the best I could do today" and move on.

Four Things Can Happen

Don't complain either. No one was holding your bow except you! No one else nocked your arrows, set your sight or made your bow shake! It was all you . . . and only you! Coaches need to be cognizant of this because any criticism of an archer's performance gets laid right in that archer's lap. There are no teamamtes to diffuse the disappointments.

Athletes shouldn't hang around with those who complain either. Try to stay at least neutral or positive until you do a real evaluation of your or your athlete's situation. I've failed in this department at times and I can tell you it never produces positive outcomes – it drags you down lower! Don't go there!

Instead, keep your thinking simple. One of four things just happened:
1. You executed well and met your goals.
2. You executed well and did not meet your goals.
3. You executed poorly and met your goals.
4. You executed poorly and did not meet your goals.

Pick the one that best fits your situation. Now, the hard part is approaching each with the same amount of emotion. Too much emotion leads you to make conclusions about your "self-worth" that are just not true. In other words, beating on yourself or gloating serves no good purpose. Remember, your dog will still love you when you get home regardless of which category fits your situation. And you'll still have to take out the trash on Tuesday morning.

Written Goals and The Day After

Notice that I am focusing on process goals here. You should have written your process goals in your notebook weeks before the tournament. You should have then worked toward those goals during your practice sessions prior to the tournament and now is the time that they are important to you.

The day after the tournament is probably the best time to review your goals and tournament performance. With some time to think behind you, better evaluations are made.

Case One You executed well and met or exceeded your goals. This is great and you are justified in feeling proud. Enjoy it for a few days but remember that you did not perform perfectly and that there are still some form or equipment issues to work on.

You may have been weak on uphill shots (always a struggle for me) or you may not have been able to see well when standing in the sun and shooting at a darker target. Perhaps you have to increase your physical conditioning to better handle the rigors of six or eight hours in the field. Identify these issues and rewrite new goals accordingly.

Case Two You executed well but did not achieve your goals. This happens – it happened to me more times than I care to remember. Nevertheless, you have to identify the reason(s) for it.

Perhaps you experienced some unexpected low arrows on well-executed shots. Was it due to bad arrows, incorrectly matched point weight, or maybe poor nock-fit? Maybe it was due to a moving nock-locator or a faulty arrow rest. Make a list of possibilities, mark your bow parts to be sure nothing is moving and test your setup for a few days. Change one thing at a time so when you cure the problem you know the reason why. Be thorough and keep notes – you may have to restore everything to your original starting point. Search for the reason!

Case Three You executed poorly and still met your goals. Aren't you lucky! It takes a little luck for this to happen but maybe you made that luck for yourself by the hard work you did in preparation. Regardless, you have to identify exactly why your performance was not what you planned.

Was it mental or physical? If it was mental then you have to examine your mental game plan, make some changes and begin practicing it.

If it's physical then you have to identify the cause. A coach can be really helpful here. If you are self-coaching then set up your camera, take some still pics and record some video. Here's where you have to be honest and also have a good form model for comparison. (Without the form model, you're playing the form lottery!)

Compare your new stills/video to what you have on file and make decisions about what needs remediation.

Case Four You executed poorly and did not meet your goals. Yep, we usually get this when we perform poorly so don't be too bummed out by it. Instead, put your energy into identifying the cause(s). You're facing the same two-edged sword again – was it mental or physical?

Whichever, you have to proceed as in Case Three. Make a new mental plan and/or get out the cameras. If this has been a reoccurring theme then maybe it's time to hire a coach . . . or find a new coach. Being honest is the hard part, but always remember that the problem can be fixed with commitment to "smart" work!

Setting New Goals

The next few paragraphs are taken from a previous chapter but they need repeating here so it's fresh in your mind.

Take out a piece of paper or find a page in your archery notebook/log and write your goals for the next tournament for which you are training. There are three types of goals you can make: performance goals, result-oriented goals, or process-oriented goals.

Result-oriented goals are those that focus on where you finish relative to your competitors. An example would be "I want to finish in the top three" or "I want to win."

Performance goals are linked to results also. An example would be "I want to average 50 Xs per round" or "I want to shoot my personal best."

A process goal would be "I want to execute at least 50 out of 60 shots with good back tension." These types of goals are for the learning archer or someone who is rebuilding form.

If your most recent tournament performance fell into Case Three or Four then you must set some new process goals. The pictures and video that you have recently taken

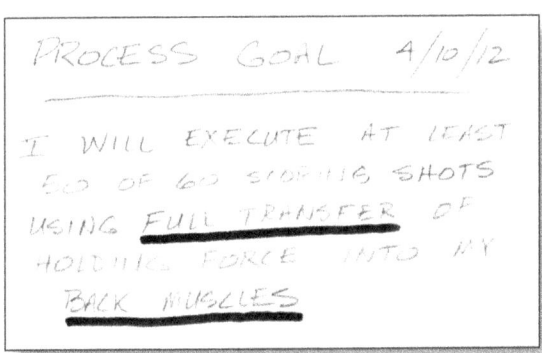

Process Goal *Having a process goal is the first thing you must do if you want to get better. Writing it and reading it frequently is a strong step toward accomplishing it. Make this goal fit into your training plan and record your progress in your shooting log.*

will point to some issues that need repair. Set process goals to deal with these.

For example "I will execute 60 out of 72 shots at 50 meters at an 80-cm target using a properly placed bow hand that is relaxed" and "I will practice five days a week for the next three weeks and use blank-bale practice to begin and end each practice session."

Identify the problem and make a specific plan to get it fixed. Again, having a biomechanically sound form model to follow is essential. Otherwise you are just making it up as you go like a ship without a compass. Get a compass and be sure it is calibrated to good biomechanics.

If your performance put you into Case One then you can set some results-oriented goals for the next tournament. Maybe now you can think about winning the next one or finishing in the top three. Don't forget to also set some process goals because that's what really puts you on the podium. Revise your goal list as you see fit and then continue to work smartly toward them – it always takes work!

A Case Two scenario usually leaves you with equipment issues. So besides reviewing your process goals you will have to do some bow tuning. Fun, fun, fun! But ya gotta do it! Do it systematically and keep good notes and you'll sort it out.

What About Your Coach?

It is nice to sit down with someone whose opinion you trust to review your last tournament performance. Coaches can be really helpful in putting your performance into perspective. A coach can keep you from being too high or too low and help guide your goal-making process.

A good coach can help you cut through the emotions surrounding the tournament conditions and results. Such a view is essential in planning your next step so that you don't waste time chasing something that wasn't really a problem – you just thought it was. A coach with skills related to the mental game can help keep you in a more balanced state of mind and that will shortcut the process to reaching your next set of goals.

Tiger Woods has come through some really down times but he is now winning again. He didn't do it alone – nobody does. Even Tiger has a coach.

Summary

The basic ideas presented in this chapter are not new ideas by any stretch of the imagination. They are, however, effective for those who choose to put them into practice so your job is to be honest with yourself, plan your work and then work your plan. You just have to get out there and try . . . but if you are smart about it you'll get better results.

Chapter 24
Fostering Young Talent

I started shooting archery when I was eight years old because I wanted to. I was interested in making arrows fly to a target; I thought it was neat. No one helped me much other than to buy me a fiberglass bow and a few wooden arrows. Other than that I was on my own . . . and the neighbors were nervous!

When I was about twelve my dad bought us both some better bows and we started shooting with some of the local guys. We joined a club in the next county and traveled there to shoot on weekends. We had a great time but none of us knew much about shooting and so we copied others and tried things on our own hoping to make ourselves better. There was no coach available and no program to help me or the adults. The only guide we had was a book called "Power Archery" by Dave Keaggy, Sr. With that bit of help we kept at it, had our fun and our frustrations, and kept shooting because we liked archery and bowhunting.

I elevated my archery interest in 1976 but found help only from some of the league shooters at the local club. Again there were no books or coaches to look to for help and so I struggled through the winter shooting fingers and then fingers with a clicker. After that I switched to a release aid and, thank heavens, I started with a two-finger back tension Stanislawski and taught myself how to shoot it in my front yard. By luck, dumb luck, I got it right and shot well from the beginning.

Being an adult and an educator I should be able to teach myself how to do things, but what about our kids? How will they learn? And if they have a real interest and a high skill level who can guide them to their highest level of achievement?

Further, what organizations are available to assist those young archers whose parents are not able to? Who will help those parents who want to provide guidance but don't have the knowledge or skill to do so? And who is able to help the dealers who need help with program structure and coaching skills?

Helping kids achieve is important – I know because I did it for 35 years in the math classroom. Helping kids achieve in archery is just as important to me. The following information will help you help your youth archers improve skill and achieve higher scores. It will also help you help parents do the same.

What Our Youth Need

So what do young archers and young athletes in general need in order to reach their full potential? That's, of course, a complicated question because there are a host of concerns that have to be addressed when dealing with a young student/athlete.

Rule One: Have Fun
It took me a while to learn this one but with the help of some of my friends I figured out that the first rule of archery is to have fun. If it isn't fun then why are you doing it? If you can't smile while you are shooting and if you can't laugh at yourself at least once every day while you're training then archery will become drudgery – it will become hard, dull work.

Your job as a coach or advisor is to be sure that every archer in your group learns to have fun while shooting so focusing on the positive is essential to that. Scheduling games and activities that relieve stress and promote group togetherness are important parts of any program that attends to the needs of the entire individual. Your athletes will thrive when a variety of activities are in front of them at each practice session. Just shooting arrows at thirty yards every session isn't very appealing and doesn't prepare anyone for much other than shooting lots of arrows, period.

Inventing new games and new team activities keeps young archers interested. A fun game I use with youth groups is the blind-man's archery team event. Choose teams of three or four archers, blind-fold the shooter and have the others direct the shooter—without-touching him or her—for an end of five arrows at eight to ten yards distance. Then switch shooters until each team member has shot their five arrows. High score wins.

Shooting this game forces the shooter to "feel" his or her full draw posture and try to repeat it. The others on the team are learning verbal skills for directing and should pick up on how to look through the shooter's sight to help him or her line up on the target. It's really fun to watch and referee this event – I can't keep from laughing out loud. And they want to play it over and over at following practice sessions.

Be creative; try different games until you find several that interest your group or individual. Keep the variety and fun level up!

Balance Athletics with Academics
As a coach or mentor to a young athlete you have to remember that they are not just athletes, they are also students. They are either in junior or senior high school or home-schooled and must maintain a commitment to their education to protect their future – very few will make a living in archery.

With that in mind, as their coach you must construct their practice and tournament schedule around their school commitments. Assignments and testing at school must take priority over archery practice and sometimes tournament participation. Other times it's necessary to leave school early, go in late or miss a school day to make it to a national level competition but in general, school should take top priority.

It's important for the coach/mentor to monitor school achievement levels. Some young archers will focus only on archery and forget their education – I saw this during my teaching career – and have to be reminded about what is most important in their lives and for their future. Some of your archery students who let their studies lapse will need to have archery suspended or limited until they readjust their priorities. I know that all of the teachers and coaches at my school worked together to make this happen and sometimes it was tough on the kids involved but it had to happen – and did.

Training Schedule Balance and Variety

Training is important, of course, but so is the daily level of training and the variety of activities used during that training. Archery is not shooting lots of arrows every day until your arms drop off. In fact, that approach will produce negative results, wear out muscles and result in archer burnout.

As I have written before you have to vary the intensity of the daily workouts and take some days off. I suggest that you use a schedule that employs a medium training level on day one, light on day two, heavy on day three and rest on day four. Over time this type of schedule can be used to increase the number of arrows shot in order to prepare for major tournaments, or reduced for a maintenance period between tournaments.

During each training session the activities can and should be varied. Shooting different distances, new and different target faces and engaging in team and individual games is a great way to keep your students interested and focused but still well prepared.

Nuitrition Needs

You are what you eat! We know that this is true, so your diet must be part of a training program. Some foods and drink have to be eliminated and others have to be introduced.

Most—and I do mean most—of my high school students did not eat breakfast. They got up in the morning and left home without eating anything at all or eating the wrong things; nothing against Pop Tarts, but they ain't breakfast!

A simple but nutritious breakfast is essential for "standing still" during archery practice. So is a good lunch and good things to drink. Soda has to be eliminated from the diet – it's just no good for you. In fact, beer would be better because it has nutritious elements in it but we don't do that for kids! You should provide water and sports drinks for your archery students before, during and after practice – keep the body hydrated for any sports activity.

Personality Differences

I've been reading and studying a golf book titled **Golf's Mental Hazards** by Alan Shapiro, Ph. D. (Simon & Shuster, 1996). The author outlines six mental hazards that golfers and all athletes face while practicing and playing their game.

The six hazards are:
1. Fear of Fear
2. Losing Your Cool
3. Getting Too Up or Too Down
4. Worrying What Others Think
5. The Need To Be In Control

6. Unwillingness to Work.

You should read this book or one like it to better understand what your athletes may be experiencing as scoring rounds and tournaments approach. I know you're not a psychologist, neither am I, but we have to be informed so we can help our young athletes better prepare for competition. You may even learn something about yourself and your own shooting.

Once you identify the one or two mental hazards of a particular student you can construct their training to attack the problem. Helping the student with their mental preparation pays big dividends when the competition starts. The book I mentioned, **The Mental Hazards of Golf**, gives you some ways to deal with each type of hazard and I'm sure you'll find other books that are very helpful in this regard. Spend a little time doing this research and you'll be better able to help your student.

Equipment Fitting

Fitting a young person with a bow is a crucial to getting their form correctly developed. If the bow doesn't fit properly they won't learn to shoot properly. This is true for compounds as well as recurve bows.

Checking the listings for recurve bow lengths you'll find overall bow lengths from 56″ to 70″. Most manufactures make risers in the two most common lengths, 23″ and 25″ and limbs ranging in draw weights from about 16# to 46#. PSE, I know, makes three lengths of their X-Pression limbs so that when matched to their two X-Appeal risers you can build bows from 64″ to 70″ long. Other manufactures make similar configurations so that you can fit your shorter/younger archers to the shorter bows and the taller/older archers to the longer bows.

For the younger/smaller archer you can take advantage of a bow like the PSE Optima that provides lengths of 56″ to 66″ in draw weights ranging from 15# to 35#. It is vitally important to get the length and weight matched to the shooter's size so that they can physically manage the bow, properly place their bow hand on the riser grip section and easily establish proper full-draw-position—straight bow arm and drawing forearm positioned in line with the arrow.

Some guidelines for recurve bow length and draw weight are as follows:

Ages	6-9	10-14	15-Adult
Length	56″	62″	64-70″
Weight	15-20#	20-30#	25-46#

On the compound side, bow lengths vary from 28″ to 42″ (measured axle-to-axle) and draw weights from 15# to 70#. The important issue here is not so much the overall axle-to-axle length but the draw weight. The weight must be matched to the shooter's strength so that he or she can raise the bow to target level and draw the bow at that level. If the weight is too great then they will most likely raise one shoulder higher than another to get the bow drawn and thereby compromise their full-draw-position. Proper full-draw-position requires that both shoulders be level and set back and down.

Your concern here for the advanced athlete centers around keeping them in a bow that fits properly so that their release hand and drawing forearm are always in line with the arrow when at full draw. As they grow in size and strength their needs will change and you'll have to adjust draw weight and draw length. Many of the compound manufacturers have a bow model that adjusts from 16″ to 26″ specifically for the growing youth. But, once they get near that 26" limit it's time to move them to a longer axle-to-axle bow and a longer draw length adjustment range.

Also consider how their hand fits the riser grip section; smaller bows have smaller grips for smaller hands. A larger hand will need a larger grip section. Mastering a properly placed bow hand with knuckles at a forty-five degree angle to the riser is difficult for adults so special attention must be paid to this essential form element when working with growing youth shooters. Getting the grip trained correctly is a prerequisite to shooting high scores.

Parental Support
Having parental support makes life easier, however it comes in various forms: most are helpful but a few are not. Certainly, having the parent on your side reinforcing what you are doing makes you a more effective teacher and coach. And we all want to be effective.

In all the years I was teaching mathematics I liked having parents who supported my efforts in the classroom by encouraging their son or daughter to try all of the activities, including homework, which my classroom and subject required. By and large, the overwhelming majority of parents fit this group.

Coaching archery is a little different. Archery is not a required subject in school and it requires some extra financial support from the parent. This puts the coach in the line of fire sometimes and, so, you have to forge a partnership of sorts in order to get the right equipment in the hands of the talented youth archer.

The money may not necessarily be there to buy all of the latest and best gear exactly when it's needed. You may have to buy used or go the "loaner" route for a while in order to get the proper fitting or better functioning equipment in their hands. There's nothing wrong with that if it keeps you and the archer focused on "form first" and scoring second.

Many archers (I've been guilty of this myself at times) get to thinking far too often that the equipment is holding them back when really it's their form or lack of commitment that is the problem. Some parents have too much money to throw at the situation and greatly enlarge this problem and you, the coach, have to be mediator between them and their child – not a good place to be. This is where having a well established and biomechanically sound form model becomes your friend and parental guiding light. Being able to visually show the parent what the student/archer needs to improve in his/her form helps you remain the authority in what needs to be done next in order to insure continued progress. This approach can help you get the right equipment in the student's hands at the right time – not too early and not too late.

A different but just as difficult problem is the parent that "knows" how to shoot archery. This is like a few parents I encountered over the years who, when their child gets home from school, remarks that they (the parent) never needed that "fancy math stuff" and their child doesn't need it either. And in a few seconds everything you've done in eight or ten weeks is totally undermined. In archery a parent may simply say that the coach doesn't know what he/she is doing because the coach can't shoot or never shot any good scores. Or that a bent bow arm works for the parent and shooting with a straight bow arm is stupid.

The answer to combating that kind of comment or influence is once again to teach a proven form model. You need to be teaching the form model promoted by the National Field Archery Association (NFAA), USA Archery, and the Archery Shooters Association through their Community Coaches Course. The USAA National Training System (NTS) methods give you the right model to teach and use to justify what you are having your students do. When I was teaching math I had the proven laws and theorems of mathematics to guide me; in archery I have the proven shooting form models taught in the Level Three/Community Coaches Certification program. With a proven form model you are never out on a limb having to resort to saying "Do it because I say so!" Instead, you always have valid reasons based on what the human body can and cannot do; it's science-based and not something you made up.

Pre-Tournament Prep

All of our archery students need help preparing for tournaments but those young archers that have that extra spark and extra talent will need to pay attention to the smaller details. And when your other students reach that level they too will have to become a little more detail oriented. The old adage, "Plan your work and then work your plan" has to be the motto for any good shooter, young or old.

This is where a student-kept notebook is essential. Kids forget things and are less organized than most adults (yeah, I know there are exceptions, boy, do I know there are exceptions) so requiring them to keep a notebook helps the learning process and builds self-reliance.

Being thorough during the weeks and months leading up to a major tournament will greatly enhance your special archer's success rate. Paying attention to and organizing their practice schedule, types of practice activities, frequency of practice, rest days, equipment preparation and exercise routine can be monitored with a notebook. You can follow some guidelines I set out in the chapter "Pre-tournament Preparation." You will have to make some age-appropriate adjustments to those guidelines but they will be very helpful.

Mid-Tournament Support

Shooting tournaments presents new and immediate problems that don't arise during practice. Extreme nervousness, misplaced or forgotten accessories, score keeping errors and "unexplained" missed arrows are just a few of the issues that arise during the tournament and you, the coach, have to solve them. Now!

Preparation heads off most of these issues but not all of them. The broken and loosened bow parts, cracked nocks and disappointment have to be handled immediately. How you do so will convey either calmness or panic to your student – I vote for calmness on your part. Even if you can't completely solve the problem you must convey calmness and confidence so your student remains relatively calm and a little confident when he/she resumes shooting.

Your younger shooters, ages 9 – 14, will usually need the most attention and closest supervision. By the time they reach the age of 15 or 16 they should have learned to be much more self-sufficient.

My favorite archery event is field shooting and when my son or daughter went with me to the NFAA Outdoor Nationals I knew they would have to be totally self-sufficient when they went out on the course because I would be shooting with the professionals on a different course and hard to find if they had a problem. Jennifer learned to do this by the age of fifteen while Todd needed to be ready at the age of ten when we went to England for the World Field Championship. I'm thankful that our preparation paid off and they didn't have any emergencies during their daily excursions onto the field course. Handling yourself on a field course for five consecutive days is a major accomplishment for any youngster; I was certainly impressed by my own kids – and thankful.

Post-Tournament Support

Sometimes you'll have to lend a shoulder for one of your students to cry on but usually after a tournament you'll need to have an open and honest discussion about the results. Your students need to make a few notes about their score, place of finish and some feelings they might be having. Most importantly they need to evaluate how they shot – not the score but how they executed.

How they executed or how they perceive their shot execution provides the basis for their practice over the next few weeks and months. Execution flaws, perceived or actual, must be remediated and that goes into the practice plan you make with them.

USA Archery and the JOAD Program

The best place to go for youth archery development is the Junior Olympic Archery Development program (JOAD for short) within the USA Archery organization (formerly the NAA). The JOAD program is designed to channel young archers, ages 8 to 18, into competitive avenues and provide the structure for them to compete against others of their age level and at age-appropriate distances. It's a local club program and maybe there is one near you or maybe you can establish one.

I interviewed Diane Watson, then National JOAD Coordinator for USA Archery, to gain insight into several important topics. She was able to give some guidelines for deciding at what age and for what reasons the recurve/compound decision should be made. She also informed me how shooting distance plays a role in this decision and, also, where parent/coaches can get support.

The biggest and most important question regarding your youth archer is what style they should shoot, recurve/fingers or compound/release. Typically I recommend that parents start their really young kids, ages 3-8, with a recurve bow and two or three arrows. The purpose here is to just have fun shooting a few arrows because their attention span is so short that doing more is not always feasible or desirable. Once they grow into more serious archery at ages 8 through 10 a decision should be made regarding what style they want to develop.

Diane recommends that a discussion with the student about a long term dream or goal can be the decision maker. She says, "Typically, JOAD youths express an interest in either winning an Olympic medal with the recurve or winning World Championships with a compound. That guides them into a bow style and the next level of competition." Diane goes on to say "Sometimes distance plays a role in the decision because some youths can only reach the longer distance for their age group with a compound. In these cases, the student can develop the necessary mental and physical competition skills with a compound and switch back to a recurve when their strength level allows." A final thought from Diane here is "some young archers are just more comfortable with one style versus the other." I agree with that because if they are comfortable they will enjoy archery more and stay interested.

If you want more information about JOAD and/or a JOAD Handbook you can check www.usarchery.org to search for more information about other programs available.

The NFAA has the After School Archery Program (ASAP) available and you may be able to find one or start one in your area. This program also supports both recurve/fingers and compound/release shooting styles. Contact the NFAA at www.fieldarchery.com or 605.260.9279 for more information.

A Voice of Experience
Cindy Bevilacqua of Media, PA, has been a long time JOAD archery coach. We met at the Lake Placid Olympic Training Center while working with our mentor Bud Fowkes – he taught us so much. Cindy coaches the JOAD group at Middletown Archery Club on Barren Road just across the street from the high school (www.middletownarchery.com). She has a wealth of experience and I asked her to share some of it for this chapter.

My first thought for dealing with a talented youth archer was "how do you recognize one"? So I asked Cindy that question. She answered, "I believe that if an archer comes with the ability to learn and listen that is half the battle. After watching how an archer shoots you can see their form and their willingness to make changes and how to make them a champion." Most importantly here she adds "you can recognize a talented archer by the way they respond to your coaching." I agree with that; you know talented students by how good their "ears are"!

Larry What special practice do you set for them compared to others?
Cindy I would set up a schedule based on their lifestyle: school, homework and other commitments. I would sit down with them and arrange a calendar of practice times and tournaments. Then we would plan how much time to spend on each area of training.
Larry How involved are the parents?
Cindy The parents are very involved with high-level elite archers. First they provide the financial support that includes equipment, coaching, practice and trans-

portation. The parents need to listen to what the archer is saying and understand that communication has to be positive and then they must provide positive reinforcement and listening support for those times when the archer is so hard on him/herself and needs to be motivated into new thought patterns.

Larry What about the financial commitment? How much is it?

Cindy Of course there is always the financial commitment and the more skilled the archer is, it seems that the financial commitment just keeps getting higher and higher. However, the archer could contact archery manufacturers to see how they might qualify as a staff shooter or request discounted rates. You are looking at thousands of dollars when you put the whole coaching-equipment-travel package together.

Larry What about extra coach's time?

Cindy I usually see archers at least once a week or every other week for a coaching session besides being involved in their target league and JOAD shooting. The archer will shoot 4-5 times a week for practice on their own if they aren't committed to a league.

Larry What about travel time?

Cindy This goes along with the archer's tournament schedule and where your travel might take you. You have to factor in how far away the shoot is and then decide if you're driving or flying. It's always best to get there one day ahead of the tournament just in case things don't run smoothly.

Larry Do you always travel with them? What about costs?

Cindy This can be either yes or no. I feel that sometimes you do need to be there as a coach to provide that support. I also think it depends on the caliber of tournament as to whether or not you go along. For some smaller local shoots it might be best to let them go on their own to get used to you not always being there. And then I think you should discuss it with your archer(s) so they can have some input. They may feel more comfortable just knowing that you are standing in the back watching and supporting them." Regarding the cost Cindy says "one should get their expenses paid for and if you are coaching more than one archer then the cost should be shared equally.

Larry Who does the equipment preparation and tuning?

Cindy I do the equipment tuning and prep work but I try to teach the archer what I'm doing so they can start doing it for themselves. That's the best way for me to see what will work best for arrow grouping.

Larry What single ingredient do your best archers have?

Cindy The elite youth archer has the dedication and the drive to be the best and will set their own goals to make that achievement a reality.

I sincerely thanked Cindy for providing such great information about her experience with talented youth archers and wish her and her JOAD group the best in the coming years.

Summary

Coaching young athletes is not easy, just as teaching them mathematics was not always easy. Most of them don't know a lot and you have to be aware of that and have the patience and willingness to go the distance with them at their pace. Cindy B. does that with her athletes and has enjoyed sharing great success with them over the years.

Planning schedules, teaching the NTS form model and communication are the keys to success when working with young and talented athletes. Spending time on all of them will make your program better.

I hope the insights that I have provided here are helpful for your efforts with young athletes.

Section 7
On Equipment

A good coach has to have knowledge across a wide variety of topics. This section contains chapters dealing with mostly equipment and bow-tuning topics. Use them to begin building or to expand your knowledge on issues vital to success with today's high-tech archery equipment.

Of course this is a never-ending process of learning as equipment design is always changing. I'd say that it is always improving but that is not always the case because in my experience technology takes two or three steps forward and then one backwards every now and then. Good ideas on the design drawing board don't always prove to be fully effective in getting arrows into the middle on the target range so keep learning and modifying your bow tuning skills.

Chapter 25
Arrows in Action:
Dynamic Arrow Spine

Spine, as we use the term in archery, refers to the bending action and recovery properties of arrow shafts. As archers, we have to learn how to control this bending to our advantage so our arrow groupings in the target accurately reflect our archery skill level. I've been launching arrows for over fifty years and I still get a kick out of watching the flight of an arrow. It's extra special if that arrow also hits the middle – it gives me that "I can still do this" kind of feeling.

Controlling an arrow shaft's dynamic spine (its in-flight bending/flexing) is something I've done for years. Controlling this three-dimensional bending involves a wide variety of details that affect the ability of the shaft to bend, recover from that bending, establish free flight and then fall into the target at the end of its parabolic arc. Knowing a little about these details and the tuning strategies that affect arrow flight will help you help yourself and others. I've outlined some concepts about spine below. Doing a better job matching a shaft's dynamic spine to the bow setup will make you and your students happier.

Static Spine The at-rest measurement of an arrow shaft's stiffness is called its static spine. This measurement is defined as the distance in inches the shaft bends at its middle when a 1.94# (880 g) weight is placed at the shaft-center while the shaft is supported across 28″ of shaft length. This measure is recorded in thousandths of an inch

Spine Measuring My friend, Moose, at Lancaster Archery is shown here measuring the spine of several arrow shafts. Measuring your arrows can show you how consistent they are in spine from end-to-end and every ninety-degrees around the shaft. Spine consistency is the main ingredient to good groups.

Larry Wise on Coaching Archery

and often appears printed on shafts. For example, the spine measure 440 would mean that the shaft would bend 0.440 inches at its center if a 1.94# weight were hung midway between those two supports placed 28″ apart (26″ and 2.00# for wood shafts).

Currently I shoot Carbon Express CXL 2-150 shafts with a 0.504″ spine rating but this static spine value is just the beginning. I have to fletch the shaft, put a nock in it, maybe a nock collar, put a point in it, nock it on the bowstring, place it on an arrow rest, draw and shoot it. Now it gets interesting because when the bowstring is released everything involved is in motion! The bowstring punches the arrow in the behind and accelerates it rapidly out of the bow (it only takes 0.015 s to leave the bow) so now we're talking about dynamic spine!

Dynamic Spine The bending and recovery properties of an in-flight shaft is referred to as its dynamic spine. We can't measure it easily but we sure have to deal with its effects on the arrow and how well our set of arrows group in the target. It's almost as if this moving, vibrating object takes on a life of its own during its time in flight and, sometimes, it defies us to find a way to control it.

However, most of the time we can control it by following a set of strategies that affect the dynamic spine. These strategies begin with the selection of shaft material, design, size, making of the arrow, arrow rest type and adjustment, nock fit, D-loop style and long-distance fine tuning. You can use this chapter as a checklist for your arrow tuning.

Spine Control Factors

Shaft Considerations Several factors affect how a shaft will act in flight. They are shaft diameter, wall thickness, shaft material, shaft length, profile, point weight, nock weight, and fletching weight.

Diameter Most aluminum shafts are marked with their diameter. An example here is a 2612 shaft where the first two digits, the 26, is the shaft diameter in sixty-fourths of an inch ($^{26}/_{64}″$). Carbon shafts don't have this marking and you may have to consult the manufacturers' charts or actually measure with a caliper to learn the diameter. Most roll-wrapped carbon shafts have the same inside diameter, 0.243″ or 0.244″, with their outside being in the range of 0.285″ to 0.300″. Some are larger in diameter to satisfy the indoor and 3-D archers while carbon-aluminum shafts, like the X10, are smaller. Consult the manufacturers' spine charts for more information.

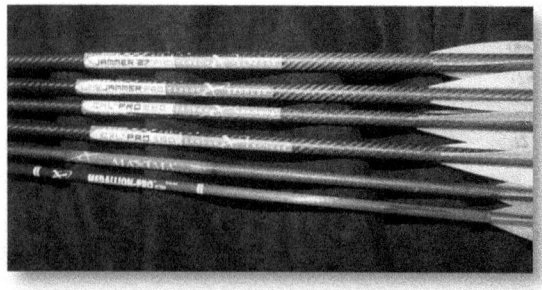

Size and Spine Labels Most arrow shaft manufacturers label their shafts with a number that can be related to the size or bending amount of the shaft. Shown here are some of my own Carbon Express arrows most having a size label that links it to a given appropriate draw weight. The 150 indicates that this shaft is suited to 45 to 55 pounds. The 530 on the Medallion Pro is a true spine value indicating this shaft bends 0.530 inches in a spine measuring tool.

In general, the larger the diameter, the stiffer the shaft and the less it flexes when launched. Therefore its spine measurement would be lower and it would be more suited to a higher draw weight bow. Shafts are just like people, the swifter the kick in the behind the more they bend!

Wall Thickness Using the aluminum shaft example of 2612 again we find that the last two digits, 12, correspond to the thickness of the aluminum wall in thousandths of an inch. In this case the 12 indicates that the shaft's walls are 0.012˝ thick. A 2613 would have a thicker wall and would be stiffer than the 2612. This would also hold for carbon shafts that are thicker walled.

Wall Thickness Wall thickness and shaft diameter are two characteristics that determine the relative bending of an arrow shaft. The material type and construction process used are also determining factors in shaft's bending characteristics.

Shaft Material The shaft material makes a big difference in how the arrow shaft bends and recovers. Aluminum is stronger and stiffer than wood and carbon is stiffer than aluminum given the same diameter and wall thickness. Not only are the strength properties different, their recovery properties vary as well. Carbon oscillates faster with less deflection-from-straight through its bending and recovery cycles than does aluminum, which means that carbon-shafted arrows can recover from their initial-thrust-bending in less time than other shafted arrows, provided that all other construction characteristics are held equal.

This recovery-rate property is also true for carbon at impact. The carbon bends less side-to-side than aluminum on impact and therefore delivers more of its energy in line. The net result is more penetration. I notice this with my target arrows in practice when I change distances and forget to change my sight – the carbon arrows penetrate all the way through the treated 2x4 lumber around my target butt while the aluminum only go half-way!

Shaft Length Most archers know that a longer shaft will act weaker, that is bend more during the initial thrust, than shorter shafts of the same size and shape. Although static spine is measured across a 28-inch span, dynamic spine affects the entire length whatever that may be. For that reason many indoor archers use full-length (and therefore weaker acting) large-diameter aluminum shafts to match their 45 to 50-pound indoor bows. (The advantage being that the larger shafts are more likely to cut the next higher scoring ring on the target face.)

Carbon and carbon-aluminum shafts have this same property—longer acts weaker—and many archers cut these shafts in ¼-inch increments while holding point weight constant to achieve a desired spine. This is a technique used mostly for long-distance shooting but you can use it for all of your archery if you want to spend the time.

Shaft Profile Type Most shop owners only deal with the cylindrical or parallel shafts. That's what most hunters, 3-D, and target shooters use. The Easton X10 and ACE shafts have a "barreled" design. That is, it has a fatter diameter just behind its center than at its ends. (I've also seen back-to-front straight-line tapered shafts.) Centuries ago the Turks used the barreled shaft to increase the distance an arrow could fly by taking advantage of the "lift" property of the barreled shape. Actually, the barreled design has less drag than a cylindrical shaft and, therefore, less velocity decay during its down-range flight and that's what interests those shooting 90 meters.

Fletching Considerations As soon as we begin building an arrow we change the dynamic spine of the shaft. In other words, we change how it bends and recovers from that bending by adding weight at various positions along the shaft. When we apply a pushing force to the back end of the arrow we must deal with what Sir Isaac Newton stated as his first law of motion: an object at rest or in motion will stay at rest or in motion unless acted upon by a force.

In the case of the arrow we are applying a force to an object at rest and that arrow will tend to stay at rest until the string begins to push it at the nock end. A weighted point now becomes an important factor as it tends to stay at rest longer than the lighter-weight nock end and, thus, the arrow shaft is forced to bend to accommodate this condition. Weights added to the point end makes the arrow act "weaker" or bend more during the initial thrust of the string for this reason. We just can't escape the laws of physics; Sir Isaac was right and every arrow we shoot verifies that fact as it bends.

Fletching Weight Adding fletching to the nock end of the shaft adds weight to that end and affects the dynamic bending of the shaft. Weights added to the nock end makes the arrow act "stiffer" or bend less during the initial-thrust of the string. Bigger fletching adds more weight: 4″ Flex Fletch vanes weigh 9.6 gr. each, 3″ vanes weigh 5.7gr. each, and 1¾″ vanes weigh 3.0-gr. each. If your purpose is to shoot broadheads then you need the 4-inch vanes or feathers for the increased surface area and you must

Vanes and Nock *The scale reads 34.3 grains for the combined weight of the nock, collar, and three 3″ vanes. Adding this to the nock end makes the arrow shaft act stiffer. Adding the 120-grain point (shown) to the front end makes the shaft act weaker (bend more when propelled by the bowstring).*

tune the arrows accordingly.

Fletch Angle You must install your fletches at an angle to the shaft. Gluing the vane or feather in place so that it is in line with the shaft will yield minimum air resistance and, therefore, less stabilizing effect. Without one side turned slightly toward the direction of flight the shaft will not be guided consistently to the target.

Consider the baseball pitcher who has a good "knuckle ball." The ball has no spin to establish a consistent direction of air resistance and neither the poor hitter nor catcher has any idea where it's going. We must install the fletching with a set angle to the shaft length in order to create directed air resistance and provide a set direction for the arrow as it recovers from its bending. Use two degrees (2°) for smaller carbon shafts and more for the fatter shafts. I use a "helical curve" fletching clamp in my fletching jig to establish as much angle as possible for those situations needing a lot of "steerage" from the vanes. I highly recommend this approach for greatest accuracy.

Fletch Shape Vanes and feathers come in many shapes and sizes. Most are "parabolic" while others are "shield-cut" having a sharp cutoff at the back end. Fletching can have a low, medium or high profile depending on how much surface area and weight you want or need on the nock end. Higher profiled fletching will have more surface area and aid the arrow in its in-flight recovery but will also

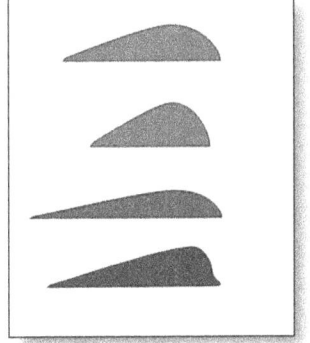

Vane Profiles *The most common shapes found on arrows today are (from the top): parabolic, high profile parabolic, low profile parabolic, and shield cut. With feathers and a feather "burner" almost any shape is possible.*

increase drag at long distance. The testing I've done shows virtually no difference in velocity decay out to fifty yards.

Fletch Clearance Certainly a top concern during bow tuning is fletching contact with the arrow rest. Any contact the fletching might have during the beginning of its flight will disturb the normal bending and recovery of the arrow down range. Spraying white foot powder on the fletched end, then shooting the shaft and checking it for any marks it might have received due to rest or arrow shelf contact is a good method for uncovering this contact or uncovering unequal contact in the case of "surround" type rests. Then make adjustments to the rest, rotate the nocks, move the nocking point location, etc., to eliminate or optimize the contact. Can be eliminated with the use of "drop-away" arrow rests, but these also have issues to deal with.

Nock Considerations (General) The nock and nock insert on the back end of the shaft adds weight. The nock also grips the string with some degree of tightness. Both of these affect the flight of the arrow during its initial bending and recovery.

There are other factors like nocking point location and release aid attachment method.

Nock Weight My Carbon Express *Maxima Blue Streak* arrows come with nocks weighing 10.1 gr. and a collar weighing 4.1 gr. Combine this with three 1¾-inch fletches at 3.0 gr. each and you have a total add-on weight of 23.2 grains. This weight at the rear of the shaft will reduce the amount of shaft bending when the bowstring applies a force to that end. In other words, the arrow acts stiffer.

The CXL nock weighs 11.9 gr. and the collar weighs 4.4 gr. while the tiny SOMA nock weighs only 3.5 gr. for a total load of 28.8 gr. with the same fletching.

Nock Fit How the nock fits to the bowstring is important in that a force is necessary to make it separate from the string at the end of the power stroke. If the nock fits too tightly then more force is required to separate it from the string resulting in the nock end's direction and bending being affected. Too loose and the separation is inconsistent at best. A "snap" onto the bowstring is desired but the nock-tabs should return to their natural spread when the nock is on the bowstring. The string should be able to be freely rotated inside of the nock groove when the arrow is on the bow.

Nocking Point Location If the arrow crosses the arrow rest with undue contact then shaft bending can be affected. The same is true if the arrow crosses the rest without contact as it does with the drop-away rests. Getting it just right so it's consistent is always a challenge. The basic rule I follow is to have the bottom of the shaft level with or slightly higher than the contact point on the arrow rest.

Release Hook-Up How the release aid connects to the bowstring is important to how the string applies force to the arrow. Release jaws that contact the nock will cause a different shaft bending than when a D-loop is used. If a release rope is attached to the release aid it will have an even different effect. I can think of dozen different ways to hook the release aid to the bowstring so testing them all to find the most consistent for a given bow setup can be very time consuming. You probably have a favorite that's most consistent for you but another method may work better – only testing will tell.

Point Considerations For an arrow to do its job effectively it must have a point. The factors that come into play when the point is added are weight, shape and how the point affects the arrow's front-of-center balance point.

Point Weight Adding a point to the front of an arrow shaft moves the arrow's center of mass forward. The heavier the point the more the center of mass is moved for-

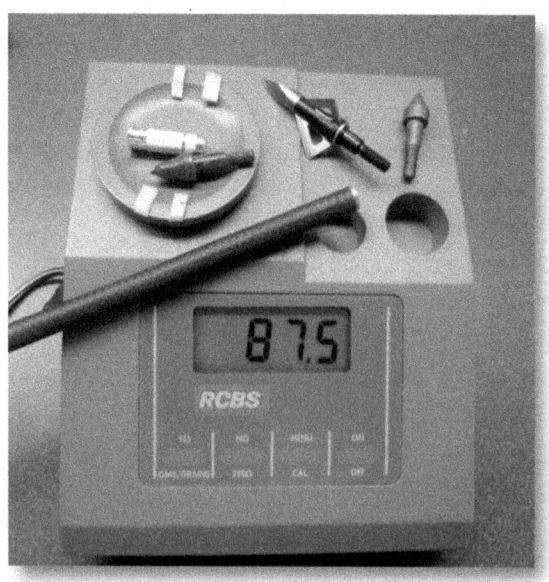

Points *Field points and broadheads may have the same weight but certainly not the same shape and weight distribution. And don't forget the insert when determining the total point weight and its affect on arrow spine. The broadhead shown extend its weight further beyond the shaft end than the field point so you must shoot test your broadheads before going hunting.*

ward and the more the shaft will bend when a force is applied to nock end. The tricky part is getting just the right amount of point weight to optimize arrow flexing and enhance its flight to the target. Too light of a point and the arrow will fly erratically and group poorly; too heavy and the arrow falls from the sky too quickly.

Lots of archers are concerned about the Front-of Center (FOC) location of the arrow's balance point but I don't ever measure that. I shoot for groups since that's what builds high scores and brings home the bacon during hunting season. Testing point weights across the range from 50 grains to 125 grains or more is the surest method to find the best grouping arrow balance.

I have some favorite combinations: my Carbon Express *Maxima* points have a base unit that weighs 60 gr. and an add-on 40-gr. weight that has 10.0-gr. break-off segments for fine tuning. My WASP broadhead weighs in at 75 gr. with a 13-gr. insert.

Point Style The shape of the point added has an effect on how the arrow flies and balances. The broadhead, for instance, extends the point weight more beyond the shaft end than the field point or target point and, therefore, moves the arrow's balance point more to the front.

Exposed broadhead blades affect the aerodynamics of a shaft in flight and it's bending/recovery cycle. For that reason bowhunters should always group test their broadheads, even the enclosed-blade mechanicals. Any change in the point configuration and the arrow will fly, bend, and impact differently because both its center of mass balance point and its aerodynamics have changed. Most bowhunters skip over this detail thinking that their broadhead arrows (of any kind) will impact the same as their field point arrows and, of course, they get a big surprise in their tree stand. Archers of all kinds must practice with the exact setup they intend to use for a given endeavor to be sure it shoots as expected.

Arrow Rest Considerations The arrow touches the arrow rest for some amount of time during its forward flight. This means the rest affects arrow bending and recovery. This makes them a rather important part of the dynamic spine equation.

"Drop Away" rests cradle the shaft for approximately the first two to four inches of flight. Remember, however, that the arrow shaft is bending during this time and is affected by its interaction with the rest, so you have to tune this interaction.

Fixed rests may sustain longer contact with the shaft and endure more of its bending and, therefore, the flexibility of its parts must be tuned to interact favorably with the shaft's flight. Launchers with various blade spring stiffnesses must be tried, centershot location must be shifted, surround-type rests must be positioned and angled for best passage characteristics and the nocking point height must be adjusted—all in an effort to synchronize the rest parts with the bending and recovery of the arrow shaft.

Cam Considerations The cams on compound bows have an effect on the launch of the arrow and, therefore, its bending. The more radical the cam design and its force-draw curve the more potential there is for radical shaft bending.

Cams that have a sudden drop-off in draw weight in the last two inches of their draw stroke will, on the power stroke, apply most of the forward thrusting power to the arrow in the same short two inches (in high-speed video this acceleration is timed at under 0.015 seconds). Matching the shaft's dynamic spine to this situation is tricky because the quicker the force is applied the stiffer the arrow acts. Consider the hammer hitting a very soft nail and applying a great force in a few milliseconds. The nail doesn't bend under the force because of the short time frame in which the force was applied. In the case of some cams most of this force is being applied in under 0.005 seconds.

Sometimes we can't tell whether the shaft is too weak or too stiff so our only option is to shoot-test them with different point weights. We can only respond to the data we can collect and that's ultimately the size of the arrow groups in the target. We only use the charts to guide us in selecting three or four shafts that "should" work well.

Hybrid (asymmetric) cam timing and single cam rotational positioning are also factors in energy delivery. The mechanical parts must operate in a synchronized manner to provide a smooth and efficient delivery of the energy available. If they don't, then arrow bending is affected and may be inconsistent from shot to shot. It is to your advantage to have your bow's cam system operating in-synch.

Tuning Considerations Bow tuning includes the basics of draw length adjustment, wheel timing, nock fit, and paper and powder testing. Of course, you must have your shooting form in order before you start bow tuning.

Here's the step-by-step procedure that leads to arrow shaft tuning:
1. Set draw length.
2. Adjust cam timing and/or rotational position.
3. Set nocking point.
4. Check nock-fit and correct if necessary.
5. Install release loop.
6. Adjust arrow rest centershot location.
7. Powder & paper test.
8. Sight setting at 20 yards, then 40 yards.
9. Group testing at 40 yards then 60 yards.
10. Redo powder test to be certain of clearance.

Now I'm ready to test different point weights in the arrows I'm shooting. For hunting and target I use field points from 50 to 125 grains. Don't forget to add the twelve grains for the threaded insert to get an accurate total if you intend to eventually install target points.

I shoot test them all with six-arrow groups from 40 and 60 yards and shoot them through paper for a little more info. Usually one or two of these will group better and that tells me what weight broadhead and/or target point I need. If several point weights work well then you'll have to make a personal decision as to which weight to use – most stay light if they're shooting target or 3-D. Regardless, you choose based on groups first, light weight second.

If none of the points group to your satisfaction then perhaps your choice of static shaft spine is not correct. Choose another shaft that is slightly stiffer and repeat the process and if that doesn't work try a shaft that is slightly weaker. The results in the target will let you know when you're right.

Summary

Group tuning is never an exact science and depends on the shooting skill of the archer. Understand that you, as a coach, have to use your own best judgment to guide your students to a reasonable arrow and point selection. Keeping your eyes and ears open to the better shooters in your area can give you good information as to what combinations are working well out of a particular bow.

In any event, you have to deal with dynamic arrow spine through observation of results in the target. The charts are great for guiding you to several shaft spines but ultimately you have to deal with real-world results so understanding a little more about what affects an arrow in flight is helpful. Use the information above to work smarter toward getting better groups.

Chapter 26
Putting Your Bow In Balance

It happens in the blink of an eye! In fact, it happens in half that time – the bowstring traverses its roughly 20-inch power stroke toward the target in a mere 0.015 seconds. The arrow gets off the bowstring and is launched to the target so quickly that the human eye cannot see it.

Although it takes only 0.015 seconds much is happening. While the arrow is propelled toward the target by the bowstring, the limbs and cams are also moving. Unseen, the bow handle is going in the opposite direction from the arrow and compressing into the archer's bow hand.

A law of physics: for every action there is an equal and opposite reaction.
(Newton's Third Law of Motion)

How the handle performs during this "blink" of time is one of the major determining factors in where the arrow lands and the consistency with which it does so. In other words, both accuracy and precision depend on the bow handle action – its dynamic performance – during the brief time the limbs and bowstring are driving the arrow out of the bow and toward the target.

Once the arrow separates from the bowstring neither the handle, bowstring, limbs nor bow hand have any effect on the arrow. Once the arrow is in "free flight" the archer has no more effect on the landing of the arrow. Therefore, great care must be taken to properly and consistently optimize the conditions of the launch and ensure that the arrow impacts the desired target. Those conditions include the following:
1. The aimed direction of the bow-arrow system.
2. The placement of the bow hand.
3. The consistency of the release technique.
4. The physical balance of the bow.
5. The arrow's dynamic spine and flight characteristics.

Please notice that all of these are within the direct control of the archer. All of them! Good form takes care of the first three while good bow tuning and arrow building take care of the last two. This chapter is about number four.

The Problem: Bow System Dynamic Performance
What is, or should be, the bow handle action as it presses back into the bow hand during that critical 0.015 of a second? That's the big question we have to deal with when we want to begin balancing the bow with stabilizers.

Here are some facts that we know and have to deal with regarding the compound bow systems we are currently shooting:
1. The bow hand center of pressure in the grip is below the center of the bow.
2. The nocking point on the bowstring is at or above center.
3. The top and bottom halves of the handle are unequal in weight.
4. Only a few handles are left-right equal in weight, most are not.
5. The bow sight and arrow rest add weight to only one side of the handle.
6. The top and bottom cams are unequal in weight on most bows.

Wow, while making this list I just realized just how unbalanced the whole bow system is before we put any stabilizers on it. Maybe a shoot-through handle really does help a little by more closely balancing the left and right sides – I'll have to get one and give it a try – regardless, after the sight is installed the bow is weighted to that side and balance can be only be returned to the system by using stabilizers.

Let's look at each of these in a little more detail:

Bow Hand When the bow hand presses into the grip section of the bow handle it is doing so below the vertical center of the bow which is just below the arrow shelf. This means that the hand is exerting a force on the lower half of the handle tending to rotate that handle about its center resulting in the bottom limb rotating away from the shooter while the top limb rotates back toward the archer.

Nocking Point The nocking point of most bows is well above the vertical center of the bowstring. At full draw this force is also trying to rotate the bow handle about its center by pulling the top limb toward the archer. The ideal bow would have the grip at the center, the bow hand at the center, the nocking point at the center and the arrow also traveling through the center . . . a piercingly painful experience to the bow hand and, therefore, not practical so we compromise in the bow design by moving both the arrow rest and bow hand a short distance away from the center. We compromise bow design so the arrow does not pass through our hand.

Handle Design The top and bottom halves of any handle are unequal in mass (weight) – some more than others. During the launch of the arrow this unequal mass plays a role in the attitude of the handle as it comes back into your bow hand.

Handle Weighting Most handles are weighted more to one side. A few of the more expensive handles have shoot-through risers that do a better job of left-right weight balance. These risers are also less prone to three-dimensional flexing during the draw and power strokes.

Bow Sight Any sighting device that is attached to one side of the bow handle adds weight to that side. The heavier the bow sight the more off-balance the bow handle becomes and the more counter weighting must be used to establish a left-right neutral balance. The arrow rest also adds weight to one side.

Cam Weight Most bows today have asymmetrical cam systems. In other words, the top and bottom cams (wheels/eccentrics) have different shapes and masses (weights). The exception to this is the "binary" system employed by several companies; the two-wheel bows of the seventies and eighties were also symmetric. These cams/wheels are thrust into motion when the bowstring is released giving them momentum and if these wheels are of different weights they will have different amounts of momentum.

Although this may be a relatively small matter it does enter the dynamic bow balancing equation.

These are some of the facts that we know regarding our bow/limbs/cams system. They are out of balance and when brought into relative balance with stabilizers the system can and usually does perform more consistently. The bottom line is this: an optimally balanced system shoots better arrow groups in the target.

My old friend, former Olympic Coach and mentor, Bud Fowkes, always said, "We add accessories if and only if they improve the arrow groups in the target!" As an archer or coach, don't you do this when you take a bow out of the box and start assembling it for a student? Some people lose touch with Bud's Rule and go way overboard with accessories and stabilizers forgetting to determine whether they improve the archers groups. I follow Bud's Rule all the time!

If the bow's purpose is to accurately and consistently launch the arrow to the target center then we would expect the bow handle to remain in its position and attitude during the power stroke. That means that during the 0.015 second that the bowstring is propelling the arrow forward, the handle should remain vertically oriented and move only horizontally a micro amount into the bow hand. In other words, the handle-top neither tips forward nor backward, doesn't tip left or right and the handle does not rotate (torque) on its vertical or horizontal axes – it only shifts back into the bow hand a microscopic amount during the power stroke (due to the increasing force upon the arrow dictated by the letoff of the bow). Following that, the entire bow system thrusts toward the target during a "rebound or recoil" reaction. But the arrow is gone by this time and unaffected by such a reaction.

The Purpose of Stabilizers
The job of the stabilizer is to dampen or eliminate all handle movement other than the horizontal movement into the bow hand. The stabilizer(s) must dampen any handle tipping and any torque rotation so that the arrow can be aimed and launched accurately and consistently to the target. In other words, the wasted energy of the power stroke (about 25% of the stored energy) and unwanted bow hand torque must be dampened or dissipated by the stabilizers during both the aiming phase and power stroke. The law of physics at work here is: an object at rest tends to stay at rest unless acted on by a force (Newton's First Law of Motion).

For stabilizers we know that a weight suspended at some distance resists movement more effectively than a weight attached directly to the bow handle – hence, the stabilizer rod.

The Construction of Stabilizers
The shape and the materials of the stabilizer(s) are very important to how well they do their job. Weight suspended at a distance and how it resists movement is one of the important features of the design process. The material of the stabilizer rod also contributes greatly to the energy damping process.

My friend Todd Reich of Beaver Springs, PA, lives over just one mountain from me here in central Pennsylvania so we're neighbors. He builds and sells stabilizers under the business name of Dead Center Archery Products.

Todd owns half interest in a machine shop business, Top Notch Machine, Beavertown, PA. That, coupled with his interest in archery, led to the development of a line of aluminum stabilizers a few years ago. Since then he has expanded his line to include carbon rod stabilizers which quickly became his major focus.

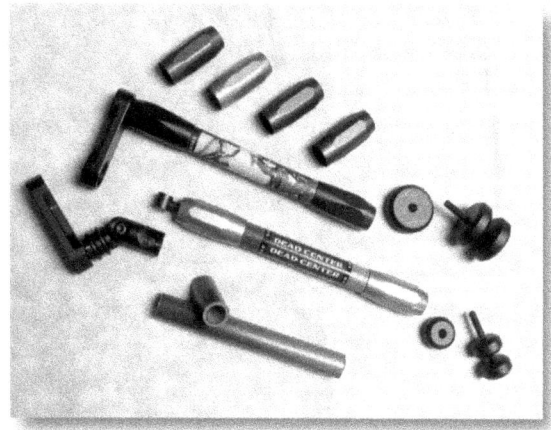

Unassembled Parts *Testing various pultruded rod diameters and wall thicknesses helped Dead Center determine the optimum rod dimensions for bow stabilizing. The colored end caps, weights, quick disconnects and angled connectors are all machined at the Top Notch Machine shop in Beavertown, PA.*

The carbon rods Todd uses are pultruded tubes. The diameter and wall-thickness determine their great strength and rigidity. The high-modulus carbon fibers that run linearly (lengthwise/end to end) oscillate at a high frequency as they dissipate the vibrations that are transferred to them from the bow system. The end-caps are machined aluminum as are the add-on weights and the quick disconnect adjustable arms.

Using the proper adhesives and preparation processes are critical to making a lasting product. The glossy surface of the carbon has to be scuffed by a sanding operation so the adhesive makes a good bond for the end-cap outserts that cover the end of the carbon fibers to prevent splitting.

The Setup of a Target Bow Stabilizer System

If we understand the purpose of the stabilizer system then we know that we must establish a starting point for attaching and balancing the stabilizers we use. This initial combination may not be the combination that gives the best arrow groups in the target so we will also need to establish a tuning process that will move us from the initial combination to the "optimum" combination.

The initial stabilizer combination that Todd and I both recommend begins with the use of the *Pro Balancer* (or similar device) that Todd manufactures. This device attaches to a work bench via screws or a "C" clamp and holds the bow at the grip section with a collar device. The balancer allows the bow to rotate on two-sets of pivots so that it can tilt freely in two planes; one pivot allows the long stabilizer to "pitch" up and down in the vertical plane while the other pivot allows the handle-top to tilt or "roll" left and right. It's simple and very effective – I wish I'd had one back in the eighties!

At the start, the bow must be ready to shoot except for the stabilizers to be added. All of the accessories you intend to use must be installed and should include the bow sight, arrow rest, peep sight, nocking point and string dampeners.

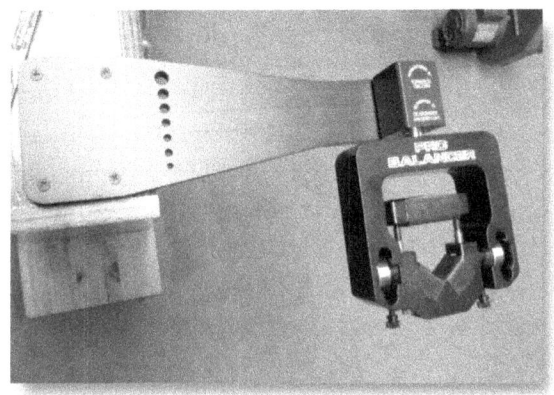

Pro Balancer *The Dead Center Archery Pro Balancer is a great way to get started with bow balancing. The device holds any bow at the grip section and allows it to pivot freely in two planes separately or in both simultaneously. The owner/inventor Todd Reich and I both like to set the long rod tip-down balance before setting the the left-right balance. Fine tuning from long range will help you optimize the long rod tip weight to get best groups.*

Step I Place the Bow in the Pro Balancer Attach the handle collar and insert the collar into the balancer unit. The collar duplicates your bow hand position as closely as possible. Keep in mind that no machine can duplicate exactly how the human hand holds the bow and that this is a starting point of a process that ends with a fine tuning and shoot test.

Step II Install The Long Rod Place the long stabilizer rod to the target-side of the bow with one small weight attached to the end. The length of the rod is a personal choice but keep in mind that the effectiveness of the stabilizer is directly related to the mathematical product of the mass/weight at the rod's end and the rod length (mass x length). This product is a measure of how well the stabilizer's weighted end resists movement generated at the bow end of the rod.

Step III Install a Short Rod to the Side Opposite the Bow Sight To balance the left-right weight of the bow system you must install a short rod-with-weight to counterbalance the weight of the bow sight. Once again the length of the rod multiplied by the end-weight is a measure of the stabilizer's effectiveness. The offset arm can also be adjusted so the stabilizer rotates further outboard from the bow handle – use this in

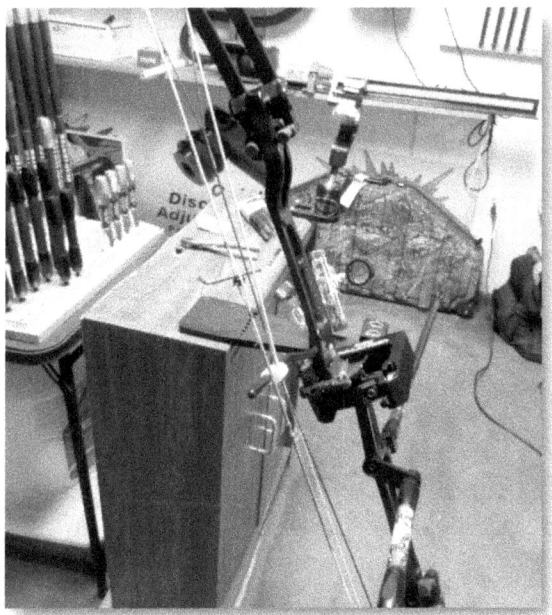

Unbalanced Bow *I have to confess that I haven't shot my bow as much as I should have this past year. Nor did I work on my stabilizer package so my left-handed bow was severely out of balance when we first put it into the Balancer – it's tipped far to the sight-side. To get it better balanced we increased the back-rod from 8″ to 12″ and added more tip weight.*

the final balancing process while the bow is in the balancer.

Step IV *Establish a Beginning Balance Between the Long Rod and the Short Rod* Balancing the bow so the handle and bowstring are vertical at this point is not the objective. Remember, the bow is not "working" when it is in the balancer unit and having an equal "static" (still or inactive) balance does not mean that the system will be optimally balanced when you have the bow at full draw and also when the bow is "working" during its power stroke. The "dynamic" balance must be found by shoot-testing for arrow groups; therefore, the starting point for the bow held in the balancer unit is arbitrary. For my own personal bows I find that when the long-rod pitches down at a 45-degree angle when the bow is held in the balancer gives the best starting point. Todd finds the same with the overwhelming majority of client bows he balances.

Front-Back Balance I recommend that you begin with the front-back balance set so the long-rod tips down slightly. Once again it's all about the weight multiplied by its distance from the bow handle. In this static position my long rod tipped down at a 45-degree angle but when the bow is "working" during the power stroke when your bow hand is pressing below the handle center the long rod tip stays level instead of instantly tipping up while the arrow is leaving the bow.

Left-Right Balance After the front-back balance is set then set the left-right balance so the handle is in a vertical plane. The Pro Balancer unit can be locked to prevent the long rod tipping down while you add weight to the counterbalance rod and also rotate it further or nearer to the bow handle using the offset bar. On my own bow I had to increase the rod length from 8″ to 12″, add 6 oz of weight and increase the offset bar length from 3″ to 4″. A small rotation change got the bow in perfect left-right balance.

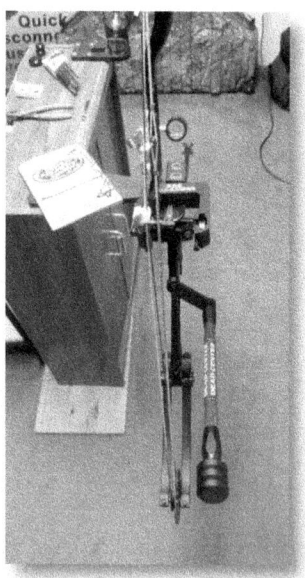

Balanced Bow *To bring my bow closer into balance we increased the offset bar from 3″ to 4″ and after a slight rotation inboard the bow balance was vertically perfect. Next we changed the tip weights on the long rod to get the desired tip-down position that will get me started with my long distance tuning (as soon as the weather warms a little). I can tell from only a few arrows that the bow aims extremely well at twenty yards already.*

Step V *Shoot Testing For Groups* Test the initial stabilizer setup by paper testing from five to eight yards. (See Chapter 25 to learn more about Powder and Paper Tuning.)

Next, choose some long distance from which to test the arrow groupings from your bow. I always prefer sixty yards – anything more than forty is good.

Begin by recording your "zero" or starting combination of balance weights. Next, add either a one-oz or two-oz weight to the target-side long-rod, record it, and shoot test for arrow groups. Add a second weight and repeat the testing.

Remove those two weights and add a one-oz weight to the counter-balance stabilizer. Test for groups then add a second weight and retest. Record each weight combination you test, how well it aimed, and the resulting arrow groups.

Add a third weight into your process if you like and/or try a longer or shorter counter-balance rod. Warning: I see some really long counter balance rods that negatively affect shooting form. When the rod extends back into your gut so far that you have to bend out over the bow while nocking the arrow then proper posture is jeopardized – you are creating extra work for yourself and you may not reestablish proper body position at full draw. Body position has to be top priority so add weights to a shorter rod or offset that rod further from the bow to get the same balance.

Finish your tuning by resetting the weights to the combination that produced best groups. Don't forget to retest periodically.

Balancing a Hunting Bow

My hunting bow is an entirely different animal from my target bow. My hunting bow is designed to do a one-shot job – at least that's the plan I always have! My hunting bow doesn't have to shoot multiple arrows at long distances either – one shot at 20 yards is the game.

My own hunting bow is very lopsided because of the two-piece bow quiver attached to the same side as the bow sight. It's better balanced than the one-piece quivers I've used. I use a short 8″ stabilizer on the target side with a four-inch offset bar so I can rotate the stabilizer several inches to the left so it helps counter-balance the quiver. I'm satisfied with how it handles but I don't use a reflex handle like most hunters; mine is a straight-line handle – neither deflex nor reflex. When I did use a reflex handle I had to install a counter balance back-bar to better balance the quiver and sight.

My hunting bow has to "carry" well and "hold" comfortably while I'm in the treestand. I spend a lot of time with my bow in my hand, waiting for that elusive buck to show himself – particularly in the heavy cover areas around my home.

It also has to shoot well on the first shot. I tune my hunting bow so it does that and if I need more weight on the rod-tip I put it on. My interest is hitting a paper plate within thirty yards near the middle on the first shot with a broadhead. I spend enough time adjusting my stabilizer balance to make that happen.

Summary

Shooting archery is a fantastic way to measure yourself against yourself. To do it well requires that you prepare thoroughly and that means covering all the bases in personal form and in equipment preparation. All too often the balance of the bow is overlooked or misapplied so help your students build the proper bow balance by adopting a systematic method like the one outlined in this chapter. Use a bow balancing device so you can find "exactly" the stabilizer weights a given bow needs and where to locate them. Be a little more scientific and you will reap the rewards.

Chapter 27
Installing and Calibrating Target Sights

From the day after the bow and arrow was first invented archers have been doing two things: inventing aiming devices and release aids. The modern results of this quest are machined bow sights and mechanical release aids. I've written lots about release aids already so it's time to tend to the bow sight.

Most every archer is using a bow sight of some kind. It makes aiming easier for the novice and more accurate for everyone. Even the highly skilled barebow shooters employ some kind of aiming system to improve their accuracy. That means that as a coach you have to understand how to install, calibrate, and use a bow sight.

Over the years I've learned to follow an installation routine to get long-range accuracy from my target and hunting sights. I'm passing these steps along to you for your consideration.

Installation Basics
You may already be aware that there are three major adjustments to installing a bow sight: vertical sight-bar plumb (first axis), scope/pin leveled to the sight-bar (second axis) and the scope lens (third axis) perpendicular to the arrow direction. This third axis has a related adjustment involving the sight extension bar being parallel to the arrow shaft flight-plane. Following are the setup steps to get all of these adjustments completed to secure long-range accuracy and reliability.

Arrow Trajectory Facts In the fully drawn and aimed position the arrow is pointed slightly uphill. It is below the line of sight when it is launched but even if it were on the line of sight the arrow must be pointed upward. (Do you know why?) When propelled by the bowstring the arrow travels up to that line-of-sight between the archer's eye and the target, rises above it and then follows a curved arc – a parabolic arc – and falls downward to the target.

The longer the distance to the target the more an arrow falls relative to the line of sight and, thus, the more it has to be aimed upward at the start. An example of this is the fact that from 20 yards to 30 yards a certain arrow flying at 280 fps will fall four inches. That same arrow will fall fourteen inches between forty yards and fifty yards. To learn about your own bow just shoot an arrow at a spot from twenty-yards using your twenty-yard pin. Then, aiming with the same 20-pin at the same spot, shoot more arrows from thirty, forty and fifty yards and measure the drop distance between arrows.

When the bow sight is calibrated correctly the arrow hits the target center. When the sight is not calibrated correctly the arrow hits high, low, right or left of the target. Getting the sight working correctly begins when you install it on the bow so here are some tips for installing sights. (Getting the archer calibrated is quite another matter – I wrote a book about that!)

Step One *Install the Mounting Block* Secure the sight-mounting block to the outside of the sight-window (right-side for right-handers). I clean all threaded holes with a correct sized tap (these are standardized and should be 10-24 threads), test the screws I intend to use for fit and so they do not "bottom out," and then attach the mounting block. This step avoids a potential thread-stripping problem that can ruin a bow riser.

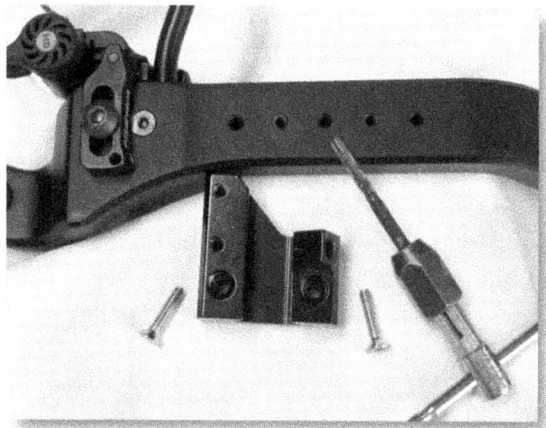

Mount Block & Thread Tap *The mounting block is the first sight part to be installed on the bow. I always clean the threaded holes in the riser with a tap to be sure of a clean installation. Damaged riser threads may require shipment back to the factory for repair.*

Step Two *Install the Extension Bar* Next, install the horizontal extension bar. The machined accuracy of today's manufacturing should make the extension nearly parallel to the side of the riser and to the path of the arrow. If you have a concern about this then shim the mount block to align the extension bar with vertical plane of the riser.

Step Three *Adjust the Sight Bar* Adjust the vertical sight bar so that it is plumb (true vertical) while the bowstring is also plumb. All of the long-range micro-

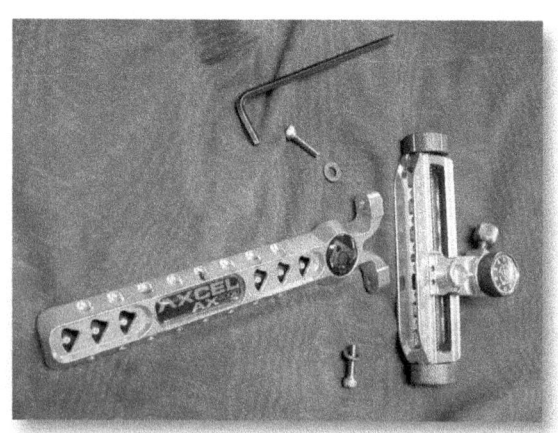

Extension & Vertical Bar *Most bow sights have adjustment screws that allow you to adjust the vertical alignment of the sight bar. Adjusted properly, your sight will generate arrows in the middle of the spot at all distances. When incorrect, it will miss to one side up close and to the opposite side at long range.*

adjustable target sights I have seen have an adjustment built in so that you can easily make this adjustment.

This is a very important step that must begin with the bow fixed in a vertical position. Some shops use a table-mounted bow vise while some use a work-mate type vise to hold the bow. Others have a tested plumb door-jamb against which they hold their bows to check the plumb adjustment of the vertical sight bar or you can use a bow-mounted leveling tool. The device I now prefer to use is the *Pro Balancer* from Dead Center Archery Products – I set the bow handle plumb and lock it in place.

Many sight bars have two screws that attach the vertical sight bar to the horizontal extension bar. Loosen these screws a small amount, hold a small level to the side of the vertical bar, adjust the vertical bar to plumb and tighten the two attachment screws. Recheck the bar with the level to be sure it stayed plumb when you tightened the screws.

Step Four *Install the Sight Block* Now its time to install the sight block to the vertical sight bar. If the bow is vertical and the vertical bar is truly vertical then the scope block will move up and down in the desired vertical plane.

Step Five *Adjust Scope/Block Level* If you intend to use a level on your scope or pin you need to adjust that level at this time. With the bow held in a vertical position and the vertical sight bar adjusted to plumb, loosen the sight block level adjustment screws and adjust the block so the level reads true level and retighten the screws.

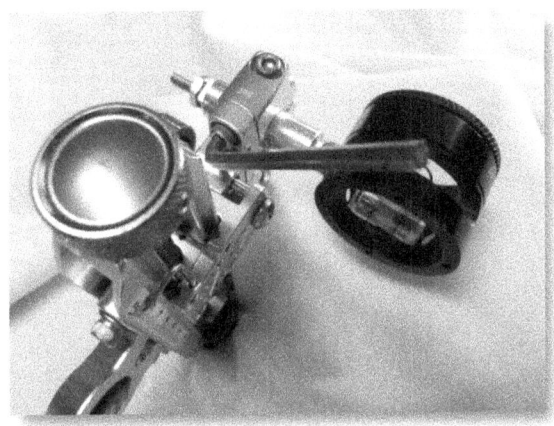

Sight Block/Level *The sight block level shown here can be adjusted using the adjustment screw on the top of the block marked "2nd" for second axis. This allows you to swivel the scope up or down a little to set its bubble level to match the vertical attitude of the bow. Double check this setting to be sure it's correct.*

Step Six *Final Check* Recheck the bow position to be plumb, the vertical sight-bar to be vertical and the sight block level to show true level. Rechecking these adjustments will save you from false and unusual results when sighting in later.

Step Seven *Third Axis Adjustment* The adjustments you've made so far prepare the sight for shooting on level ground. However, much of 3-D, field archery, and treestand hunting involve shooting upward and downward angles so there's more to do to the sight.

The third axis adjustment involves adjusting the plane of the scope/level relative to the arrow-trajectory plane. If the scope/level is not perpendicular to the arrow trajectory path then it will not read correctly when the bow is aimed uphill or downhill. A misaligned scope will be canted off-vertical when the bow is aimed uphill, let's say top-to-the-right, even though the bubble indicates true plumb status. This same bow will cant the opposite way, top-to-the-left, to center the bubble when the bow is aimed downhill. This leads to arrows missed to the right on uphill shots and arrows missed to the left on downhill shots.

You can test this by keeping the bow plumb while tilting it uphill and downhill and note if the bubble moves out of its center lines. If the scope lens is not perpendicular to the arrow line (as seen from the top view) then the bubble will move one direction when the bow is tilted upward and the opposite when the bow is tilted downward. (Example: bubble left when aimed uphill and bubble right when aimed down.)

The correction for this is to adjust the plane of the scope as seen from the top view. If you imagine the bow in the aiming position, the scope has to be either rotated slightly toward your eye or rotated slightly away from your eye. The photo shows an overhead view of an exaggerated situation where the scope is rotated too far away from your eye and is clearly not perpendicular to the arrow trajectory path. The correction is, of course, to rotate the scope so that it is at a right angle to the arrow path.

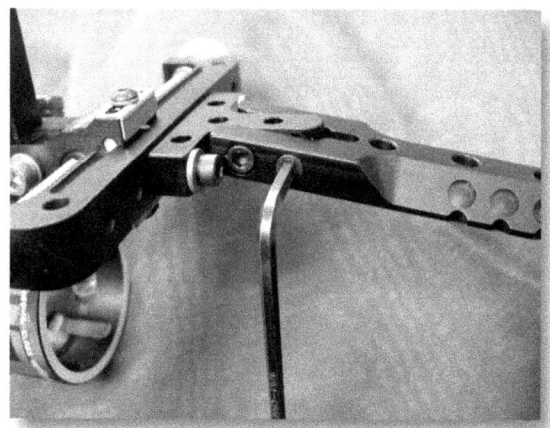

Misaligned Scope/3rd Axis *This scope is clearly not perpendicular to the arrow path. Using the screw on the front you rotate your scope in the horizontal plane to get it perpendicular to the arrow path. Correctly adjusted it will place good shots in the middle for uphill and downhill targets.*

Most sight manufacturers have designed an adjustment feature into the scope attachment block so you don't have to bend the scope rod or sight extension like I had to do back in the early 1980s. On this demo sight you need to loosen the top two-screw adjustment nose piece, rotate the scope a few degrees and retighten.

Reset the level as in Step Five above and redo the upward and downward tilt-test. Be sure to hold the bow plumb while doing this. Continue adjusting the 3rd axis until the bubble stays in the middle while being tilted both upward and downward. Now, any left or right missed arrows at uphill or downhill targets will be due to shooter error and not a misaligned scope lens.

Bow Canting The above steps will get a sight close to perfect and ready for initial testing. Poor bow hand position, unnecessary bow arm tension, some grip designs, as well as a person's anatomy may lead to left/right errors even when the sight setup is "perfect."

A well-balanced bow can help minimize these kinds of errors. Balance your bow so that it stays plumb during aiming. Beyond that, you will have to learn how to manage the bow in the vertical plane or tilt the vertical sight-bar out of plumb to compensate (not recommended).

Long & Short Range Testing

So when is it right for you? It's correct when you can shoot arrows in the middle from long and short range without having to change your windage adjustment. I test often at eighty yards, walk up to twenty yards and test there. If I don't get arrows in the middle at both ranges then I continue adjusting the third axis and/or the vertical angle of the sight bar. I test on side hill, uphill, and downhill shots, to be sure I get arrows in the middle under all conditions guaranteeing a correctly installed sight.

Sight Leveling Tools

There are tools on the market now that simplify the leveling process and get good results in just a few minutes. I've tested two of these that use a level that attaches to the vertical slide bar just above the arrow, make a few setscrew adjustments and your sight is ready for long-range testing.

The Sure Loc *Leveling Tool* also helps deal with the cable guard torque in the handle when the bow is at full draw. It's at full draw when the cable weight load gets high and applies side torque against the cable guard. This torque has an effect on where the arrow shoots through the bow handle and, consequently, where the sight lines up over the arrow shaft and with the target.

Following Step Four above, install the sight-leveling device to the bottom of the vertical sight bar. Slide the level extension left or right so the level is over the arrow and tighten in place. Next, pull the elastic cord from the tool level, around the bowstring and fasten with some tension to the sight bar on the anchor post opposite the tool level. Prop the bow so that it is pointed horizontally and the tool bubble reads level. With the bow held in this position adjust the scope bubble to read level.

Simulate shooting up and down hills by tilting the bow up or down about 30 degrees, prop it so the tool bubble reads level and check the scope bubble. If it is not centered then adjust the third axis of the scope so that its bubble reads level.

The Hamskea *Third Axis Leveler* device enables you to set your third axis easily. Mount it to the bow as per the directions and then raise the bow upward and downward to compare the tool level to the scope level. The long vertical pin helps you keep your sight in line with the bow string during the process. Adjust the lens/scope angle relative to your arrow (from the top view) until the scope bubble reads "true level" when the bow is aimed at an upward angle, downward angle and when aimed at a level target.

Don't forget to test your setup at both long and short range to be sure the arrows are hitting the center at both distances. No matter how the sight is setup, the final test is always done by shooting long and short.

Building a Full Set of Sight Marks

A target sight is no good to you until you have a good set of sight marks on it. That process seems to be a mystery to some shooters but it is really quite simple, especially with the aid of computer programs. I follow a process to get a few sight marks for reference and then use the computer to calculate and print a full sight-mark tape to place on the vertical slide bar. I never shoot 3-D or field archery without a printed sight tape marked in yards on my bow sight. Never!

Step One Set a short-range reference mark by shooting some arrows at twenty yards. Once you've adjusted your sight and shot several arrows into the spot at twenty yards then record the value from the sight bar reference scale. The scale is usually a twenty-four-turn scale that provides a three-digit reference number similar to tenths of a millimeter or hundredths of an inch. Also place a pencil mark on the sight-tape side of the slide bar as an extra reference.

Pencil Marks *Before computer programs we had to use pencil marks for every yard placed on the paper tape. I still do that along with using the twenty-four turn scale reference numbers. I always place a pencil mark for my 20-yd and 60-yd reference.*

Step Two Now move to a longer range to determine another reference mark. If your maximum shooting distance is fifty yards then sight in there. Shoot enough arrows to get an accurate sight mark from the sight bar reference scale. Once again, place a pencil mark on the sight-tape side of the slide bar. Shooting at a third distance can add accuracy to your sight tape so if the program you choose directs you to do that then obtain a sight reference number at an intermediate distance like forty yards. I prefer to use 20, 40 and 60 yards for my own personal reference points – I always shoot-in my 80-yd mark.

Step Three The pair or triplet of three-digit reference numbers you have recorded can be used in one of several computer programs for establishing a full-length tape of sight marks. The program that I've used for years is by Archer's Advantage and available online at www.archersadvantage.com. Some others also available online are www.thearcheryprogram.com and www.pinwheelsoftware.com.

The programs require you to supply information about your arrows, sight extension, and peep height. That along with the reference sight marks you have obtained will be used to develop a mathematical function that will calculate sight reference numbers for every single yard distance from ten yards to one hundred yards or meters.

The most important accessory you need is the computer print-out of a complete sight tape. When you go to the field archery course or the 3-D range you must have this sight tape mounted to the side of your sight bar – don't leave home without it! This is the only reference you need while shooting – disregard the other reference scale on the opposite side of the sight bar. Install the tape on the sight bar matching the pencil marks you made earlier.

Your sight tape marks can be calculated mathematically because the arrow trajectory is parabolic in shape due to the effects of gravity. Other examples of the parabolic arc can be seen in the path of a thrown baseball, a shot basketball, a shot bullet or in the curvature of all of those roof-top satellite-receiving dishes.

Preprinted Sight Tapes
The two or three pencil marks you have placed on the side of the slide bar can be matched to preprinted sight marks. These sight aids are available at many pro shops and provide a series of sight tapes of differing lengths. Faster bows will need the marks that are spaced close together while slower bows need wider spaced marks since slower arrows drop more over a given distance. By comparing your two or three pencil marks to the same marks on the

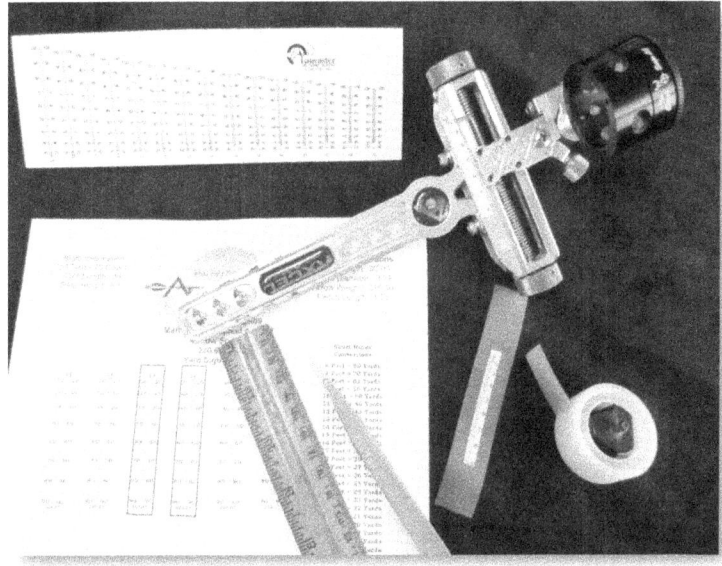

Printed Sight Marks *The Archer's Advantage computer program and the others available print out really neat sets of sight marks that can be cut out and taped to your sight bar. Lancaster Archery sells peel-off preprinted pages of sight marks that can be easily matched to the speed of your bow and taped to the slide bar. Each system requires at least two good sight-in marks for reference. I slice the sight mark strip from the printout, cover it with clear tape for water proofing and attach it to the slide bar using my 20- and 60-yard pencil marks for reference.*

preprinted sight tapes you can select the one tape that best matches. If you don't have a perfect match you can always micro-adjust the draw weight of your bow to increase or decrease the speed of your arrow to match the sight marks on the tape.

Or, you could sight in the old-fashioned way – I've done it many times – by shooting in a mark at each five- or ten-yard interval. When you are done, check the spacing between marks to be sure that as the distance from the target increases so does the spacing – remember that as the arrow flies down range its velocity decays and the arrow drops more and more until it hits a target or drops to the ground. (I've tested a wide range of arrow types and fletching combinations between twenty and fifty yards and found the decay to be about twenty feet per second for all of them over that distance.)

Step Four Last, I test my set of marks by shooting at several distances. To begin, I shoot at twenty yards and adjust my sight so that I get arrows in the middle. I then set the sight indicator needle to match the twenty-yard mark on the sight tape.

Next, I move to a longer distance, set my sight to that mark and shoot some arrows – they should be in the middle if I make good shots. I continue shooting longer distances through eighty yards. If my original two reference marks were correct my good shots should hit the middle at all other distances. If they don't then I may have to rebuild those original reference pencil marks.

Sight Pin and Shaft Alignment

On most bows you'll find that the arrow shaft and the sight pin don't line up as you look down across the undrawn bowstring and shaft. The pin is slightly off to one side of the string/shaft line due to the torque that develops on the cable guard when the bow is brought to full draw. As the draw force on the bowstring decreases at full draw the weight force on the cables continues to increase all through the draw stroke. That high force against the cable guard results in torque applied to the bow handle. A bow with shoot-through cables has little torque on the cable guard and should have its pin, string and shaft align closely at brace position.

Multiple Sight Pin Alignment
Many bowhunters use fixed, multiple pin sights, as do those who choose to shoot tournament archery in the bowhunter-pin styles (BHFS and BHFSL). These archers are, therefore, concerned with their vertical pin alignment and spacing.

The spacings should match the spacing of the computer-generated or preprinted tapes already mentioned. The alignment of the pins should, in a perfect world, be vertical when the bow is held vertical (plumb). This is similar to having the sight-bar vertical on a target sight as described above.

Once again, if you have a student who cannot hold the bow in a true vertical position then his or her pin alignment will be slightly off vertical. The pins will be in line but not the same line as the handle. For instance, the lower fifty-yard pin may extend further to the left than the top or twenty-yard pin with the other pins falling in line between these two. What's important here is for the shooter to be aiming with the pins in a vertical line as the bow is slightly canted.

I'll remind you here that some centershot and/or form flaws can cause pins to be misaligned. An arrow rest set too far to the left of bowstring alignment (right-handers) will cause the long distance pins to be further to the left than the shorter distance pins. Any contact, slight or otherwise, between the lower bowstring and your body will cause arrows to impact to the left (for right-handers). Proper bow hand technique is also a must if you hope to establish good pin alignment.

Another problem for some bowhunters involves the misuse of their peep sight. Some get a little sloppy with their aiming through the large peep sight hole they're using. Failing to look through the peep center and/or to center the sight pin arrangement in the peep for every shot will result in errant arrows. This is a skill I have to practice for hunting season every year as I use a scope and small peep hole most of the year but pins and a large peep for hunting. Proper head position, peep height, practice and having a brightly colored ring around the pin housing helps me consistently center the pin cluster.

Movable Hunting Sights
Some bowhunters prefer a sliding sight for hunting. It allows them to use just one pin, the one color that they can see the best, so they always know what pin to use when its time to make that hunting shot.

The setup steps are the same as for any sliding sight. Mount it to the side of the bow, check to be sure that the slide is vertical when the bow is plumb, set the level and then shoot test. I find that this works well for me but I have to do a good job of holding the bow vertical for all of my shots, even those out of a treestand.

Recommendation Not everyone needs a high-end sight for their target shooting especially if it is their first sight. Too many adjustments may confuse them or they may only want to shoot in their back yard. These archers can make do with a simple, inexpensive target sight – or just a simple pin sight.

I know at my own club there's a group of young guys and gals who like to shoot the winter league and need a mid-range sight. A sight with a 4X scope and micro-adjust windage and elevation is enough to match their skill level. Several of these archers are shooting 295 to 300 on the Vegas three-spot target. This caliber of sight works well on 3-D as well.

Shooting serious outdoor 3-D and long-range archery requires the top-of-the-line ($300-$350) sight—and a good scope, too (another $100-150). The third axis adjustment feature of the best sights is needed if you plan to shoot up- and down-hill targets beyond twenty yards. The permanent reference scale also makes the sight-in process easy.

These high quality sights also travel well. The extension bar can be removed and the sight block detaches easily but both can be reattached with accuracy. Packing your sight and bow in towels in the bow case keeps them protected from the "luggage gorillas" during travel. I have no suggestions for handling the extra luggage fee!

Summary

I find that many beginning archers and some who only shoot to prepare for hunting season forget how to adjust their sight. They forget that the sight is wrong and want to adjust as if the arrows in the target are wrong. Once they see my point they can do a better job of moving the incorrect sight to match the arrow impact point so their next shot is closer to the middle.

No matter how well you get your system sighted in you have to maintain it. I do that by constantly shooting at a long distance and then moving to a short distance to be sure my sight system windage is correct and the mark spacing matches my arrow speed. I also test up- and down-hill shots.

I also developed a sight-setting routine when I approach any target: Approach the shooting position, determine the distance, set my sight, double check distance and sight setting, set my stance and run my shooting form to make the shot(s). Here's where concentration and focus become all important so you do what you should be doing and do it correctly. But that's another topic.

Chapter 28
Powder and Paper Testing

The Facts Ma'am, All We Want Are The Facts!
That's a great line from *Dragnet's* Joe Friday, remember him? (If you do, you are older than you look!) But that's just what bow tuning needs if you're going to make a difference for yourself or your students. So here's what to do to get the facts and how to use them when you get them.

Knowledge about arrow flight as the arrow leaves the bow is essential if you want the best arrow flight and best groups possible. If you're a coach, you must have an effective method for collecting and showing the facts about arrow flight if you expect your students to believe in what you're doing for them.

In order to improve flight you must first identify the flight problems and that means powder testing and paper testing arrow flight. A can of white-powder spray, a picture frame, some sheets of newspaper, and some test arrows are all that you need to get started.

Powder and paper tests tell you exactly what the arrow is doing as it passes the arrow rest and travels the first eight yards down range. With this knowledge you can make tension adjustments to your arrow rest, adjust nock fit, adjust nocking point location, and alter the centershot location of your rest just to name a few critical tuning parameters.

Powder Testing

The powder test is best done using an aerosol can of white powder (foot spray); make sure it is white powder and not a clear liquid spray. To do the test, spray powder on the last six or eight inches of the fletched end of an arrow and shoot the arrow into a relatively dense backstop (you do not want anything close to being a "pass through" which would disturb the powder). Next, check the fletching for contact marks because those marks came from contact with the arrow rest, sight window of the bow, or even the cables.

Since that contact disturbs the arrow's flight you must take steps to eliminate it or dampen it as much as possible. As long as the contact exists you can't proceed with other tuning steps because of the likelihood of false indications created by the contact.

Adjusting Nock Orientation You can often eliminate contact between the arrow

Powder Test To make the powder test effective, use a common athlete's foot spray on the fletched end of the shaft. Be sure that it is the "powder" type and not clear liquid so that any contact marks can be easily seen. Any contact marks of the arrow rest can be seen as streaks in the powder on the vanes.

rest and the fletching by rotating nocks to reposition the fletching. Rotate the nock on one arrow a few degrees and retest with powder to note improvement or lack thereof. If you get clear flight set all of the other arrow nocks to match the test arrow.

The most common nock position for right-handers has the index fletch pointing upward on the bow. This allows good clearance over a launcher-style arrow rest and also through a drop-away rest. Regardless of the rest, if arrow fletching is making contact you rotate the nock a few degrees and retest until you eliminate the contact.

Adjusting The Arrow Rest If nock rotation doesn't eliminate the contact then examine the arrow rest. Many rests can be repositioned to allow more space for the fletching as it passes through or over it.

Tuning Adjustments Occasionally, some simple adjustments can correct fletch contact. Raising the nocking point can eliminate contact on the bottom fletch while changing the tension on the cushion plunger or side spring will help eliminate contact with the sight window and cushion plunger. Adjusting the rest for centershot (left-right position) can also make a difference.

When a launcher blade is too weak the arrow tends to ride low across it allowing the bottom fletch to strike it on the way by. Using a stiffer launcher can help raise the fletched end of the arrow and eliminate contact. This will also help tighten arrow groups that have been vertical in shape.

Some popular rests surround the arrow with bristles. These bristles hold a hunter's arrow in place at all times and guide the arrow through the rest but don't give clear results with powder test. You may give the powder a try looking for equal contact all around the fletched end of the shaft but this is often difficult to ascertain.

Powder Testing Drop-Away Rests

Shooting a drop-away rest requires some extra powder testing. The front-end of the arrow shaft should contact the rest for only about three or four inches before the rest falls away from under the shaft. About the only way to check this is with a high-speed camera. We did this at one of my shooting schools at Lancaster Archery using their high-speed camera and obtained some very interesting results. It's incredible how many bow and rest parts move, bounce and shake. That was a real eye opener.

Sometimes the drop-away rest can fall down and then bounce back up making contact with the shaft or fletching near the back of the shaft. To check for this you have to spray powder on both the rest and shaft and look for contact. To combat the bounce-up you may have to place a rubber dampener device under the rest or raise the rest location upward to allow it to drop further downward, well below the passing arrow shaft.

The high-speed video showed arrows launched with a low nocking point whose fletching contacted the fallen rest. Some of these arrows bounced upward causing a nock-high paper test. Talk about confused! You can uncover this problem by powder testing the fletching and the rest. The solution is simple, raise the nocking point – the opposite of what the paper test indicated. (See Paper Testing below.)

Adjusting Nock Fit Nocks that fit too tightly tend to act stiff as they leave the bow. In other words, they leave nock-right for right-handers and sometimes strike the sight window or arrow rest. Nocks that are too loose may leave nock-left or nock low and result in fletch contact with arrow rest.

To get the proper fit you may have to change strings and/or center serving. When the fit is correct you can easily pull the nock from the string with index finger and thumb and the nock should slide, but not too easily, up and down the string when pushed. Paying attention to this detail will improve arrow flight and groups greatly just because contact has been eliminated.

Adjusting Arrow Size If none of the simple adjustments work then you'll have to get radical and change the arrow and fletching combination. The easiest to change is the fletching angle. Contact may be due to the size/length or angle of the fletching on the shaft and reducing it slightly may help eliminate contact. Don't put fletches on straight down the shaft since some angle is necessary to stabilize the arrow, especially when shooting broadheads.

The very last resort is to change arrow sizes. Arrows that are too stiff or too weak won't clear the rest as well as an arrow whose spine is matched to the draw weight and arrow rest. As a coach you should have a selection of test arrows (I know this can get expensive) so you can quickly sort out which size shoots and clears best.

Adjusting Shooting Form Some archers have form flaws that cause bad arrow flight. Before you correct arrow flight you should be correcting form issues. For example, bow draw length has to correctly match the archer in order to enhance the release technique and followthrough. String finger placement, if they shoot with fingers, must be corrected to prevent twisting the string to the side at full draw.

The most significant flaw is the archer's bow hand placement. 99% of the archers who attend my shooting schools or come for private coaching do not have correct bow hand placement. They, instead, grip the bow handle in some way, fail to rotate their knuckles to a forty-five degree angle, tense their hand and fingers or do some combination of all of these. This, of course, means that during the power stroke when the arrow is crossing the arrow rest the bow handle is being torqued is some direction instead of being free from torque.

When these form flaws are corrected your student is going to get more reliable test results from powder testing. With more reliable results it is easier to decide which adjustments are really necessary.

Paper Testing

Paper testing is the practice of shooting arrows through a piece of paper from close range. This creates a hole in the paper that tells how the arrow was oriented in three-dimensional space as it passed through the paper. Since that arrow is a flying projectile, reading this orientation means determining if the arrow has any pitch or yaw. Making adjustments to dampen either of these conditions can improve arrow flight and arrow grouping by better positioning the arrow's nock-end behind and in-line with the point-end.

To start paper testing, you need a picture frame or similar wooden frame about 15″ x 15″ or bigger. Hang it three or four feet in front of your target and cover it with newspaper. You can use a roll of plain paper if it has the same density as newspaper; heavy paper can alter the arrow's flight and give false readings.

Paper Test *A picture frame covered with some newspaper or wrapping paper is all that is needed for paper testing. The one shown has been around for . . . well, a long time. Be sure to hang it about two to three yards in front a dense backstop so the arrows pass completely through the paper but stop quickly with the powder marks undisturbed.*

Stand at least three yards away from the paper frame when shooting your arrows through the paper. I find that five to eight yards gives the best readings because that is where your arrows are usually at their worst and if you get good results there you can be sure that your arrow flight is good at any distance. You should have completed all powder testing at this point and have uninhibited arrow passage since contact with the arrow rest definitely affects arrow flight and how the arrow passes through the paper.

Shoot several arrows through the paper making sure that you or your students are using good relaxed hand position on the bow handle. Test at several distances back to about eight yards before you jump to any conclusions about arrow flight.

A typical hole looks like the one on the left in the photo. This hole shows the

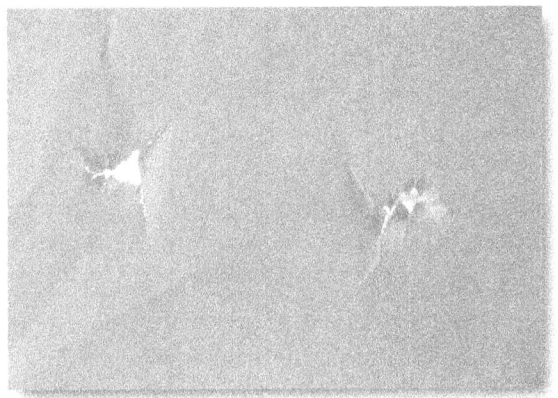

Test Holes The left-hand hole shown is from my PSE MoneyMaker and shows a slight nock-right tear. To improve this stiff-acting arrow flight I will test heavier points in the same 0.500 spine Maxima shaft. The hole on the right is from a Mathews Apex and shows a slight nock-left and low tear. This setup needs a slightly stiffer shaft and a higher nock point.

point entering on the left (where some small short tears appear on the low left). The vanes tear to the up and right making bigger and more irregular tears. Once you read the hole you then must decide on a course of corrections to improve the arrow flight.

Adjusting Nocking Point If the arrow holes have any high or low tearing then you must adjust the nocking point location. Do this first. If the tear is high then the arrow is pitched point down. In other words, the fletched-end is passing through the paper higher than the point and the vanes are creating paper-rips that are above and larger than the tiny rips created by the point. To correct this condition move the nocking point down the bowstring a small amount and retest.

Continue lowering the nocking point and retesting until you get good results through the paper or until the nocking point positions the bottom of the shaft level with the arrow rest. Generally, you don't want the nock-end setting lower than the point-end but sometimes that's what it takes to get good flight. Be careful however, as this may create contact between the fletching and the arrow rest and give false results – powder test again to be sure.

If the fletched-end rips lower through the paper the arrow is pitched upward. Correct it by moving the nocking point up the string a little and retest.

Don't knock yourself out trying to get a perfect hole. Instead, look for a hole that has crisp vane slices through the paper. Another caution, if you have to move the nocking point below level then start looking for another solution to the high knocking point indication. Sometimes an ultra-stiff launcher will keep the arrow tearing high through the paper and changing it to a slightly weaker launcher blade will solve the problem.

Arrow tears of less than a half-inch are good, just be sure that the vane slices are crisp which indicates a stable arrow. Perfect holes are great if you can get them but the "proof of the pudding" is always the groups you get in the target. Paper testing is going to help you most with eliminating arrow sizes that don't work well and getting that correct shaft closer to good arrow flight; it's not the last step in tuning.

Single Cam Bow Tuning Arrow spine can affect the high/low ripping of the paper test for one-cam bows. My good friend Dietmar Trillus of Canada and 2007 World Target Champion instructed me that weak-spined arrow shafts out of his Mathews bow will tend to tear nock-high when paper testing. The stiffer spined shafts will tend to show a low nock tear through the paper. That's one reason why some bow setups continue to tear nock high no matter where you adjust the nocking point location – the arrow is acting weak and needs to be switched for a stiffer shaft.

Once Dietmar set me straight on this tuning indicator I was able to greatly improve my setup of my Mathews *Conquest 4*. Mostly I was getting a slightly low nock-left tear through the paper so I switched from 90-grain to 108-grain points making the shaft act weaker and immediately improved my paper test, arrow flight, and arrow groupings. Remember, the bottom line is always about the groupings!

Adjusting For Arrow Yaw/Left And Right Arrow Tears Correcting arrow flight for nock-right and nock-left tears through the paper is more difficult than correcting for up and down. An arrow tears left or right because its spine is not properly matched to the bow system. (Remember, we already eliminated arrow rest contact.) These adjustments are numerous and don't always get results if the arrow isn't the proper spine or something major is wrong with the bow system.

Nock-left holes in paper (for right-handers) can result from weak-acting spined arrows. The corrections for weak arrows are:
1. Less draw weight
2. More horizontal plunger tension
3. Less point weight
4. Move centershot of rest slightly left
5. Replace with a stiffer (lower static spine value) arrow shaft.

When your arrows are indicating "weak spine" it may take a combination of these adjustments to correct the flight but try one at a time so you can identify which one made the change and make a note for future reference.

Nock-right holes in paper (for right-handers) can result from stiff-acting arrows. The corrections for stiffness are:
1. More draw weight
2. Less horizontal plunger tension
3. More point weight
4. Move center-shot of rest slightly right
5. Replace with a weaker (higher static spine value) arrow shaft.

Again, make a combination of these adjustments to correct stiff arrow flight but make them one at a time.

I remind you again that this is not a perfect world and you should not beat your head against the wall trying to get a perfect hole. Close is good especially if the vane slices through the paper are crisp and all test shots produce the same hole. A little high-left or a little high tear, less than a half inch from eight yards, is very acceptable and tells you that the arrows are flying well. All that remains is to shoot for groups from some distance that matches your or your student's ability level.

If your student-archer continues to get mixed results with nock-right and nock-left tears then his bowhand position needs inspection and improvement. Torque on the bow handle from the bowhand can cause wide variations in how the arrow leaves the bow and until hand placement is addressed and improved the paper testing won't yield consistent results. My guess is that you'll have lots of coaching to do in the area of hand placement.

Some archers I know spend hours and hours paper testing. I use it to determine if I'm close on shaft selection. Spending a lot of time on it isn't my idea of tuning. Group shooting tells me more and, after all, that's where good scores come from. Paper testing is a great timesaver if you use it properly.

Chapter 29
Getting Looped

Think back to the day after the first bow was invented. Can you imagine that first ever archer looking for some different method of holding the bowstring because his fingers were sore? I can see that very clearly and so he invented a strip of leather to hold the string, or the bone ring or some other device. What he also discovered was that his shooting was more accurate and so, today we have all kinds of release aid devices from fancy five- and six- part tabs to machined metal contraptions that have a hundred parts.

One thing they all have in common is that they must all be hooked to the bowstring. How they make this hookup has a great impact on the accuracy that today's archers can achieve. These days the D-loop is the most popular method of release aid attachment. Does hooking the loop directly above and below the arrow nock group better than using nock locators above and below the nock and then tying the D-loop above and below the locators? As a competitor I have to ask these kinds of questions if I hope to excel at my game and as a coach I have to ask these same questions so my students reach their potential.

There must be a hundred ways to hook a release aid to a bowstring but some are better than others. Years ago we hooked our release aid rope directly under the arrow nock. Today very few do that because the nock styles, stored energy levels and string materials have changed and you get the best groups by "trapping" the nock on the bowstring so it can't slide up or down during the power stroke.

This article is an overview of the most common and very effective methods of utilizing D-loops and nock locators. Which variations of these shoots the best groups on a given bow is something you and your students will have to find out by actually shoot-testing them. History's first archer never envisioned this, did he?

Tied-On Nock Locators
I can imagine that several days after the first bow was invented history's first archer was also figuring out how to position the arrow nock at the same point on the bowstring. Surely he recognized that placing the nock at the same string-point would give better accuracy so he tied a small amount of sinew, hair, or vine-thread on the string. This gave him a consistent reference point to which he could attach the arrow nock and, even with his crude device, he could begin shooting with a higher degree of success. Simply put, he wanted to "get the bear" and not become the bear's dinner. (Remember, we're offspring of the survivors!)

To show you how far we've come in the fifty thousand years since then, we are, this very day, tying small amounts of cord onto the bowstring to give us a consistent nocking point! Wow, we've come so far, haven't we? Or is it just that a good idea stands the test of time?

The only difference in all these years is the materials being used. Today we use man-made fibers like Dyneema™, Dacron™, and polyester to mention a few. My preference is the Polygrip material made by BCY but others are just as popular. The requirement for me is ease of installation and removal, as well as resistance to wear. Polyester has all of these properties.

Here's how I install a tie-on nock-point locator:
1. Locate nocking point with a bow square and mark it.
2. Tie a single overhand knot above this mark and make it snug.

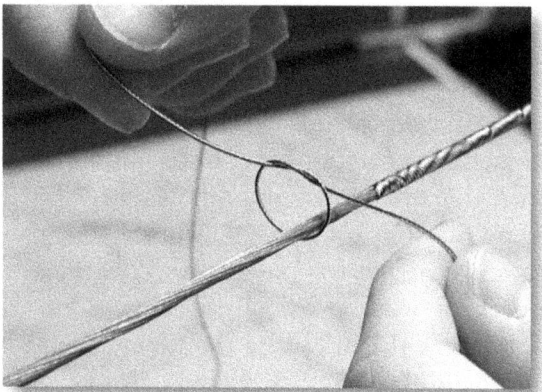

First Knot *Begin a tied-on nock locator with a single overhand knot as shown. Cinch it tight over the center serving.*

3. Tie a second knot on the opposite side of the string and above the first knot, snug.
4. Continue alternating single knots up the bowstring until knot #9 (or #11 if you wish). Do not snug up this knot.
5. Slip a separate loop of bowstring material (I use *Dyneema*™ like BCY 8125 because it is slippery) upward through this knot so a one-inch loop sticks out above the knot and its loose ends hang down over the first eight knots. Now snug that last knot (#9 or #11).

Extra Pull Through Loop *Slip an extra loop of bowstring material (yellow) under the ninth (or eleventh) knot. Tighten the ninth knot and then tie and tighten knot ten on the opposite side of the bowstring. Slip the loose thread ends through the extra loop (yellow) and pull the extra loop and the thread-ends tight.*

6. Tie one more single knot on the opposite side of the bowstring and snug it.
7. Pull the two loose nock-locator ends through the separate one-inch loop installed in step 5.

8. Pull the loose ends of this separate loop until the nock-locator loose ends pull under and through that last knot (#9 or #11). The separate loop material will pull free at this point and can be discarded.

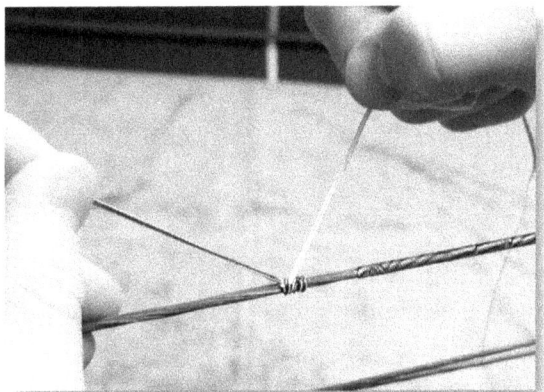

Pull Through Ends *Pull the extra loop until the thread ends pull under the ninth knot. You may have to wiggle the extra loop in order to get it to pull under the ninth knot. Cover the entire ten-knot locator with fletching glue and let it harden for an hour before using.*

9. Pull the nock-locator ends tight and cover with fletching cement (not quickset glue). Use fingernail clippers to clip off the loose ends.
10. Allow one hour for drying and it is ready to hold an arrow nock under it for thousands of shots.

This same knot tying technique can be used to tie on ten-knot locators above and below your peep sight to hold it in place. They can be moved up and down the bowstring if you need to adjust the peep height and/or flip strands from side-to-side to adjust peep rotation. Many archers tie knotted locators of different sizes above and below their arrow nock in conjunction with a D-loop as described later in this article. Other archers use a locator knot above and below the arrow nock and hook their release aid directly on the bowstring below the bottom locator. There are lots of applications for these knots.

Crimp-On Metal Nock Locators

The little metal ring called the "Nok Set" is a wonderful invention. All you have to do is crimp the metal ring around the bowstring just above the arrow nock, or above and below the nock, and you've established a durable nocking point locator. Special tools have been made for just this purpose (avoid the cheapest varieties).

Be sure to leave a small space, say one millimeter, between the nock and the two Nok Sets so the arrow nock isn't pinched at full draw. Nock pinching causes some inconsistent arrow flight and some false tuning information when paper and group testing.

Many archers use the Nok Sets in conjunction with their D-loops. The loop can be installed above and below the Nok Sets or the Nok Sets can be installed above and below the loop to provide location security.

The D-Loop

The most popular method of setting a nocking point on today's bows is with a small-diameter (2 mm) rope loop tied to the bowstring. The rope used is the same as the release rope used on most mechanical release aids a decade ago and more. This rope is made from the same materials as used for tie-on nock locators but is a larger diameter and of braided construction. Once again I prefer braided polyester rope because of its high resistance to wear, gripping ability and its uniform melting characteristic.

Regardless of the material used, the installation procedure is the same. Here are the installation steps that I follow:

1. Select the loop material and diameter preferred. Cut at least five inches for the loop. Melt a bead on one end by "flowering" the end before heating it with the flame of a butane lighter. Don't allow the material to catch on fire, as this will make it brittle.
2. Allow the bead to cool for about five seconds then flatten it by pressing the side of the lighter to the hot bead.
3. Tie the loop to the bowstring (above the top nock locator) using a double overhand cinch knot as shown. The melted bead will prevent the knot from pulling through under tension. Pull it tight by hand.

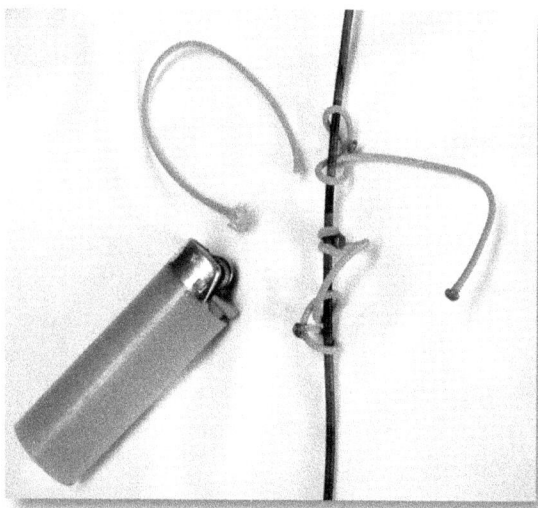

Cinch Knot *Tying a D-loop begins with a bead melted on the "flowered" end of the 4 to 5-inch loop rope. Then tie two overhand knots as shown on top in the example and pull tight. The lower cinch knot should be tied in the same manner but from the opposite side of the bowstring as shown on the bottom example.*

4. Tie the other loop-end below the arrow nock location using the same overhand cinch knot. Make a mirror image of the first knot by approaching the bowstring from the opposite side. This prevents the finished D-Loop from rotating around the bowstring through repeated use.
5. Measure the loop's length from the bowstring. To adjust the desired length untie one end and cut off a small amount.
6. Flower the end and melt an end-bead as before.
7. Retie the knot and pull tight by hand or using a release aid.
8. Slide the loop knots to their final locations allowing about one millimeter extra space around the arrow nock to avoid pinching.
9. Shoot several arrows. Recheck the loop location and length. Reset the loop location or length if needed.

Six D-Loop Attachment Possibilities

There are six basic D-loop arrangements that I see on bows. The differences lie in where the loop knots are located relative to any nock locators you wish to use. They are as follows (where (A = above (the nocking point), B = below, L = locator):

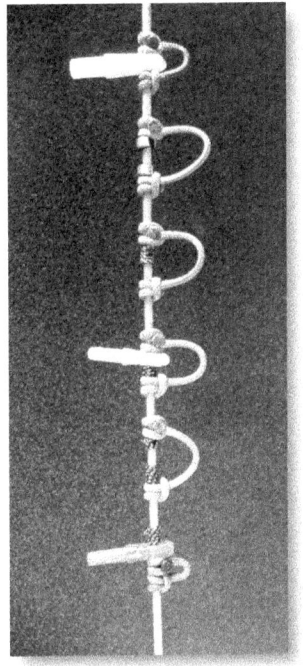

Six D-Loops *Here are six variations for tying the D-loop. The top shows the loop tied directly above and below the arrow nock. The second example uses the loop tied above and below two nock-sets. The third uses only one nock locator above the nocked arrow while the fourth and most popular uses the locator below the arrow nock. Next to the bottom is an example of a having larger bottom nock locator than the one above the arrow nock. The bottom example shows the D-loop with both ends tied below the arrow nock and a locator above it.*

1. A/B: Tie the D-loop knots directly above and below the arrow's nocking point.
2. (A+L)/(L+B): Install nock locators directly above and below the nock with the D-loop knots tied above and below the locators.
3. (A+L)/B: Use a single nock locator above the arrow nock.
4. A/(L+B): Use a single locator below the arrow nock.
5. (A+L)/(LL+B): Use a longer locator knot length on the bottom than on the top, then tie the D-loop ends above and below the locators. This is similar to #4.
6. L/(B+B): Use a locator above the arrow nock and tie both D-loop ends below the nock.

So which is the best? That's a good question. My standard answer that applies to any accessory we add to our bows (which is in the form of another question) is: "What groups the best?" Sometimes I use style #6 because it groups best with a particular bow setup.

Most of the time I use either style #4 or #5. I can tell you that at all the major tournaments I see these two styles on over half of the bows, maybe even 75%. The advantage of these two styles is how they allow the release hook to pull directly behind the arrow nock. You might think that style #1 or #2 would do that but the tendency is for the release hook to pull high in the D-loop because most nocking points are above the middle of the bowstring; being closer to the top wheel makes the release aid pull higher in the D-loop. So, using a nock locator under the arrow nock compensates for the above-center nocking point and the release hook pulls directly behind the nock.

Shoot testing for groups is the only way to know for sure. Getting both the arrow nock and release aid to escape cleanly from the bowstring is of utmost importance.

Metal Loops

I've seen several makes of metal D-loops over the years. T.R.U. has one on the market now called the Tru-Nok that uses two screw-on side plates to hold it onto the string around the nocking point. Obviously this lightweight aluminum loop will not wear as fast as some fiber loops do. It also utilizes a small crossbar that slips into the nock-throat to align the loop and peep the same direction for each shot.

This metal loop, though, is subject to imparting a twist to the bowstring depending on the type of release head you hook into it. If the release head fits tight then torquing the release in your hand can cause it to twist the loop and the bowstring. Smaller release hooks work well with it and provide long-time accuracy.

Loop Tools

Recently at the Pape's Dealer show in Louisville, KY, I saw the Viper Loopset Pliers. This tool slips in place after you tie on one loop-knot and assists you in making the D-loop the same length each time you make one. It also stretches and tightens the loop securely onto the bowstring preventing it from moving or rotating.

Viper also has a small cutting tool that quickly removes loop-knots from the string. I spend more time taking old loops off than it takes to put a new one on so this little cutter caught my eye. All you have to do is lay the tool's flat side on the bowstring next to the knot and then rotate the cutter. This action cuts the knot next to the center serving without cutting the serving.

Eliminator Buttons

These little rubber buttons slide onto the bowstring from the bottom and under the arrow nock. It creates a buffer between the nock and the release jaws for those archers who hook their metal release jaws directly to their bowstring but don't want to damage or wear their nocks. The button prevents the release from twisting against the nock when you torque the release head on the bowstring.

Whether you use the eliminator button or not, if you hook your release aid jaws directly onto the bowstring you should be using a release with a swivel head. The swivel head will not torque against the bowstring like a fixed head will. Some release aid models have a freely swiveling head that automatically adjusts to the bowstring when you turn your release hand at an angle to the bowstring.

Other release aids have an adjustable head that can be set to any angle. The screws holding the head in place can be loosened and the head set perpendicular to the bowstring while the archer is at full draw. Once set, the head can be locked in place by tightening the screws.

Proper Release-Hand Angle

At all of my shooting schools and during all the private lessons I give, questions about the release hand angle arises. The answer can be found in the natural angle of the forearm when you are in proper full-draw-position and that angle is about 30 degrees from the horizontal. The main ingredients here are a relaxed wrist and relaxed forearm muscles that allow the release aid to position itself at the same 30-degree angle at the end of your arm.

At full draw, many archers torque their release aid to a near-vertical angle and that requires tightening forearm muscle. With that tension in their forearm they are applying torque to the release aid at the moment of discharge and inconsistently affecting the flight of the arrow. Holding the release aid in a vertical position also places your hand against the side of your face and most shooters I see doing this generate way too much pressure between their hand and face which also negatively affects the shot.

Further, the forces at work during the proper use of back tension are acting in the 30-degree plane and a proper followthrough is in that same 30-degree. Back tension applies a rotating force on your elbow and your elbow rotates easiest in the 30-degree. The easiest and most consistent way to get a back tension release, or any other release, to discharge is to hold it in the same 30-degree.

The Proof is in the Pudding

Which of these hook-up methods is the best for you or your student? The answer, as I mentioned before, is the same as it is for so many tuning questions, "What groups the best?" We're in this game to shoot the best we can and to get our bow systems grouping the best they can. To do so you have to experiment with different types of release-to-bowstring hook-ups until you find the one that groups the best. Yes, it takes time but accuracy and consistency are important so invest the time to get it right.

About the Author

Larry Wise is an archery coach (USAA Level 4-NTS Certified Coach, NFAA Master Coach) and the author of five books on archery. In 2004 Larry retired from 35 years of teaching math and now concentrates on coaching archery, writing, and volunteer work. Larry was one of four coaches of the USA Archery team for the World Indoor Championships in Denmark in 2005. The team won 13 medals including seven golds. As well as giving private coaching lessons, Larry conducts two-day **Core Archery** shooting schools at clubs and archery pro shops. The school concentrates on proper shooting form for using back tension and provides each participant a written individual plan for practice and form improvement.

Larry was a champion archer before he was an elite level coach. He was the 1986 World Field Archery Champion (in Scotland), Five-Time World Team Champion, many-time Pennsylvania State Champion and had many professional wins including Atlantic City, Big Sky, Ann Marston Open, Milwaukee Sentinel Open and Long Island Open.

The Watching Arrows Fly Coaching Library

There are lots of books about archery—about archery form, archery execution, archery equipment, even archery history; but there weren't any books in print on archery coaching ... until now. Finally there is a book on coaching for beginning to intermediate archery coaches. In **Coaching Archery** you will learn not *what* to teach (which you can get that from those other books) but *how* to teach it and much more you won't get from certification courses. Topics include:
- tips on running programs
- the styles of archery
- the mental side of archery
- an exploration of archery coaching styles
- helping with equipment
- coaching at tournaments
- plus, advice on becoming a better coach from some top coaches

There are even seven whole pages of resources for coaches! If you are an archery coach looking to increase your coaching skills, this is the book for you!

128 pages • ISBN 978-0-9821471-0-8 • US $19.95

For Beginning Coaches!

The Watching Arrows Fly Coaching Library

Following up on his first coaching book, **Coaching Archery**, which was written to help beginning to intermediate coaches, Steve Ruis has a new offering to archery coaches everywhere. This time, the topics are on the full gamet of coaching topics which range from the role of emotion in the making of an archery shot, to teaching the shot sequence, to biomechanics, and how coaches should treat their athletes (and one another) as well as five major chapters on what is missing from the archery coaching profession.

If you are thinking of becoming a coach or already are an archery coach and are looking for some new ideas and help with dealing with the logistics of coaching, this is the book for you.

Get your copy of **More On Coaching Archery** today!

280 pages • ISBN 978-0-9821471-8-4 • US $24.95

For All Coaches!

The Watching Arrows Fly Coaching Library

Following hard on the heels of **More on Coaching Archery**, which was written to help all archery coaches, Steve Ruis has a new offering to archery coaches everywhere. As in MOCA, the topics are on the full gamet of coaching topics including form recommendations, biomechanics, coaching students based upon their personality type, how to "look" at students (what to look for), archery drills, watching out for words that don't instruct, and many, many more. Two chapters are even devoted to adapting standard form, that is how to make adjustments to the textbook form you are taught in coach trainings.

Each topic is covered in a short chapter which is easy to digest but which provides a great deal of food for thought. If you benefited from reading **More On Coaching Archery**, expect more of the same!

Get your copy of **Even More On Coaching Archery** today!

244 pages • ISBN 978-0-9848860-7-4 • US $24.95

For All Coaches!

The Watching Arrows Fly Coaching Library

A book for beginning-to-intermediate archery coaches and those coaching outside their area of expertise.

For archers there are all kinds of "how to" books available in print and on the Internet, but for coaches there is hardly anything. Even the coach training courses focus on what to teach instead of how to teach it. So where should coaches go for ideas as to how to introduce various pieces of archery equipment or new elements of form and execution? If you don't hasve an elite coach as a next-door neighbor, this book may help fill you in on a few things you don't know how to do.

Get your copy of **Archery Coaching How To's** today!

218 pages • ISBN 978-0-9913326-0-1 • US $14.95

For All Coaches!

Notes

Notes

Notes

The Watching Arrows Fly Coaching Library

Larry Wise on Coaching Archery (2014)
Archery Coaching How To's (2013)
Even More on Coaching Archery (2013)
More on Coaching Archery (2010)
Coaching Archery (2008)

www.ingramcontent.com/pod-product-compliance
Lightning Source LLC
Chambersburg PA
CBHW080537170426
43195CB00016B/2587